THE OCCULT TRADITION

From the Renaissance to the Present Day

David S. Katz

JONATHAN CAPE
LONDON

1/20316543

Published by Jonathan Cape 2005

2 4 6 8 10 9 7 5 3

First published in Great Britain in 2005 by
Jonathan Cape
Random House, 20 Vauxhall Bridge Road,
London SW1V 2SA

Random House Australia (Pty) Limited
20 Alfred Street, Milsons Point, Sydney,
New South Wales 2061, Australia

Random House New Zealand Limited
18 Poland Road, Glenfield,
Auckland 10, New Zealand

Random House South Africa (Pty) Limited
Isle of Houghton, Corner Boundary Road & Carse O'Gowrie,
Houghton 2198, South Africa

The Random House Group Limited Reg. No. 954009
www.randomhouse.co.uk

A CIP catalogue record for this book
is available from the British Library

ISBN 0-224-06165-8

Papers used by The Random House Group Limited are natural,
recyclable products made from wood grown in sustainable forests;
the manufacturing processes conform to the environmental
regulations of the country of origin

Typeset in Ehrhardt by Palimpsest Book Production Limited,
Polmont, Stirlingshire
Printed and bound in Great Britain by
William Clowes Ltd, Beccles, Suffolk

In memory of Richard H. Popkin
1923–2005

CONTENTS

ILLUSTRATIONS

Pages from the first edition of the *Corpus Hermeticum*, 1471 (*J. R. Ritman Library, Bibliotheca Philosophica Hermetica, Amsterdam*).

Portae Lucis, the Latin translation of the kabbalistic writings of Joseph ben Abraham Gikatilla, 1516 (*J. R. Ritman Library, Bibliotheca Philosophica Hermetica, Amsterdam*).

Page from the *Sefer Raziel*, seventeenth century (*J. R. Ritman Library, Bibliotheca Philosophica Hermetica, Amsterdam*).

Paracelsus (*J. R. Ritman Library, Bibliotheca Philosophica Hermetica, Amsterdam*).

The Paracelsian cosmos, from Joannes D. Mylius' *Opus Medico-Chymicum*, c. 1618–30 (*British Library, shelfmark 1033.l.4*)

Joseph Wright of Derby, *The Alchymist in Search of the Philosophers' Stone Discovers Phosphorus*, 1771 (*Derby Museum & Art Gallery*).

Johann Valentin Andreae (*J. R. Ritman Library, Bibliotheca Philosophica Hermetica, Amsterdam*).

John Dee, by William P. Sherlock, after unknown artist (*National Portrait Gallery, London*).

Michael Maier (*Science and Society Picture Library*).

Francis Bacon under an angel's wing: frontispiece of the official history of the Royal Society, 1667 (*Science and Society Picture Library*).

Descartes' view of the universe (*Library of Congress*).

The Duke of Montagu presenting the Roll of Constitutions to Philip, Duke of Wharton, 1723 (*Grand Lodge of British Columbia and Yukon*).

The first degree tracing board (*Grand Lodge of British Columbia and Yukon*).

The third degree tracing board (*Grand Lodge of British Columbia and Yukon*).

Adam Weishaupt (*Grand Lodge of British Columbia and Yukon*).

'A Masonic Anecdote' (Alessandro, Count of Cagliostro) by James Gillray (1786) (*National Portrait Gallery, London*).

The Book of Mormon (*Library of Congress*).

American outdoor religious meeting, 1839 (*New Bedford Whaling Museum*).

Sir William Crookes with the medium Florence Cook (*International Survivalist Society*).

Photograph taken by Crookes of Florence Cook (*International Survivalist Society*).

Madame Blavatsky and Henry Steel Olcott in London, 1888 (*copyright © The Regents of the University of California 2005*).

John Nelson Darby, after Edward Penstone *(National Portrait Gallery, London)*.

ACKNOWLEDGEMENTS

This book is dedicated to the memory of Richard H. Popkin (1923–2005), who was one of the most original and creative intellectual historians of the last fifty years. Dick and I shared ideas, hunches, and photocopies since the day we met in Tel Aviv early in 1980. Apart from his nearly annual conferences – what he liked to call 'clambakes' – and our archival jaunts, we kept in constant touch, at first through letters and faxes, and then via e-mail. Dick's intuition was extraordinary, and even when it didn't pan out, somehow it seemed like the fault of history rather than his own miscalculation. In the last years of his life, Dick was confined to a wheelchair, nearly blind, relying on oxygen tanks. Despite these inconveniences, Dick carried on with his research, producing new work, while continuing to send me updates about his views on American politics. The occult tradition was one of his favourite subjects, and I am sorry that he won't read this book. Dick Popkin was one of a kind, and he is greatly missed by his many acolytes.

As usual, I thank the staff of the Upper Reading Room at the Bodleian Library in Oxford. I have been sitting at Seat U151 since Harold Wilson was prime minister, and I still take notes with a fountain pen. Special thanks to Vera Ryhajlo, my favourite librarian there.

Once again, I owe a debt of gratitude to Peter Robinson, my agent at Curtis Brown. Many thanks as well to the people at Jonathan Cape, Will Sulkin and Jörg Hensgen, and the copy-editor, Alison Tulett. Joan Lessing kindly helped with the proofs, as did my research assistant, Sylvie Kraus. But my greatest debt is to Professor Amy Singer, *en can dostum ve hayat arkadaşım*, which will come as no surprise to anyone.

INTRODUCTION

There are only three drawings among the many pages that comprise the manuscripts of Sir Isaac Newton. We might expect them to be sketch maps of the stars or diagrams illustrating the laws of gravitation. In fact, they are detailed plans of the Temple of Solomon, based on the measurements given in the Book of Ezekiel, chapters 40–46.[1] Newton had a theory: when Moses installed a perpetual flame in the desert tabernacle of the Hebrews, he was in fact restoring the original biblical religion, that of Noah, now purged of Egyptian superstition. When the Jews finally built their temple under Solomon, they worshipped in a sanctum that reproduced God's creation, for it had a fire in the centre, representing the sun, and was further illuminated by seven lamps around it, symbolising the seven planets. As Newton explained,

> Now the rationale of this institution was that the God of Nature should be worshipped in a temple which imitates Nature, in a temple which is, as it were, a reflection of God. Everyone agrees that a Sanctum with a fire in the middle was an emblem of the system of the world.

In other words, the temple in Jerusalem was a sort of divine planetarium, and, after its destruction, knowledge of the true arrangement of the heavens disappeared. A misreading of the heavens goes along with a misreading of religion.

Among Newton's papers are several dozen full boxes of manuscripts devoted to understanding occult, or hidden, esoteric knowledge. That the man who is often credited with being the first modern scientist should have devoted so much effort to studying the occult tradition is itself a paradox that demands more careful examination, but, as we shall see, it is only part of a story that begins with Plato and travels along a winding path that brings us even to American Fundamentalism in our own time.

The occult tradition is a coherent intellectual stream that has roots in metaphysics, cosmology and religion and which has tried to bring together widely disparate aspects of God's Creation within a complex structure of connections, sympathies and affinities. Within its realm are numerous sub-systems such as magic, astrology, demonology, Kabbalah, numerology, pyramidism, divination, theurgy and much else. An occult quality is one that is hidden from the senses, as opposed to a manifest quality that is readily apprehended. As such it would come to include the more supernatural elements of normative religion, such as providence, prophecy and millenarianism. At the bottom of all this was the firm conviction that there is a plan to the universe, an underlying structure, and if only we understood it, not only would that knowledge make us happy, but we might even be able to manipulate its operation.

The celebrated German–Jewish philosopher Theodor W. Adorno (1903–69) made a study of the astrology column published in the *Los Angeles Times* during the winter of 1952–3. Adorno's starting point was his firm belief that the 'modern occultist movements, including astrology, are more or less artificial rehashes of old and by-gone superstitions, susceptibility for which is kept awake by certain social and psychological conditions while the resuscitated creeds remain basically discordant with today's universal state of enlightenment'. One of the advantages of studying astrology rather than other aspects of the occult, Adorno explained, was that it represents a kind of occult-lite world view: 'It is certainly not one of the extreme occultist trades, but puts up a façade of pseudo-rationality which makes it easier to embrace than, for example, spiritualism. No wraiths appear, and the forecasts pretend to be derived from astronomic facts. Thus astrology might not bring out so clearly psychotic mechanisms as those fashions indulged in by the real lunatic fringe of superstition.'[2]

Yet despite Adorno's disparaging remarks, even he recognised that a belief system like astrology was worth a good deal of study and thought, not least because so many intelligent and rational people swear by it. The question for us remains, however, how to approach a subject like the occult, which has numerous different paths of entry, most of them quite removed from Adorno's scornful assessment of its component ideas. In purely historiographical terms, the study of the occult tradition attained unquestioned academic respectability in 1964, when Frances Yates (1899–1981) published her classic study of Giordano Bruno.[3] There will be much to say about her ground-breaking work below, but the point to be made here is that in the mid-1960s, Frances Yates's book seemed to promise a glimpse into an alternative tradition, a path not taken that led to a spiritual philosophy – a religion, even – that was less dogmatic and more attuned to Nature and the universe than the usual Western religions on offer at the time.

During the past forty years, there has been a huge expansion in the study of Hermeticism and other esoteric Renaissance philosophies. At the same time, the historical study of witchcraft became a growth industry after the publication in 1971 of *Religion and the Decline of Magic* by Keith Thomas (b. 1933), which rooted the phenomenon in the particular social conditions of post-Reformation England.[4] Even earlier, Hugh Trevor-Roper (1914–2003) contributed an exciting essay about 'The European Witch-craze of the Sixteenth and Seventeenth Centuries'.[5] For Trevor-Roper, the key to understanding early modern witchcraft lay in the failure of the Roman Catholic Church to penetrate certain areas of Europe. The demonisation of these recalcitrant territories as being 'bewitched' then provided the model later for attacking non-conformists and other perceived enemies of the faith.

There is no doubt that the works of Frances Yates and the seminal book by Keith Thomas had an enormous influence on jump-starting the field of occult studies. These two scholars came out of different traditions: Yates from the rarefied history of philosophy as practised at the Warburg Institute in London; and Thomas from the study of radical religion as taught by Christopher Hill (1912–2003) at Balliol College, Oxford. But at some point the study of the occult tradition merges with social history, and we need to draw a line and content ourselves with looking cheerfully over the fence. Witchcraft, it seems to me, does not fall within the purview of the occult tradition, and it will therefore be omitted from this book.[6] Hermeticism, on the other hand, falls squarely within our brief, and the ideas expressed by that term fuelled a powerful conceptual engine that helped propel the occult tradition over the centuries.

One difference between the two subjects is that Hermeticism is much more a body of ideas – if that is not an oxymoronic phrase – than a historical phenomenon, like witchcraft. Arthur Oncken Lovejoy (1873–1962) was the famous American historian who has a claim to having invented the academic field called 'the history of ideas'. Lovejoy used the term to describe a process of enquiry that 'cuts into the hard-and-fast individual systems and, for its own purposes, breaks them up into their component elements, into what may be called their unit-ideas'. Lovejoy is often accused of having initiated and promoted a method of study in which the historian denigrates context, but in fact he insisted that it 'is in the persistent dynamic factors, the ideas that produce effects in the history of thought, that he is especially interested'. Furthermore, Lovejoy explains, 'any unit-idea which the historian thus isolates he next seeks to trace through more than one – ultimately, indeed, through all – of the provinces of history in which it figures in any important degree'. Lovejoy emphasised that he understood the history of ideas as being 'especially concerned with the manifestation of specific unit-ideas in the collective thought of large groups of persons, not merely in the doctrines or opinions of a small number of profound thinkers or eminent writers'. Finally, Lovejoy warned, the history of ideas 'is pursued with some difficulty in an age of departmentalised minds'.[7]

Lovejoy was undoubtedly correct that in order to trace the progress and development of a particular 'unit-idea' one needs to become proficient in many different disciplines, such as history, philosophy, literature, art and so on. It was his own wide knowledge that enabled him so well to study Plato's principle of plenitude – the 'Great Chain of Being' – from ancient times up until his own day. Contemporary scholars of the occult tradition often complain that people who work in the field plough their solitary furrows in separate departments of history, philosophy, literature and art, oblivious to the fact that there are colleagues out there whose academic company could be mutually beneficial and creative.

Professor Wouter J. Hanegraaff, for example, calls for greater organisational cooperation among scholars of esotericism, but at the same time condemns those who come to see the occult tradition as having a deep meaning in their own lives outside of academia:

Certainly, scholars of hermeticism or esotericism, no less than their colleagues in other domains, should be free to feel personally inspired by the traditions they study. However, not all of them have realized that the very future of the study of western esotericism as an academic discipline may be seriously endangered, for obvious socio-political reasons, if a considerable part of its representatives refuses to respect the distinction between research and the expression of personal beliefs.

According to Hanegraaff, the 'discipline is therefore internally divided into a religionists and an empirico-historical camp, without this distinction being always immediately evident to outsiders'.[8]

These are very instructive remarks by a scholar who in many ways is representative of the sociologists who have done some fascinating work in the field. The researchers who become personally affected by the occult tradition are referred to as 'religionist', as opposed to the scientifically neutral people in the 'empirico-historical camp'.[9] Yet the same call for emotional distance would hardly be appropriately addressed, say, to historians of Christianity, many of whom are believers who would explain that it was their faith that drew them to the subject in the first place. Moreover, this distinction between religious faith and the occult tradition is much more problematic than my own exclusion of witchcraft from the present discussion. We shall see that apocalyptic and millenarian Protestantism is an integral part of the supernatural world view beyond conventional Christianity and needs to be seen as part of the occult tradition.

George Orwell (1903–50) understood the social environment of radical beliefs when he complained that as 'with the Christian religion, the worst advertisement for Socialism is its adherents':

> In addition to this there is the horrible – the really disquieting – prevalence of cranks whenever Socialists are gathered together. One sometimes gets the impression that the mere words 'Socialism' and 'Communism' draw towards them with magnetic force every fruit-juice drinker, nudist, sandal-wearer, sex-maniac, Quaker, 'Nature Cure' quack, pacifist and feminist in England.

The end result was that to the ordinary person, 'a crank meant a Socialist and a Socialist meant a crank. Any Socialist, he probably felt, could be counted on to have *something* eccentric about him.'[10]

Thirty-five years later, Orwell's concept resurfaced among sociologists of religion as the principle of 'the cultic milieu', proposed by Colin Campbell in 1972. He posited that 'cults must exist within a milieu which, if not conducive to the maintenance of individual cults, is clearly highly conducive to the spawning of cults in general.' As Campbell defined it,

> The cultic milieu can be regarded as the cultural underground of society. Much broader, deeper and historically based than the

contemporary movement known as *the* underground, it includes all deviant belief-systems and their associated practices. Unorthodox science, alien and heretical religion, deviant medicine, all comprise elements of such an underground. In addition, it includes the collectivities, institutions, individuals and media of communication associated with these beliefs. Substantively it includes the worlds of the occult and the magical, of spiritualism and psychic phenomena, of mysticism and new thought, of alien intelligences and lost civilizations, of faith healing and nature cure. This heterogeneous assortment of cultural items can be regarded, despite its apparent diversity, as constituting a single entity – the entity of the cultic milieu.

Almost paraphrasing Orwell, Campbell also noticed that 'individuals who "enter" the cultic milieu at any one point frequently travel rapidly through a wide variety of movements and beliefs and by so doing constitute yet another unifying force within the milieu'. As for the survival of occult beliefs in a disenchanted scientific world, Campbell suggested that 'it could be that the very processes of secularisation which have been responsible for the "cutting back" of the established form of religion have actually allowed "hardier varieties" to flourish, or possibly created the circumstances for the emergence, not of a secular scientific society, but of a society centred on a blend of mysticism, magic and pseudo-science'.[11]

One of the central themes in this book is that it was the creation of an occult milieu that provided a fertile environment for the development of such schools of thought as Swedenborgianism; a religion such as Mormonism; and individuals such as Nostradamus, Isaac Newton, Madame Blavatsky and Pat Robertson. That some of these groups and people are usually discussed in the context of religion rather than as part of the occult tradition should frighten us not a bit. As we shall see, American Fundamentalism, for example, developed a detailed mythology about the End of Days based on an esoteric reading of an exoteric text, the Bible. This book attempts to restore the supernatural elements of radical religion to the history of the occult tradition. In many ways, the occult itself is religion's supernatural shadow.

One of Adorno's most penetrating insights in his essay on astrology is the concept of 'secondary superstition'. By this he means that 'people responding to the stimuli we are here investigating seem in a way "alien" to the experience on which they claim their decisions are based'. Most people who profess confidence in predictions based on the stars 'take astrology for granted, much like psychiatry, symphony concerts or political parties; they accept it because it *exists*, without much reflection'. Indeed, Adorno writes, they 'are hardly interested in the justification of the system. In the newspaper column . . . the mechanics of the astrological system are never divulged and the readers are presented only with the alleged results of astrological reasoning in which the reader does not actively participate.' Astrology, in other words, is a belief system, a kind of faith.

Adorno admits that 'organised fortune-telling has for time immemorial had the character of "secondary superstition"' in that for thousands of years there has been 'a division of labor that admitted only priests into the esoteric mystery'. But in more modern times we need to pay attention to a more pronounced

> detachment of large groups of believers from the 'working' of superstition, and to their interest in net results rather than in supposedly supranatural powers. They don't even see the sorcerers at work any more nor are they allowed to listen to their abracadabra. They simply 'get the dope.' . . . The sharp division between alchemy and chemistry, between astrology and astronomy, is a comparatively late achievement.

In former times, even scholars at the cutting edge of cosmology might believe that the stars influence events on earth no less than we accept that the moon regulates the tides: 'Today, however, the incompatibility of the progress of natural sciences, such as astro-physics, with a belief in astrology is blatant. Those who combine both are forced to an intellectual retrogression which formerly was hardly required.'[12] As we shall see, Adorno was quite wrong to think that border disputes such as that between astrology and astronomy ended at the dawn of the modern era five hundred years ago. The boundary between faith and what came to be called science has been drawn and re-drawn most especially in the history of the occult tradition. For example, these issues will be critical when discussing spiritualism and telepathy, particularly during the early days of psychology and psychoanalysis when Freud and his followers were desperate to place themselves on the scientific side of the fence, without excluding disputed territories such as hypnotism and the uncanny. Adorno himself admitted:

> Modern science, which has replaced more and more categories which once interpreted events as though they were meaningful, tends to promote a kind of opaqueness which at least for the uninitiated is hard to distinguish from an equally opaque and non-transparent thesis such as the dependence of the individual human fate on stellar constellations.[13]

There is a huge element of faith in modern science.[14] Just as a refusal to accept the existence of God was an absurd proposition in the medieval world, so too is disbelief in unseen atoms and molecules not an option today.

In other words, the people who studied and promoted the occult tradition were not lunatics. It is true that in retrospect – the historian's dirty trick – many of them found themselves in the territory of faith when they so dearly wanted to be full citizens of science. What unites these seekers is what Adorno called 'the readiness to relate the unrelated'. It may be, as he says, that the occult tradition looks at the 'fears that are produced by the conditions of the present' and

> takes care of this mood by translating it into a pseudo-rational form, thus somehow localizing free-floating anxieties in some definite symbolism, but it also gives some vague and diffused comfort by making the senseless appear as though it had some hidden and grandiose sense while at the same time corroborating that this sense can neither be sought in the realm of the human nor can properly be grasped by humans.

Adorno claims that the occult 'represents a threat and a remedy in one, just as certain psychotics may start a fire and at the same time prepare for its extinction'.[15]

Yet, at the same time, the search for meaning and patterns in nature is a worthy goal common both to science and to religion and not the exclusive methodology of the occult tradition. Apart from charlatans and mountebanks, who exist in the fields of science and religion as well, scholars of the occult tradition did not consciously attempt to deceive 'by making the senseless appear as though it had some hidden and grandiose sense'. In the history of ideas, we need to go up many blind alleys and not confine ourselves merely to the paths that lead up to broad highways, a map that can be drawn only by retracing our steps. Not even the most empirical and positivistic historian would claim that the history of the occult tradition is simply a mapping of dead ends.

This book is a study of the occult tradition from its flowering during the European Renaissance, through its manifestations up to and including the American Fundamentalist movement. The main theme that should emerge is that it is possible to speak of a unified occult tradition with ancient roots, which crystallises in the period of the Renaissance and continues to grow and remain extremely viable until our own day. This is not an easy subject, and trashy books on the occult fill shelves of used bookshops everywhere. Most of these rather dubious works recycle information with an emphasis on the uncanny and the bizarre, with a tilt to the pornographic, like exhibits at a carnival sideshow. Nostradamus is an ever-popular favourite, accompanied by free-floating potted summaries of astrology and alchemy. The problem with such parasitic books is that if you want gobbets of third-hand knowledge about Nostradamus you can get it elsewhere more efficiently and for free – that's what the internet is for. This book traces the growth and meandering path of the occult tradition over the past five hundred years and shows how the esoteric world view fits together.

Adorno had a flash of insight when he singled out the defining characteristic of the occult tradition as 'the readiness to relate the unrelated'. We will need to cover a lot of ground to survey the history of the occult as a body of knowledge. Fortunately, the wonderful thing about history is that one thing happens after another, which gives it a kind of basic order, and, even better, history is made by people, whose dates of birth and death provide us with helpful signposts. At the risk of typographical clutter, these dates (when known) appear the first time someone is mentioned in the following pages.

The history of the occult tradition demonstrates the mathematical principle that a line can be drawn through an infinite number of points, as the unrelated becomes surprisingly related. This could have been an encyclopedia instead of a single volume. Instead, this book aims at providing a big picture, a view from above of an enormous and rich landscape. Some rivers of thought will disappear over the horizon at a certain point. This will be especially true when discussing subjects that have traditionally been understood within the purview of theology or religious history. At the same time, emphasising a supernatural or occult element in the theology of a contemporary religion (such as Mormonism) is not meant to denigrate the sincerity of belief or the validity of any denomination. But, once having seen where a piece of the occult puzzle fits, the rest is easy.

In Umberto Eco's novel *Foucault's Pendulum*, the main characters contemplate setting up a whole series of books covering the occult tradition, to be called 'Isis Unveiled':

> 'Well,' Garamond said, 'would you try to sell readers something they knew nothing about? The Isis Unveiled books must deal with the exact same subjects as all the others. They confirm one another; therefore they're true. Never trust originality.'

Eco's book is a brilliant satire of the occult world, and, as he suggests, it is very nearly a complete system of ideas which vibrates across the centuries.[16] *The Occult Tradition* aims to be a different sort of work: the cartography of a secret esoteric body of knowledge that has had an indelible influence on Western culture.

ONE

Religion, Magic and the Occult Tradition

I

'Roughly speaking, all men in Australia are magicians, but not one is a priest.' Thus, in characteristic blind self-parody, did the great James George Frazer (1854–1941) illustrate the distinction between magic and religion at the core of his great work, *The Golden Bough*, which appeared in various editions between 1890 and 1915. His reference, of course, was to 'the aborigines of Australia, the rudest savages as to whom we possess accurate information', the primitive inhabitants of the Victorian anthropologist's carefully classified dream-world. Frazer shared in the belief that 'recent researches into the early history of man have revealed the essential similarity with which, under many superficial differences, the human mind has elaborated its first crude philosophy of life.' Just as Darwin had demonstrated the evolution of the human body from simpler organisms, the new science of anthropology hoped to learn about the evolution of the human mind from proving that the same 'motives have operated widely, perhaps universally, in human society, producing in varied circumstances a variety of institutions, specifically different but generically alike'.[1]

Frazer's background was Free Church of Scotland; he was an undergraduate at Trinity College, Cambridge, and once he entered he never left, although his fellowship had to be renewed three times until it was confirmed for life at the age of forty-five. It was there that Frazer became friends with William Robertson Smith (1846–94), the celebrated and often notorious fellow Scotsman who was trying to apply anthropological methods to the study of Scripture. Robertson Smith was also one of the chief editors of the superb ninth edition of the

Encyclopaedia Britannica, which was being published in alphabetical order during those years. Smith met Frazer by the time they had reached the letter 'T', a fateful letter in the anthropologist's dictionary. Brushing aside Frazer's objections that he really didn't know anything about the subjects, Smith assigned him to write the articles on 'Taboo' and 'Totemism'. The first article would be the embryonic draft of *The Golden Bough*; the second for his two works on totemism, the last of which would inspire Freud to make his own contribution to the field.[2]

But of course it was Frazer's *Golden Bough* that had the greatest influence on so many aspects of European intellectual life. Robertson Smith died in 1894, and by then Frazer had rejected his mentor's emphasis on religion as a *social* institution in which the group was the prime unit. Frazer had come to see religion as more of a *philosophical* system actually devised by individuals and based on supernatural sanctions. This religious system would endure until it was replaced by a better one, science. Robertson Smith had been content to draw his anthropological data only from the world of the Semites; Frazer cast his net much wider, but everything he said was meant to apply to the biblical peoples as well.

Frazer sharpened up his general thesis for the second edition of *The Golden Bough,* published in 1900. The original subtitle of the book, 'A study in comparative religion', was changed to read, 'A study in magic and religion'. Frazer argued that these terms reflected two very different world views. Magic 'assumes that in nature one event follows another necessarily and invariably without the intervention of any spiritual or personal agency. Thus its fundamental conception is identical with that of modern science; underlying the whole system is a faith, implicit but real and firm, in the order and uniformity of nature'. Frazer called magic 'the bastard sister of science'. So far, so good – but he was aware that any definition of religion, on the other hand, would be fraught with difficulties. He had a stab at it anyway:

> By religion, then, I understand a propitiation or conciliation of powers superior to man which are believed to direct and control the course of nature and of human life . . . Thus in so far as religion assumes the world to be directed by conscious agents who may be turned from their purpose by persuasion, it stands in fundamental antagonism to magic as well as to science, both of which take for granted that the course of nature is determined,

not by the passions and caprice of personal beings, but by the operation of immutable laws acting mechanically.

The magician-scientist is very unlike the priest: 'He supplicates no higher power: he sues the favour of no fickle and wayward being: he abases himself before no awful deity.' Indeed, 'If he claims a sovereignty over nature, it is a constitutional sovereignty rigorously limited in its scope.' Frazer saw mankind as going through definite stages: 'an Age of Religion has thus everywhere, as I venture to surmise, been preceded by an Age of Magic'. Primitive man first tries to compel nature, and when that fails, he begs. This, in turn, is followed by a more efficient kind of compulsion, called science.[3] Frazer's distinction between magic and religion was seminal, and according to his most recent biographer is 'Frazer's single most important contribution to the anthropology of religion.'[4]

As Frazer himself admitted, all this waffling about the golden bough was 'little more than a stalking-horse to carry two heavy pack-loads of facts'.[5] Nevertheless, Frazer had an enormous influence on all historians of religion and biblical scholars. His distinction between religion and magic; his notion of the magician being closer to the scientist than to the priest; his use of anthropological data from a wide variety of sources – all this shows Frazer to have been himself a 'stalking-horse' for much later historical works, especially the studies of religion, magic, witchcraft and the occult, which were published in the 1970s.

It is especially telling that Frazer should use the notion of a magician-scientist as a kind of constitutional sovereign, as this is the very same image that Isaac Newton employed two centuries before in speaking of God, when devising his famous and enduring synthesis between religion and science. Newton stressed the image of a Deity with absolute power, a God of Dominion, who nevertheless demonstrated his gracious authority by obeying the very laws that He himself had established. The law of gravity was posited by God and would continue to operate as evidence of his constitutional rulership as long as the earth survived, which, incidentally, would not be for ever. Among God's promises, and this in the Book of Revelation, was to create 'a new heaven and a new earth: for the first heaven and the first earth were passed away'. Having been promised, God's word becomes law, capable of being relied upon no less than the gravitation of the earth.[6] The way in which God would accomplish this cosmic destruction and millennial rebuilding was certainly *supernatural*, quite literally. But it was also *magical*, in the 'Harry Potter' sense, including wonderful beasts and aerial battles. The millennium was at the centre of a religion made magical, and stretches Frazer's definition beyond the breaking point.

Names and things usually go together, although sometimes we can have one before we have the other. The terms '*l'occultisme*' and '*l'ésotérisme*' seem to have been popularised by 'Eliphas Lévi' [Alphonse-Louis Constant (1810–75)] in his book *Dogme et rituel*, published at Paris in 1856. The word '*l'ésotérisme*' had already appeared in an earlier book published in 1828, and '*l'occultisme*' was probably suggested by Cornelius Agrippa's *De occulta philosophia* (1533).[7]

The great historian of these weighty matters, Frances Yates (1899–1981), had a simple definition for what she called 'the occult philosophy' of the Renaissance: 'This philosophy, or outlook, was compounded of Hermeticism as revived by Marsilio Ficino, to which Pico della Mirandola added a Christianized version of Jewish Cabala. These two trends, associated together, form what I call "the occult philosophy".'[8] Hermeticism plus Kabbalah: we shall shortly delve into those subjects, but what is interesting about the Yates definition is its simplicity and its historical basis. The situation has become vastly more complicated in the past few decades, not least because of the more recent work of Antoine Faivre and his associates.[9]

When discussing the occult tradition, Faivre prefers to use the word 'esotericism'. For him, 'occultism' is something quite different, and refers to the attempt in the eighteenth and nineteenth centuries to adapt esotericism to a disenchanted world. He sees 'occultism' as a new subcategory of esotericism, a synthesis of magic and science. Allowing him the privilege of word colonisation, then, we need to look at what he calls 'esotericism', which he argues is a distinct form of thought complete by the Renaissance, and exhibiting six characteristics, the first four of which are intrinsic to its definition, that is, they all have to be present for a movement or a corpus of texts to qualify as 'esoteric'.

The first characteristic is that it needs to promote the notion of *correspondences*, symbolic or real, seen or unseen, which are said to exist among all parts of the universe. This is the ancient idea of macrocosm and microcosm; everything is signs, codes and hieroglyphs, a huge theatre of mirrors; every object conceals a secret.[10] There are two kinds of correspondences: (1) those that exist in nature, seen and unseen, such as correspondences between the planets and parts of the human body, which is the basis of astrology; and (2) those between nature (that is, the cosmos) and the revealed texts (including the history of humankind), which is the basis of Kabbalah and *physica sacra*.[11]

The next characteristic involves a belief in *living nature*. If correspondences and sympathies exist throughout the universe, then there must be a world-mind or a world-soul that causes this to happen. Nature, in other words, is essentially alive in all its parts, a sort of huge living creature, and all components of the universe are invested with mind (or God, if you prefer). This living nature has circulating within it a light or a hidden fire. Magic is the knowledge (*gnosis*) of the networks of sympathies that connect material nature, and how they might be influenced by special plants and stones, which is the basis not only of practical magic but of alchemy.[12]

The third defining characteristic is an emphasis on *imagination and mediations*, which is implied by the first, the idea of correspondences. There must be a mediation between the higher and lower worlds, by rituals, symbols, angels and intermediate spirits, but above all by *imaginatio*, a word related to *magia, imago* and magnet. This has nothing to do with fantasy, for *imaginatio* is an organ of the soul. While the mystic tries to suppress images or intermediaries because for him they are obstacles to union with God, the esoterist adopts exactly the opposite strategy and uses the power of his imagination to focus on the intermediaries, the symbols or images, in order to decipher the hieroglyphs of nature and understand how this material world is connected to the divine one above.

The fourth and last intrinsic characteristic in Faivre's lexicon notes the *experience of transmutation*, the effect of the practical application of the ideas of imagination and mediation. Esotericism is not merely a speculative activity, but a type of knowledge whereby perfect *gnosis* can be attained, a sort of second birth, like alchemical laboratory experiments that show a process of transmutation in a series of stages.

Faivre appends two optional characteristics of esotericism: (1) *the praxis of the concordance*, the tendency to look for similarities between secret doctrines in order to reach an even higher stage of understanding; and (2) *transmission*, of esoteric teachings from master to disciple by means of special initiations, including the notion of a historical genealogy of 'authentic' spiritual knowledge in a well-defined tradition.

You say esoteric; I say occult. There is no doubt that we could fill many pages with a learned discussion of what constitutes the occult tradition, and in what way it might differ from esoteric bodies of knowledge and supernatural manifestations. According to the *Oxford English Dictionary*, the occult is the 'realm of the unknown; the super-natural world or its influences, manifestations, etc.'. Let us keep our options open, and accept for the time being what I said in the intro-duction: 'An occult quality is one which is hidden from the senses, as opposed to a manifest quality which is readily apprehended. As such it would come to include the more supernatural elements of normative religion, such as providence, prophecy and millenarianism.' The time has come to dive directly into the issues that the occult tradition has tried to resolve.

II

Why is there anything? And what is it? There may never be answers to these questions, but any study of the occult tradition has to start with the Greeks, for not only were they the first ones to tackle issues such as these in ways that we would recognise as systematic, but the philosophers of the Renaissance saw themselves as conscious revivers of the glory that was Greece. The Greek view of the universe thrived in fifteenth-century Italy, first and foremost in the general conception of the world of Nature as *alive*, an unimaginably huge organism, a colossal animal with feelings and senses, a gigantic creature with a mind and a body. The 'world soul', the mind of this organism, was the source of regularity and order in the natural world, of which mankind is one small part. The notion of the universe as alive was accepted by European thinkers well into the seventeenth century, and remains even today an absolutely critical occult theme in New Age religion.

From at least the seventh century BC, Greeks wanted to know what was the basic material from which the universe is made. This was the key question for the Ionian pre-Socratics. Thales (c.630–546 BC) thought it was water, especially because life itself begins in a liquid environment. In his universe, a flat earth floats on an ocean of water.

Anaximander (*c.*610–547 BC), his contemporary, objected that since water was one of the differentiated four elements of our own world, it was not likely to be a basic substance on its own. There was probably some other substance that lacked what we might recognise as elemental qualities. This substance was in itself a creative force, God, and the process of world-making began with self-generated vortices in this primary matter, which in turn differentiated into other substances. Our own world is only one of these worlds, a solid cylinder floating in primary matter. Anaximenes (584–528 BC), who was a bit younger than the others, saw this primary matter as a kind of vapour, not air exactly, but something else. He explained how this substance could turn into the elements with which we are familiar by a dual process of rarification and condensation: its rarification produced fire; its condensation wind, water and earth. Like Thales, Anaximenes's earth was flat, floating in the primary matter. From our point of view, what is particularly interesting is that Anaximenes emphasises the *process* of change, and wonders why different things behave differently, despite having a common origin.

The Pythagoreans took the subject one step further. Pythagoras (*c.*572–497 BC) actually wrote nothing himself, but he has remained an almost supernatural figure in the occult tradition. Like Anaximenes, Phythagoras and his followers saw the world as floating in an infinite ocean of vapour with the earth at the centre, the motion of which generated everything else by separating out the different elements. Pythagoras, however, argued that the earth was not a cylinder but must be in the form of a sphere, the most perfect shape in Nature. Like Anaximander, Pythagoras believed that primary matter cannot be made up of one of the four basic elements. We can never know what this material is: all we can say about it is that it occupies *space*. Indeed, we do not really need to know what primary matter is. The important point is that something that occupies space can be defined geometrically, in mathematical terms, which express knowledge of the most clear and certain kind. In other words, the nature of things is not the material of which they are made, but their *structure*, their *form*.

And the word 'form' brings us to Plato (427?–347 BC). Every schoolboy knows about Plato's theory of forms: pure, 'real', absolute Ideas, which provide the models upon which the world is based. In the *Republic*, Plato himself uses the example of a table, which is recognisable to us as such only because the Idea of a perfect Table pre-exists any individual table that mankind ever constructed. Any table we build will someday be destroyed and lose the qualities that make it a table at all. The only 'real' and absolute table is the one of the mind, the Idea that will never decay and remains eternal. The Idea is 'real' in the same sense that we might describe a coat as being made of 'real leather'. Nothing in our world of change is ultimately completely real, just as any circle we draw, no matter how exactly, will never reproduce precisely the theoretical mathematical form. In the end, Platonic philosophy conceived of a world of forms, somewhere apart from our world of Nature.

Plato's major work on cosmology is his *Timaeus*, and as far as many Renaissance thinkers were concerned, this dialogue was the subject's starting point. Parts of the *Timaeus* were translated into Latin in Roman times by Cicero (106–43 BC) and Chalcidius (fourth century AD), and it was Plato's most widely known work throughout the medieval period. Plato accepted the pre-Socratic conception of the world as a living organism, and agreed with Pythagoras that form was the key concept, rather than matter and its nature. Plato's view of space and time followed from these premises. Space exists only in the world of Nature as that out of which copies of the eternal forms are made, a kind of place to deposit those copies. Time also exists only in the world of Nature, since time implies change, and this is not a feature of the eternal world of forms. God initiated space and time when the world of Nature was created. Why did God create the world in the first place? Because He is Pure Good, the form of Good itself, and the nature of Goodness is to be expressed and to reproduce itself. The creation of the world followed logically from the nature of God.

Plato also had something to say about the body of the created world. He knew it must be 'extended', that is, 'three-dimensional', tangible, solid. The world must be visible, which implies fire or light. Somewhere between solid and fire/light must be intermediate forms of matter: liquid and gas. These are the four elements, and, like Pythagoras, Plato thought that their totality must form a sphere, the only uniform solid, any deviation from which being caused by some sort of external influence such as pressure or attraction. This spherical material world is enveloped by the 'world soul', which serves as the intermediate between our own material world and the world of forms.

Aristotle (384–322 BC) amplified the Platonic cosmology by

emphasising final causes. His doctrine identified four different varieties of causes, which explained each individual object in the material world: (1) *material*: the matter out of which it is made; (2) *formal*: the shape and arrangement of its parts; (3) *efficient*: the moving force; (4) *final*: the purpose or ultimate end for which the object exists in the first place. Aristotle argued that everything had a *nisus*, a tendency for change in a particular way, a built-in potentiality as each object strives to become the Platonic form of which it is a copy. In more dramatic terms, the Platonic form is the goal of the object's desire. Pure matter in this sense can never actually exist, since it would be pure potentiality with no *nisus* at all, at the ultimate negative point of Nature.

Aristotle also had a somewhat different conception of the Platonic forms themselves. Plato had tended to see God as an external thinker or mind completely separate from the world of forms. Aristotle, on the other hand, argued that the forms are themselves the thoughts of God, whose contemplation of Himself is itself a form, the model for all other thinking. When we think, we are not only imitating the divine cogitation, but fulfilling our *nisus* for reproducing this higher activity. This upward contemplation is Aristotle's definition of love: his God could hardly love the world since it is not in His perfect divine Nature to direct His attention down below.

Nevertheless, according to Aristotle, God's thinking is literally what makes the world go around. As God contemplates himself, this perfect activity is copied by the *primum mobile* (the outermost stellar sphere of the heavens), which rotates in a perfectly uniform motion. The planets, in turn, imitate the imitation in motions, which depart even more radically from perfect uniformity.

As we shall soon see, it was in the Renaissance that the occult tradition began to gel, and, in the most general and superficial sense, Renaissance philosophy represented a revolt against Aristotelianism, especially the teleological concept of *nisus* or tendency, as 'final causes' almost pulled forward the changes that were occurring in Nature. Aristotelian Scholasticism was a by-word for everything that was wrong in medieval philosophy. It was now Plato who was seen as the philosopher who represented all that was great in the Greek intellectual tradition. His all-powerful philosopher-kings had strong appeal for the upstart dictators of Renaissance Italy. Platonic cosmology, with its emphasis on form and structure, meshed well with the emerging axiom that, as Galileo (1564–1642) expressed it, the universe is a vast book 'written in mathematical language'.

Only since the nineteenth century have historians distinguished the later devotion to the author of the *Republic* as 'Neoplatonism'. Strictly speaking, Neoplatonism is the system of Platonic thought developed by Plotinus (AD 205–270), and amplified by his successors Porphyry (AD 232–305) and Proclus (*c.* AD 410–485) in the Platonic Academy at Athens. Its most recognisable feature is the emphasis on the One, the Good, the First Principle, which radiates love to all souls, which in turn seek mystical union with this source of all things through intellectual and moral labour. The Neoplatonic One transcends Being and Thought and is unknowable; unity with the One can only be reached through mystical experience. Neoplatonism worked well with what we might call religion, especially because of the supremacy of the interior experience as a mystical technique. Not only was God immanent, all around us, but our sense of Him within confirmed His existence and His work in the world.

Neoplatonism was regarded as an important tool for explaining and systematising Christianity ever since Origen (AD 185?–254?) responded to the anti-Christian attacks made a hundred years earlier by the Platonist Celsus. Origen himself was a great influence on the so-called fourth-century Cappadocian fathers (Basil 'the Great' of Caesarea, his brother Gregory of Nyssa, and Gregory of Nazianzus), whose views were crucial for John Scotus Eriugena (fl. 847–877). Proclus was a key authority for the fifth-century Christian theologian Pseudo-Dionysius the Areopagite.

What did the Neoplatonic world look like, and what was mankind's place in it? As we have come to expect, the universe in the Neoplatonic system was a living organism, with all parts linked and connected. At the very top, of course, was the One, which in the Christianized Neoplatonism of the Renaissance became the Divine Mind, the seat of the Platonic Forms, the Eternal Ideas. Its location was the Empyrean of God, the highest part of Heaven, beyond the Sphere of the Fixed Stars (including the zodiac). Below the stars could be found the *primum mobile*, the sphere that is the source of the daily rotation of the heavens. Underneath this level were the spheres of the seven planets, filled with ether, and, yet further, the moon and finally the earth. On the earth were to be found the four elements of water, earth, air and fire, which mixed together to form the animal, vegetable and mineral kingdoms.

In one sense, from the vantage point of the earth, God's Empyrean looked impossibly distant. But there was a direct connection, and this made life possible in the universe. The Divine Mind was the source of the *anima mundi*, the world soul, which was everywhere present and was quite literally the life of the cosmic animal that we call Nature. The actual link between the world soul and the world body (the earth itself) was the *spiritus mundi*, the world spirit. Mankind, then, was not quite at the bottom of the cosmic totem pole, being himself a kind of miniature replica of the celestial spheres, a microcosm to the macrocosm of the universe. He was therefore vulnerable to celestial influences of various kinds, especially to the planets of the zodiac, each of which governed a part of his body. The force of mutual attraction, which was active in the cosmos and which held it together, might be described as a kind of love.

The most wonderful feature of this love is that it went both ways: not only was mankind influenced from on high, but a person adept at the ways of the universe – a *magus* – could actually make Nature do his bidding. This could be done by understanding the nature of 'occult' or hidden qualities, those opposed to properties that were visible or 'manifest'. Manifest features of matter consisted of primary qualities (hot, cold, dry or moist) and secondary qualities (soft, hard, sweet, sour, etc.) and derived from combinations of the four elements. Occult qualities ultimately derived from the stars, and were injected into seemingly ordinary objects by the world spirit. An occult property operated by generating its like, making natural objects more like themselves, or, in the contemporary parlance, applying 'actives to passives'.

A Neoplatonic *magus* had the knowledge that enabled him to spy out these occult properties in seemingly ordinary plants and animals, and to use these things to make some other natural object more like the desired quality. For example, applying the heart of a brave animal like a cock or a lion would help promote bravery. The breast of loving creatures like sparrows or turtles would induce love. These things possessed the desired virtue in a particularly strong form, and might be used not only to generate like, but to drive away the opposite characteristic, in this case, cowardice and hate. These virtues were occult in that they could neither be seen nor be measured, and they adhered to the said plants and animals rather than being intrinsic parts of their nature, having their source, as we have seen, in the world soul and ultimately, in the Divine Mind of God. The mystical homeopathic physician Paracelsus (1490–1541) argued that Nature has left 'signatures' so that the occult virtues of a plant or animal would be revealed by some external sign: a root that looks as if it is wrapped in armour might provide protection against weapons, for example. This entire body of knowledge fell under the purview of 'natural magic', utilised by the *magus* to link what is above with what is below and thereby to manipulate Nature according to his will.

Pessimistic Judaeo-Christian Gnosticism was part of that same supernatural world, based on the notion of a Higher God with which the soul strives for unity. The supreme God had no part in Creation, which is the bungling work of an evil lesser deity, perhaps the god of the Old Testament. Our bodies are physical but our souls consist of a spark of the divine, trapped within our flesh. Salvation involves the escape of the soul from the body by means of knowledge (*gnosis*), insight achieved through mystical contemplation. Our souls can rise above this world, passing through the realms of divine beings who dwell among the stars and planets. In this sense at least, God is within us, and by emphasising our religious experience, Gnosticism points the way towards much later theologies.

The Gnostics had their own scriptures, found by two peasants in southern Egypt at a place called Nag Hammadi in 1945, two years before the Dead Sea Scrolls were discovered in Palestine. We have over fifty texts written in Coptic, which is native Egyptian written using mostly Greek letters, although it is clear that they had been translated from the original Greek. Altogether there are about a thousand pages of highly important documents, texts buried for safe keeping in the middle of the fourth century when orthodox Christianity was being created under the newly converted Emperor Constantine. Those who held different views on key issues, such as the Gnostics, suddenly found themselves to be heretics.

Along with Neoplatonism and Gnosticism, the third important strand of occult thought that was available to Renaissance thinkers was Hermeticism, rather an optimistic view of looking at the world, claiming to represent a primordial wisdom known as the *prisca theologia*. This was said to have originated with Hermes and Zoroaster and been communicated through Plato, a process emphasised in the sixteenth century as the *philosophia perenis* ('perennialism').[13] In the case of the Hermeticists, it was an attempt to return to sources of wisdom believed to be older than the civilisations of Greece and Rome, to the original wellspring of knowledge, Egypt. At the same time, they hoped to get behind Judaism, the source of Christianity, and arrive at an even older and more original philosophy.[14]

The key (mythic) figure here was Hermes Trismegistus ('thrice-great Hermes'), taking his name both from Hermes (Mercury), the giver of the divine word to mankind, and the ancient obsession with the magical number of three. According to the story, Hermes Trismegistus was an Egyptian priest who was a contemporary of Moses. Indeed, some people suggested that he and Moses were the same person. Hermes Trismegistus also appears in the Koran as Idris.[15] In any case, he was privy to the secret traditions current in Egyptian temples, and the wisdom of his times, codified in a number of texts. The first was the *Asclepius* ('Perfect Discourse'), written in a missing Greek original but known in Latin translation as early as the second century.[16] Hermes Trismegistus was also supposedly the author of the Greek treatises in the official *Corpus Hermeticum* numbered 1–18, and various other hermetic writings.

Despite their ancient pedigree, in fact, all of these texts were written in the first two centuries after Christ, in Egypt, in the city of Alexandria, and were further edited during the eleventh century in the Byzantine world: we know this because before the eleventh century there is no sign of the *Corpus Hermeticum* as such, although individual treatises were evidently in use as early as the third century.[17] In other words, none of them was a translation from the Egyptian at all; they were originally written in Greek to begin with in about AD 200 and passed off as something much more ancient.

One of the reasons for the success of hermetic writings is that they had something for everyone, and all were vaguely concerned with the occult sciences. There is a good deal about astrology, which was a perfectly acceptable Christian occupation, providing information rather than being completely deterministic. After all, the Magi were led by the stars to the baby Jesus. One also finds material concerned with alchemy, which also made a good deal of sense, accepting Aristotle's contention that all matter was formed from a *prima materia*, and that each substance owes its specific form to being impressed by some combination of the four elements of earth, air, water and fire, so that with the right agent, one could even turn base metal into gold. Hermes Trismegistus was also thought to be the author of that chief medieval alchemical text, the Emerald Tablet (*Tabula Smaragdina*), a well-known collection of thirteen alchemical maxims, including the famous tag-line, 'All that is above is like that which is below'.[18] There were also sections in the hermetic writings that discussed the secret virtues of plants and stones used in sympathetic magic, and the making of talismans.

But the highlight of the *Corpus Hermeticum* was the philosophical treatises, only sixty-odd pages in the modern edition, not concerned much with astrology, very little with magic and not at all with alchemy. These were true speculative works, dealing with the origins and nature of man and the universe. One can see the clear influence of Greek philosophical teaching, mainly Platonic and Stoic, which circulated in the first centuries of the Christian era. Jewish traces are also present, and perhaps there are even some genuine ancient Egyptian traditions witnessed, and others that were edited out by pious Byzantine scholars in the eleventh century as unfit to appear in serious philosophical treatises.

Hermeticism, then, was one of the bodies of thought that emerged during the first centuries AD in Egypt that reserved true knowledge (*gnosis*) for the élite. The others, as we have seen, were Neoplatonism and Gnosticism, to which we might add Scepticism, and its most famous exemplar, Sextus Empiricus (AD *c.*150–*c.*225). Hermeticism, however, was defiantly pagan, and gave pride of place to Egyptian wisdom, from a source not only pagan but outside the Greek and Roman classical tradition.

How did the Hermetic tradition become such a large part of the Renaissance world? We all learn that the Renaissance began with the recovery of the *Latin* classics, which was the first part of the great humanist movement. The *Greek* classics followed, especially in Florence, particularly through the patronage of Cosimo de'Medici (1389–1464) and his humanist court scholar, Marsilio Ficino (1433–99), whose life assignment was to translate all of Plato from Greek to Latin.

There was a change of plan in 1463. In that year, a Balkan monk named Leonardo da Pistoia (aka Leonardo Macedone) appeared in Florence with a manuscript in his bag. It was written on paper, measured 210 x 145 mm, and comprised about 225 pages. On folios 123 to 145 was the first copy anyone in the West had ever seen of the *Corpus Hermeticum*.[19] Almost thirty years later, in the preface to one of his books, Ficino gave a brief account of his career and recounts the following:

> But later in 1463, he [Cosimo de'Medici] charged me with translating first Mercury Trismegistus and then Plato. I finished Mercury in a few months while Cosimo was still living, and then I began work also on Plato.

In other words, so important was the Hermetic tradition to the Renaissance humanists, that they wanted to have the *Corpus Hermeticum* translated into Latin even before Plato! A readable copy of the works of Hermes Trismegistus was more urgently required than the *Republic* or the *Symposium*.

Ficino immediately set to work. Indeed, we can still see signs of his industry on the manuscript itself: little semi-circles protecting a wavy arrow pointing downwards signify the beginning of an important passage, which ends at a spot marked by another semi-circle with a wavy arrow pointing upwards. Ficino finished his project at top speed, and on 18 April 1463, Cosimo de'Medici gave him a villa as a gift of profound thanks. By September of the same year, Tommaso Benci finished translating the *Corpus Hermeticum* into Tuscan Italian.

Sadly, the copy of the text that the Balkan monk had brought to Florence only contained the first fourteen treatises of the *Corpus Hermeticum*. Although Treatises 16–18 were later found, the fifteenth remains missing. Ficino's Latin version of Treatises 1–14 was published at Treviso in 1471 – two years after the Latin *Asclepius* was printed for the first time, appearing in Ficino's text as a kind of appendix. Later editions appeared at Ferrara (1472) and Paris (1505). Ficino's edition became the most influential presentation of the hermetic writings until the nineteenth century, known as the *Pimander*, which was in fact the title only of the first treatise, more correctly 'Poimandres', a speaker who identifies himself as the divine mind, and whose revelation comprises a cosmogony and a plan of salvation. Curiously, even when Treatises 16–18 turned up, some editions continued to be published which included only Ficino's first fourteen. A Greek edition of the original text was published in 1554.[20]

Why was Cosimo de'Medici so keen on the hermetic writings, and like him so many of the Renaissance humanists? As it happens, scholars had been very anxious to get hold of texts by Hermes Trismegistus long before the Macedonian monk appeared in Florence. Their taste had been whetted by the *Asclepius*, which was the only hermetic writing known to the West before 1463, and was copied many times. Hermes Trismegistus himself had been known to the classical world, even if his writings had been lost. He appears in the works of Cicero and Clement of Alexandria (*c*.150–215). Hermes shows up in Augustine (354–430), even if he is described as living after Moses:

> As far as concerns philosophy . . . pursuits of that kind did dawn in Egypt around the time of Mercury, whom they called Trismegistus – certainly long before the sages or philosophers of Greece, but nevertheless later than Abraham, Isaac, Jacob and Joseph, and undoubtedly also later than Moses himself.[21]

Hermes Trismegistus had a revival in twelfth-century France, and was cited by Peter Abelard (1079–1142) in his famous book *Sic Et Non*. Even before 1463, there were some citations from Hermes by a bishop of Carthage named Quodvultdeus who was contemporary with Augustine and who used hermetic writings to prove the Trinity. At the same time, the Latin *Asclepius* was copied many times in the eleventh and twelfth centuries, for this was the text that attracted most interest, especially in relation to Plato's *Timaeus*. Thomas Bradwardine (d. 1349) was also a great student of *Asclepius*, as was Petrarch (1304–74).

There was a lot of talk about Hermes Trismegistus at the Council of Florence in 1439, thanks to the presence there of the Byzantine scholar George Gemisthus Plethon (*c*.1355–1452) – about whom more later – whose brilliance inspired Cosimo de'Medici to found a new academy in his honour. It was to get this academy off the ground that Cosimo hired Ficino in the first place. Ficino began to learn Greek only in 1456, trying in the meantime to round up every Latin hermetic manuscript he could find. When the Macedonian monk turned up in Florence in 1463, Ficino was prepared for action and Cosimo had the resources to make the hermetic revolution happen.

Ficino promoted the concept of an 'ancient theology' (*prisca theologia*) represented by the 'ancient theologians' (*prisci theologi*), whose teachings are largely in agreement. He placed Hermes Trismegistus at the head of the list, followed chronologically by Orpheus, Aglaophemus, Pythagoras, Philolaus and finally Plato.[22] Ficino and his patron Cosimo de'Medici wanted to have the hermetic writings translated before those of Plato because they believed that Hermes Trismegistus came first, that his work was more ancient, the oldest revelation of the truth, a very ancient theology that was passed on to those who came after, including Plato.

Even better, there was no problem with Christianity, since Hermes was prophetic in this area as well. As Ficino himself said, Hermes Trismegistus 'foresaw the ruin of the old religion, the rise of the new faith, the coming of Christ, the judgement to come, the resurrection of the race, the glory of the blessed and the torments of the damned'.[23] Echoes of Genesis in the *Corpus Hermeticum*, probably due to Jewish influence, made some scholars think that Hermes Trismegistus lived before Moses, who was the author of Genesis; mention of a 'son of God' was also seen as a prophetic utterance concerning Jesus.

What was so attractive about the Hermetic philosophy for Renaissance man? The writings of Hermes Trismegistus appealed to him not only because they provided interesting Greek philosophical puzzles, but because they promoted the concept of a person who was such a powerful individual that he could even bend Nature to his will. The ideal Hermetic man is a *magus*, a kind of very powerful magician who could put Nature under his control. Although vulgar medieval magic and sorcery were banned in the Middle Ages, hermetic magic was seen as part of an intellectual and philosophical tradition.

When Renaissance hermetic man spoke of magic, he was more interested in *gnosis*, knowledge, rather than practice. Magic for him was the knowledge of the dynamic network of sympathies and antipathies within the body of living nature, and the influence of these networks on special plants and stones. Although it is true that a Renaissance magician could manipulate material objects to attract the higher immaterial powers – such as the zodiac and planetary conjunctions – with which we are all joined through the soul, a magical spell works in a completely mechanical way, resulting automatically from the correspondences and sympathies that bind living nature together. Plotinus compares the cosmos to a dancer: the changes in the cosmos are like the movements of a dancer's body, and the configurations of the stars and planets are like a dancer's gestures. The stars no more cause the events in the cosmos than the dancer's gestures decide what her body will communicate: the true cause of events and meanings are the cosmos itself and the dancer herself. In brief, this was *spiritual magic*, non-demonic magic utilising the powers of the *spiritus mundi*, even if its subgroup *natural magic* concentrated on the interpretation and manipulation of physical phenomena.[24]

Having understood these occult magical connections, we can manufacture a working talisman, an *imago*, which ideally would be related in form to the higher thing we wished to attract. For example, if we wanted to effect an improvement in the areas of creativity, love, sex or games of chance we would need to catch the attention of the constellation of Leo, which controls these areas. We could obtain an especially conducive gem and carve it with the figure of a lion, which might do the trick.

On the other hand, adepts at Renaissance magic were much more wary about theurgy, using magic to induce the presence of a divine or supernatural being. The impulse may be strictly religious rather than magical, even if the techniques are similar or even identical. In the case of theurgy, the aim is to achieve union with the divine. This magical approach to divinity was emphasised by Porphyry, whose ideas were carried forward into Neoplatonism, although in its later manifestations Neoplatonists began to argue that natural objects have magical power only because they are demonic tokens that are activated automatically, and that therefore there could be no purely natural magic. This was *demonic magic*, which came dangerously close to heresy as it catalogued a hierarchy of intelligences in the sublunary world that might be seen to be personalised and polytheistic.[25]

Hermetic philosophy ruled from 1463 until 1614, when it should have come crashing down. Throughout the century and a half of its heyday, there were always scholars who worked for its demise, arguing that the occult tradition is not an acceptable occupation for sophisticated people. Among these opponents of hermeticism were Marin Mersenne (1588–1648), Pierre Gassendi (1592–1655), René Descartes (1596–1650) and Gabriel Naudé (1600–53). But it was the Protestant thinker Isaac Casaubon (1559–1614) who made all the difference, in the course of a long polemic against the church history of Cardinal Cesare Baronio (1538–1607).[26]

Casaubon rejected the notion that the pagan seers had predicted the coming of Christ, and one of his targets was Hermes Trismegistus. Casaubon subjected the *Corpus Hermeticum* to the sort of close reading that was so common during the Renaissance, and unearthed a number of serious textual problems. First of all, one finds a significant amount of biblical phraseology – both Jewish and Christian – in the texts, especially in Treatises I and IV. Furthermore, the Greek language used there was far too abstract to be as early as the text was supposed to be. There were Greek etymologies and puns, which would be impossible in a supposed translation from the ancient Egyptian. Hermes Trismegistus gives historical references and holds doctrinal views that appeared only at a much later date. Finally, it is astonishing that the hermetic texts were completely unknown to scholars until the Middle Ages.

Therefore, Casaubon concluded, Hermes Trismegistus could not possibly be a contemporary of Moses, and could not be a source of the *prisca theologia*, an ancient tradition of gentile theology older than biblical revelation and confirming it as well. Based on the philological evidence of the hermetic texts themselves, these writings dated not from the time of the ancient Egyptians, but from the first centuries after Christ.[27]

Casaubon was correct, but why did it take until 1614 for someone like him to say it? After all, the technique of close reading and philological analysis had been available at least from the days when Lorenzo Valla (1405–57) studied the Donation of Constantine and proved it to be a forgery. Furthermore, having disproved the antiquity of the hermetic writings, why did Casaubon's discoveries have so little effect? Important scholars such as Athanasius Kircher (1601–80) and Ralph Cudworth (1617–88) carried on as usual, even though most people (and certainly most Protestants) were convinced that the hermetic writings were forgeries. At best, it could be said that despite the text having been written down in the first centuries AD, they were in fact re-edited Greek versions of genuine Egyptian wisdom, but even that argument was rarely made.

According to the Yates thesis, we can now understand why Giordano Bruno (1548–1600) was burned alive at Rome. We had once thought that he was executed for being the great rational champion of Copernicus, Frances Yates tells us, but now we know that his much greater crime was in going too far in defence of the Hermetic tradition. Bruno's interest in heliocentrism was based on his obsession with the Egyptian world picture, which focused on the sun as the source of life and as the chief divinity; Copernicus merely provided some additional mathematical backing for this preconceived idea. Copernicus was aware of hermetic concepts and may have been influenced by them in his own scientific research.[28] Bruno's problem was that he went further by arguing that Egyptian wisdom was not only earlier than Moses but actually superior to that of the Jews as codified in the Bible. The Jews, he argued, 'are without doubt the excrement of Egypt'. Hermetic Egyptian religion is the true faith, not just the ancient theology that foreshadows Christianity.[29]

Yates insists that the origins of modern science should not be sought in the works of so-called rational men, since early modern man was thoroughly religious anyway. We should look at the Hermetic tradition for the wellspring of science, since hermetic writings encouraged man to use his powers for the domination of Nature. Yates reminds us that astrology gradually became astronomy; alchemy became chemistry, and indeed the 'hermetic seal' was a term first used by alchemists who wanted to protect their tinctures from outside agencies. People like Bruno were organised in seventeenth-century England, Germany and France into societies of like-minded people who studied the hermetic texts and advocated the direction of society by an élite of enlightened individuals who possessed scientific (and magical) knowledge. This was the concept of the 'invisible college', which eventually became institutionalised in England as the Royal Society.

There are many examples of how the world of the occult often dovetails nicely with what we would consider serious science. Take the accidental discovery in 1669 of phosphorus by Hennig Brand of Hamburg (c. 1630–92), the isolation of the first element unknown to the ancient world as it is not found free in nature, even if widely distributed in minerals. Trying to make gold, Brand had the idea of letting urine stand for several days in a pot, and then boiling it down to a sort of paste, which was then heated to a high temperature, producing vapours, then drawn down through water and condensed. Contrary to expectations, the resulting product was not gold but a white waxy substance that glowed in the dark – phosphorus. It was an amazing phenomenon, not only because of its glowing properties, but because it burned spontaneously when exposed to air, and so was often called 'cold fire'. Brand sold the secret to the German chemist Daniel Krafft, who went on the road with it, dipping his finger in a mixture of the stuff, and writing glowing words on paper. On 15 September 1677, Krafft performed before Robert Boyle (1627–91) and the Royal Society, and, with the help of Robert Hooke (1635–1703) and some loose talk from the performer, by 1680 the Englishmen figured out how to produce phosphorus themselves. Thus begins the prehistory of the match, which was produced in Britain until 1997, when Bryant & May closed its last factory.[30]

Isaac Newton (1642–1727) was also enamored of Egyptian wisdom, as we shall see in the next chapter, even if it is not clear that he accepted the Hermetic tradition. It was essential for his theory of gravitation to have an accurate measure of the world's circumference, and for that he needed to calculate exactly a single degree of latitude. Newton was convinced that there was no need to send a team of surveyors to plot distances on the ground, as the French were doing. It was rather easier to determine the exact length of an Egyptian cubit, which ancient authors insisted was directly related to a degree of latitude. This information could be obtained from the dimensions of the Great Pyramid, which was always believed (perhaps rightly) to enshrine perfect units of length, area and volume, as well as pi. Sadly, the results of the Pyramid experiment did not fit Newton's calculations, but, instead of scrapping the theory, the great scientist blamed the surveyors instead. As luck would have it, the French astronomer Jean Picard (1620–82) succeeded in 1671 in measuring perfectly a degree of latitude in Sweden, so Newton could prove his theory of gravitation without the Egyptians.[31]

Respect for Egypt continued well into the nineteenth century, and, if the argument of Black Athena has any merit, then it might have continued for much longer.[32] It may have been the worst kind of Orientalist imaginary Egypt, but nevertheless, in contemporary eyes, Egypt had acquired a status almost equal to that of Greece and Rome. In any case, the entire saga of the rise and non-fall of the Hermetic tradition reminds us that we must not see people like Bruno and Newton as modern men in fancy dress, but instead – following the insights of distinguished historians like Johan Huizinga[33] – try to recognise the tremendous mental gap between us and them in order to attempt an understanding of their motives and world view. Newton's laws of gravitation were seen as irrational and un-scientific in his own time, an occult mystical extravagance, and so they were by contemporary standards. Especially in the history of science, teleological history is never helpful.

III

Hermeticism had enormous resonance throughout the entire history of the occult tradition, but we need to go back now to the beginning of the Renaissance in order to complete the picture. We have already talked a bit about the traditional occult sciences – astrology, alchemy and magic. There are also the occult ideologies of prophecy, millenarianism and Christian Kabbalah, whose importance will become even more apparent in later generations. But it is essential to look at the origins of the environment in which occult and esoteric ideas could flourish, in the revival of Greek learning in the Renaissance.

It was the great historian Edward Gibbon (1737–94) who pointed out that the West really missed its first chance in the thirteenth century for a revival of classical Greek language and literature. European Christians during the Fourth Crusade (1202–4) got involved in a Byzantine dynastic dispute and ended up conquering Constantinople and creating a Latin Empire there. It survived until 1261, when Constantinople was retaken by the Byzantine Emperor Michael VIII Palaeologus (1259–82), the first of the Palaeologi, the last dynasty to rule Byzantium. Gibbon was puzzled that

> If a similar principle of religion repulsed the idiom of the Koran, it should have excited their patience and curiosity to understand the original text of the Gospel; and the same grammar would have unfolded the sense of Plato and the beauties of Homer. Yet, in a reign of sixty years, the Latins of Constantinople disdained the speech and learning of their subjects; and the manuscripts were the only treasures which the natives might enjoy without rapine or envy. Aristotle was indeed the oracle of the Western universities, but it was a barbarous Aristotle; and, instead of ascending to the fountain head, his Latin votaries humbly accepted a corrupt and remote version from the Jews and Moors of Andalusia.[34]

Indeed, this lost opportunity is hard to understand, but lost it was.

Nevertheless, it was another invasion that had the side effect of introducing Greek learning to the West, that of the central Asian warlord Tamerlane (1336–1405), who swept down on Anatolia and defeated the Ottoman sultan Beyazit I (1389–1403) on 25 July 1402 at the fateful Battle of Ankara. The Byzantines realised that, unlike the Crusaders, the Ottomans were here to stay, and their defeat was only a temporary reprieve. As the celebrated modern historian Steven Runciman (1903–2000) put it:

> This was the moment when, had the powers of Europe been able and willing to come swiftly together in a great coalition, the Ottoman threat to Christendom might have been broken for ever. But, though the dynasty might have perished, a Turkish problem still would have remained. Historians who blame Christians for missing a heaven-sent opportunity forget that there were already hundreds of thousands of Turks settled firmly in Europe. It would have been a formidable task to subdue them and almost impossible to expel them. Indeed, Timur's intervention had added to their strength; for families and even whole tribes fled before his armies to the safety of the European provinces, the Genoese making a handsome profit out of the ferrying services that they provided. In about 1410, so the historian Ducas believed, there were more Turks in Europe than in Anatolia.[35]

Constantinople sought help from the West, already full of admiration for ancient Greece. The Byzantine world transformed itself and changed its own self-definition. Previously, they had used the word *Hellene* to describe a pagan Greek, as opposed to a Christian; now they started calling themselves Hellenes, even though their Empire was still in theory the Roman Empire. Gradually the word *Romaioi*, by which they had referred to themselves in the past, faded away. In its last decades, Constantinople became a Greek city.[36]

It was here that Cosimo de'Medici came into the picture, less as a projector than the target of a sophisticated marketing campaign. Byzantine Emperor John VIII Palaeologus (1425–48) tried to get support for his doomed city at the Council of Ferrara-Florence (April 1438–July 1439), even agreeing to a union between Eastern and Western Christianity. He took famous Greek scholars with him to Florence, including George Scholarius Gennadius (1405–73) – who would become the first Patriarch after the Turkish conquest and who was very much against any union with the Roman Catholics – and a man we have already met, George Gemistus Plethon (who managed not to sign the agreement of union). We have already seen that Plethon was feted as a leading Platonic scholar, and in fact it was in his honour that Cosimo de'Medici founded the famous Platonic Academy in Florence. Gradually, many leading intellectuals and churchmen left for Italy, so that the Emperor had a difficult time in getting anyone to take over the Patriarchate of Constantinople, especially as three-quarters of the bishops were opposed to the union at any cost.

Here, too, Steven Runciman has some very interesting things to say:

> In the days when historians were simple folk the Fall of Constantinople, 1453, was held to mark the close of the Middle Ages. Nowadays we know too well that the stream of history flows on relentlessly and there is never a barrier across it. There is no point at which we can say that the medieval world changed itself into the modern world . . . Byzantine learning played its part in the Renaissance; but already for more than half a century before 1453 Byzantine scholars had left the poverty and uncertainty of their homeland to seek comfortable professorial Chairs in Italy, and the Greek scholars that followed them after 1453 came for the most part not as refugees from a new infidel rule but as students from islands where Venice still was in control.[37]

Furthermore, Runciman writes,

> The notion of Byzantine scholars hurrying to Italy because of the fall of their city is untenable. Italy had for more than a generation been full of Byzantine professors; and of the two great intellectual figures amongst the Greeks living in 1453 the one, [John] Bessarion [Metropolitan of Nicaea, later Cardinal], was already in Italy and the other, Gennadius, remained on at Constantinople.[38]

It is surprising how many people still believe that the Renaissance began with the Fall of Constantinople to the Ottomans on 29 May 1453, and the reason for this is probably not entirely straightforward.

Which brings us back to Marsilio Ficino, the heroic humanist in Cosimo de'Medici's court who translated the first fourteen hermetic discourses from Greek to Latin at breakneck speed. But Ficino had his sights on even higher things. He was still quite a young man when he translated Hermes Trismegistus, barely thirty years old, and the odd thing is that in later life he hardly mentions Hermeticism and never cites these treatises in his mature writings on magic. Despite its popularity, in many ways the *Corpus Hermeticum* was a big disappointment or, in the words of its modern translator, the treatises were 'banal expressions of a spirituality', and philosophically uninteresting. Perhaps Ficino felt that way, and continued to work mainly on Neoplatonic sources.[39]

Ficino's most interesting work comes in his commentary on Plotinus, especially when there is a discussion in the text about the ability of the soul to animate cult statues, that is to say, making ensouled figures. Ficino wrote a long excursus, which appeared separately in 1489 as *De vita coelitus comparanda* ('on arranging one's life according to the heavens').[40] What we have here is the most comprehensive philosophical theory of magic produced during the Renaissance, and a fascinating interpretation of the concept of mediation between this world and that above.

'Nature is a magician,' Ficino announces, and the philosopher-magician who understands natural science is like a farmer, who 'likewise implants heavenly things in earthly objects by means of certain alluring charms used at the right moment'. The key to this process, he says, is that 'all the power of magic consists in love'.[41] Ficino also deals with Plotinus's idea of 'seminal reasons', the role of the soul as the intermediary between the mind and the body. The *world*-soul has as many 'seminal reasons' as there are ideas in the divine mind and they are connected to an infinite number of species. Therefore, each species through its own seminal reason is connected to a particular divine idea. The philosopher-magician can manipulate species of material objects to attract the higher immaterial powers – such as the zodiac or conjunctions of the planets – with which they are joined through the divine soul and the seminal reasons.

Plotinus thought that all magic was natural magic, that is, simply a realisation of cosmic sympathies, and never discusses the issue of theurgy, the practice of actuating the divine. Ficino was well aware of the two passages in the Latin *Asclepius*, the first known hermetic document, which discusses making statues to attract demons. Although Ficino did not doubt that it could be done, he rejected the technique on religious grounds, citing Thomas Aquinas (*c.*1224–74), who said that pictures might be used as talismans, as long as words were not employed, which would imply actually addressing intelligent spiritual agents, dangerously close to demonolatry.[42]

Ficino also dealt with the concept of *spiritus*, something somewhere between matter and spirit whose function it was to bridge the gap between the material and immaterial elements of man's nature. The Neoplatonists believed that the soul had a spiritual garment, an astral body, which attached itself to the soul as it descended downwards through the stars and planets until it became a fully fledged earthly body. This astral body or spiritual garment was our means to communicate via the imagination with that world above. Many of Ficino's ideas were developed by Henry Cornelius Agrippa von Nettesheim (1486–1535), whose presentation was rather more popular than scholarly, and by his own disciple Johann Weyer (1515–88), who emphasised the temptations of demons and the presence of the Devil in Nature, although he also wrote against the current obsession with witchcraft in his *De praestigiis daemonum* (1563).

After Ficino came other adepts, and their views formed the body of knowledge that remained part of the occult tradition. Historians of the Renaissance certainly no longer have much cause to complain that the occult arts have been either ignored or deliberately written out of the narrative. Nevertheless, it seems sometimes that the supernatural exists on the historiographical plane on two levels, manifest and occult, that is, both confronted and ignored. The figure of Pico della Mirandola (1463–94) is a good case in point. His celebrated 'Oration on the Dignity of Man' (1486) is still read as a tribute to the power of human endeavour in an era that placed the individual centre stage. Modern readers with no knowledge of the occult tradition continue to misread the text as part of an historiographical view that proclaims the Italian Renaissance the birthplace of modern European civilisation. The great nineteenth-century Swiss historian Jacob Burckhardt (1818–97) saw Pico as a modern pioneer, and so did the émigré German professors, many of them Jews, who brought European culture to America after the Second World War.[43]

Amazingly, Pico's 'Oration' was published in English for the very first time only in 1944, in the pages of *View*, an avant-garde Surrealist literary periodical edited by the American poet Charles Henri Ford (1913–2002). *View* appeared in thirty-two issues between September 1940 and March 1947, with William Carlos Williams (1883–1963) and

Aaron Copland (1900–90) on the advisory board, and had an enormous influence in the cultural world of that era, billing itself as 'The Modern Magazine'.[44] That Pico's 'Oration' in English should first appear in *View* is an extraordinary indication of the role that this Renaissance polymath was expected to play in post-war America, and a fine illustration of how his legacy has been distorted.[45]

At any rate, the transformation of Pico into a modern man is especially surprising, since the Neoplatonic and kabbalistic vocabulary virtually jumps off the page. There are references to 'the universal chain', 'Intelligences beyond this world', 'celestial spheres', the *Timaeus*, Hermes Trismegistus, *Asclepius*, and much else. Pico's 'man who, on the ground of his mutability and of his ability to transform his own nature' was so worthy of praise, was not some imaginary Renaissance liberal humanist but a *magus*. Pico's *Oratio* and his *Conclusiones* are in effect advertisements for the occult tradition.

Seven years later, in 1493, Pico was already much more explicit about the place of natural magic and its role in the universe. In his *Disputationes adversus astrologiam divinatricem*, Pico explained that 'the wonders of the art of magic do not exist except by unifying and activating those things sown and separated in nature'. Pico praised the Kabbalah, and posited man as a 'lesser world' that mirrors the macrocosm. If he applies himself to this body of knowledge, Pico argued, human understanding can reach the 'occult alliances and affinities of all of nature'. As is well known, Pico opposed astrology, but not in order to defend the notion of free will: his intent is to explain that the effects of the stars are felt on material objects alone, which certainly include man's body but not his mind. The soul of man, moreover, is in effect a microcosm of the world soul; we are structurally linked to the rest of the universe by means of these 'occult alliances'. In a sense, Pico enjoyed the best of all worlds, both earthly and celestial, in that he saw magic as enhancing human powers, which at the same time were not limited by astrological barriers to the expression of free will. His nephew Gianfrancesco Pico (1469–1533) also saw astrology and natural magic as special threats to religion.

At the other end of the scale from Pico was Pietro Pomponazzi (1462–1525), who argued that the stars rule not only nature, but history itself, including sacred history as told in the Bible. In fact, everything that happens on earth is caused by celestial changes. God himself uses the stars in order to make the jump between There and Here. At the same time, in his *De incantationibus* (1520), Pomponazzi rejected the existence of demons, and insisted on astrological causation for everything that appears to be extraordinary and without rational explanation.

Johannes Trithemius (1462–1516) was another turn-of-the-century participant in the discussion of the principles of the occult, going into rather greater detail. In his *De septem secundeis* ('the seven secondary intelligences'), he described the seven angels governing the seven planets, each one holding power for 354 years and 4 months. History, he argued, was made up of three cycles of these seven reigns, so that time is scheduled to come to an end in the year 2235. He based this prediction on a careful examination of the star Algol (Beta Persei), in the constellation of Perseus. In fact, the name is Arabic – al Ghul – and means 'the demon', the ghoul. The star marks the Medusa's head, and was generally considered to be unlucky. Trithemius believed that when that star reaches a certain point in conjunction with the constellation Gemini, then the world will come to an end. He also wrote on the subject of *Steganographia* ('secret writing'), published only in the early seventeenth century, giving 'conjurations' or codes, various scripts that cause the angels to act on our behalf. Another of his interests was the art of drawing spirits into crystals.[46]

An even greater figure in the history of the occult tradition was Philippus Aureolos Theophrastus Bombastus von Hohenheim, who found it more convenient to go by the name of Paracelsus (1493–1541). To say that he was a Swiss alchemist, physician, mystic and philosopher would hardly do him justice. Paracelsus claimed to have discovered the very building blocks of the universe, and the key to their construction, which was chemistry. He agreed with the generally accepted occult idea of the macrocosm and microcosm, differing in dimensions but not in their inherent natures. Anything true in the laboratory must be equally valid in the universe at large. That being so, Paracelsus argued, we should understand the universe as one gigantic chemical laboratory. Creation itself should be seen as a chemical operation whereby God had distilled the pure from the impure of chaos. For the physician, this meant that the human body – the microcosm – was in its essence a chemical system that could be cured of disease by chemical treatment, by the adjustment of basic components. This was an approach to illness radically different from the prevailing Galenic theory of the four humours whose imbalance caused disease. Paracelsus, on the other hand, believed that disease was caused by living parasites in the body, and therefore used homeopathic remedies and detoxified poisons to make the medicines that killed them. He also invented 'laudanum', the opium-based painkiller so popular in the Victorian era, and ether, which at the very least eased the suffering of his patients.

Paracelsus was fond of citing Malachi 4:5: 'Behold, I will send you Elijah the prophet before the coming of the great and dreadful day of the Lord.' From this we learn, he said, that Elijah would return as 'Elijah Artista', Elijah the Alchemist, who would show us how to turn base metal into gold and bring forward the End of the World. Contrary to popular belief (and the New Testament), this would not be a great battle at Armageddon, but rather a sort of Creation in reverse, a chemical act of separation. The millennium, in other words, would be chemical, an alchemist's utopia.

In one sense at least, Paracelsus reminds us of more modern man, in that he emphasised that we need to observe and to read nature, a process that will give us *scientia*, genuine knowledge. But he believed that everything emanates from the stars and defines the object of study as particular. The identification and manipulation of such earthly products of the heavens is natural or spiritual magic, and helps us to understand God. Mankind stands at the boundary or the centre between the heavens and the rest of creation as a sort of medium. Only mankind could find and unleash the hidden virtues of stones, plants, and even words or pictures. A true *magus* was a kind of saint, whose faith enabled him to direct the forces within nature without any kind of miraculous powers or help from divine intelligences.

Paracelus had a great influence in many fields, not only in medicine, and among his followers was Jean Baptiste van Helmont (1577–1644), who developed these ideas further. Van Helmont identified the *archeus* as the organiser of the specificity of matter, and the motivator of the *semina*, the living and developing seeds within matter that were the active and moving principles that allowed things to develop and to reach their fullness. The world is made up of myriad *semina*, each with its own purpose and activity. What Aristotle thought was a final cause is in effect an efficient cause, a quality that promotes development in a certain predetermined direction. These views were continued by his son Francis Mercury van Helmont (1614–98), and Anne Conway (1631–79). Many of these ideas were synthesised by

Robert Fludd (1574–1637), who combined Neoplatonism with both the naturalist and vitalist traditions.

The most celebrated astrologer of all time, however, was of course Michel de Nostradamus (1503–66). Both of his grandfathers were Jews, but when Provence became a French possession in 1488, his family became Catholic, and in that faith he was raised. He graduated from Montpellier in 1529 as a physician, but from the middle of the century he wrote astrological works, especially the immortal book, *Les Prophéties de Maistre Michel Nostradamus*, which was first published at Lyons in 1555. It consisted of 350 rhymed quatrains arranged in groups of 100, and for that reason often appeared under the title of *Les Centuries*. In 1564, Nostradamus was appointed physician to King Charles IX.[47]

Despite his work being put by the Catholic Church on the Index of Prohibited Books in 1781, it remained and still remains a phenomenal best-seller and a potent source of speculation. Indeed, it is the spectacular malleability of Nostradamus's quatrains that has kept people coming back for unending interpretations. Take the twenty-fourth quatrain in Century Two, for example:

> Bestes farouches de faim fleuves tranner,
> Plus part du champ encontre Hister sera.
> En caige de fer le grand fera treisner,
> Quand rien enfant de Germain observera.

> [Beasts wild with hunger will cross the rivers,
> The greater part of the battlefield will be against Hister.
> He will drag the leader in a cage of iron,
> When the child of Germany observes no law.]

It is no use explaining that the Latin name of the River Danube is 'Ister'; everyone, including Hitler himself, recognised the name of the Nazi dictator thinly disguised therein.[48] Presumably there are people today who are pondering the ninety-seventh quatrain of Century Six:

> Cinq & quarante degrés ciel bruslera,
> Feu approcher de la grand cité neufve,
> Instant grand flame esparse sautera,
> Quand on voudra des Normans faire preuve.

[The sky will burn at forty-five degrees,
Fire approaches the great New City.
Immediately a huge, scattered flame leaps up,
When they want to have proof of the Normans.]

New York City is located at 40 degrees 47 minutes latitude, which is close enough for this prophecy to refer to 9/11, especially as the perfidiousness of the French seems to be implied as well. Many more examples could be given – 348 more, in fact – but the universal applicability of Nostradamus should by now be perfectly clear.[49]

A number of other sixteenth-century thinkers contributed greatly to the occult tradition as it was understood in later centuries. Among this group was Girolamo Cardano (1501–76), the physician from Pavia who went to Scotland in 1551 and treated the bishop of St Andrews for asthma. While in London, he cast a horoscope for King Edward VI. In 1570 he was imprisoned by the Inquisition for heresy, recanted, and went to Rome the following year where he was awarded a pension by Pope Pius V. His most important occult work was *De subtilitate*, in which he argued that all things had a secret 'subtle' property that could be revealed by analogy. Cardano established correspondences between planets, colours and tastes. Black, for example, was connected with bitterness and Saturn; blue was tied to salty taste and Mars.[50] Other contemporary occultists included Christopher Cattan (fl. *c.* 1550), who wrote on 'geomancy', divination by drawing figures on the earth, and Kaspar Peucer (fl. *c.* 1550), whose *Commentarius de praecipiis generibus divinationum* (1553) was an encyclopaedic study of fortune-telling. More important was Gian Battista Della Porta (1550–1615), the Neopolitan physician whose *De humana physionomia* (1586) was the first proper study of physiognomy, the 'science' of judging character from facial features, which would remain important almost until our own times. He also wrote a fifteen-volume encyclopaedia of natural magic.

Bernardino Telesio (1509–88) was another pivotal figure. Telesio saw matter as the receptacle of the divine forms at the conclusion of their struggle of opposites. The primary binary opposition has to do with heat: hot/cold generates all of the other dialectics, beginning with sun/earth, and carrying on to dark/light, dense/rare, mobile/immobile, and so on. Telesio's emphasis on contraries was extremely influential, especially among his fellow Neopolitans Campanella and Bruno.

Tommaso Campanella (1568–1639), like many others, saw the universe as alive, and believed that plants and metals were creatures with sense and feeling. The sun was the source of heat, and therefore of motion, change being the result of the opposition of active contraries. His dictum that 'the world is a feeling animal' would prove to be one of the legacies of the occult tradition.

Among the occultists whose influence has been most persistent was certainly Jacob Boehme (1575–1624), shepherd, shoemaker, linen draper and mystic. He also emphasised the importance of the interaction of opposites, which emanate from and lead back to a primal perfection. Creation in his view was *ex deo*, from God Himself, or more accurately, from an undifferentiated primal unity, which then separated into opposites. Adam at Creation was composed of a perfect balance of opposing qualities: light/dark, male/female. Boehme learned from the hermetic texts of Adam's first love, the Virgin Sophia, the heavenly Nature. Adam fell for the first time when he split into separate male and female components. The expulsion from the Garden was in fact the second Fall.

Boehme's work made much more explicit the fact that the Hermetic Creation is *creatio ex deo* not *creatio ex nihilo* as the Book of Genesis tells us. That is to say, matter was created not from nothing, but from God Himself, in a series of separations or divisions, as light emanated from the primal divine intelligence and divided into light/dark, being transmuted into fire/water, out of which all of the elements separated to become the ordered world as we know it. In this view, there is no fundamental opposition between matter and spirit; divine spirit is the original *prima materia* from which the entire universe sprang.

IV

Lastly, it is important to emphasise the Jewish sources that were part of the occult tradition from the Renaissance onwards. Pico della Mirandola was the first to introduce the Jewish mystical tradition, the Kabbalah, as a Christian tool for biblical analysis. Pico began to study Hebrew, Aramaic and Arabic in the early 1480s at Perugia, and developed an interest in the Kabbalah before 1486, the year of his famous 900 theses, of which forty-seven came directly from kabbalistic sources and a further seventy-two were his own conclusions based on kabbalistic research.

One of his theses proclaimed that 'no science can better convince us of the divinity of Jesus Christ than magic and the Kabbalah'.[51] Indeed, the kabbalistic techniques of gematria (whereby each letter stands for a significant numerical value) and notarikon (whereby words are seen as abbreviations) efficiently served Christian needs. The first three letters of the Hebrew Bible, *beth-resh-aleph*, for example, could easily be an abbreviation for *ben-ruach-av*, son-spirit-father. The placing of the Hebrew letter *shin* in the median position of the tetragrammaton produced an approximation of the name 'Jesus'. As the unspeakable word becomes pronounceable, so too is the ineffable made tangible, the spirit made flesh. Even the vertical arrangement of the four letters of the Hebrew tetragrammaton seemed to produce the stick figure of a man.[52]

Pico's determination to use the Kabbalah in the context of Christian theological discussion promoted the first genuine scholarly interest in this important Jewish tradition, and at exactly the same time that the Jews were being expelled from Spain. Iberian Jews were instrumental in raising the study of the Kabbalah to new heights in Italy, for one of the intellectual effects of the Expulsion from Spain was to turn the entire mystical tradition around from being focused on the origins of the world to the contemplation of its eventual apocalyptic destruction. The flight from Spain was the birthpangs of the messiah, and the Kabbalah was reinterpreted during the sixteenth century to reflect these new pessimistic orientations in an era of holocaust. Pico and his spiritual descendants, then, were latching on to a Jewish philosophy in the process of rapid development, as a contemporary Jewish intellectual movement came to influence Christian theology. Furthermore, since Kabbalah was fundamentally biblical, it was not a *prisca theologia*, and thereby was spared the suspicious scepticism that might be connected with the parallel hermetic interest in the Egyptian tradition.

Pico's influence is justly celebrated. Jacob Burckhardt (1818–97) proclaimed that 'He was the only man who loudly and vigorously defended the truth and science of all ages against the one-sided worship of classical antiquity.' Indeed, 'Looking at Pico, we can guess at the lofty flight which Italian philosophy would have taken had not the Counter-Reformation annihilated the higher spiritual life of the people.'[53] So too did Frances Yates stress Pico's notion of the 'dignity of Man as Magus', noting that the idea of man 'having within him the divine creative power and the magical power of marrying earth to heaven, rests on the gnostic heresy that man was once, and can become again through his intellect, the reflection of the divine *mens*, a divine being.' Through Pico's influence, Johannes Reuchlin (1455–1522) was led to kabbalistic and Hebraic wisdom, which he studied in Italy under Jacob ben Jehiel Loans, the Jewish court physician of Frederick III. Reuchlin produced in 1506 the first Hebrew grammar in Latin, and published the first full treatises on Kabbalah written by a gentile, and, as we shall see, was not without his detractors.[54]

Certainly, to some extent, the fascination that Pico and Reuchlin had for Hebrew and Kabbalah was part of Renaissance eclecticism, the notion that the truth could be found scattered in a wide variety of sources. Yet, more importantly, there was also the belief that the Kabbalah was part of the original divine message given by God on Mount Sinai, and that it had remained pure, untainted by the intervention of the rabbis and their obfuscating Talmud. Those drawn to Jewish sources were in dire need of guidance, such as could only be had from living Jews. Many Jewish rabbis and even medical doctors found themselves sought after by their intellectual Christian neighbours as purveyors of whatever Hebrew knowledge they might have had, no matter how haphazardly it had been acquired. Eventually, their monopoly would be weakened both by the printing of kabbalistical works and by the rise of Lurianic Kabbalah, the new variety of the mystical tradition that was being developed at Safed in Palestine, but for nearly a century Jewish teachers were much in demand.

Pico had his Rabbi Yohanan Isaac Allemanno, whom he met in Florence in 1488 and engaged as his teacher. We know little about Allemanno, but it appears that he was acquainted with Lorenzo de' Medici as well. Allemanno's son Isaac taught Pico's nephew Giovanni Francesco.[55] Flavius Mithridates, that mysterious Sicilian Jew who converted to Christianity, translated kabbalistic texts for Pico, and taught Hebrew, Aramaic and Arabic not only in Italy, but in France and Germany as well. He also translated the Koran into Latin for the duke of Urbino, and preached a sermon before the Pope on the suffering of Jesus.[56]

Indeed, the entire direction of translation was altered. Before the Renaissance, many philosophical treatises were translated into Hebrew by Jews for the use of other Jews. From the beginning of the fifteenth century, on the other hand, Jews and converts from Judaism were translating Hebrew works into Latin or Italian and writing themselves in these languages.[57] It has been argued that (apart from a Judaised Plato), contemporary Jews were little interested in the Renaissance notion of two sources for ancient theology, pagan and Christian, preferring the single path that led from Mount Sinai.[58] Yet the example of Abraham Yagel (1553–1623), physician and tutor to moneyed Jewish families in northern Italy, shows that many Jews were drawn to classical authors, as he compared them with Jewish sources and concluded that his own tradition was superior to that of Greece and Rome.[59] A great scholar like Azariah de' Rossi (*c.*1511–*c.*1578), whose masterpiece *Me'or Einayim* [*Enlightenment of the Eyes*] was written in the mid-1570s, demonstrated that Jews might participate fully in the intellectual ferment of the Renaissance.

The Reformation strengthened this interest and respect for Jewish learning, not so much in the kabbalistic vein, but more directly for the Jews as the guardians of the Old Testament, which came to be seen as their most important historical function.[60] The Word of God was His legacy to mankind, and His word was in Hebrew. The principle of *sola scriptura* demanded a mastery of the Hebrew language. Yet even in rationalistic Protestantism, Hebrew soon acquired mystical signification and kabbalistic intonations. Hebrew was the vernacular of Adam and Eve in the Garden of Eden, when Adam gave names to the animals and there was no poetic ambiguity between words and the things to which they referred. The Bible tells us that God created the universe by speaking, and the language He spoke was almost certainly Hebrew. There was always the hope that one day mankind might recreate this entire technology by a study of the intricacies of the Hebrew language, and thereby take part in the divine process.[61]

During the first half of the sixteenth century, then, both Protestants and Roman Catholics alike were united in the belief that in order to reach full Christian understanding it was necessary to study the Old Testament, the Hebrew language, and even the Jewish mystical tradition, the Kabbalah. The Jews of Europe, and especially in Italy, were therefore given positive associations, and a number of Jewish intellectuals found themselves popular and in demand as representatives of an entire people.

The great humanist scholar Desiderius Erasmus (1469–1536) tried to learn Hebrew 'but stopped because I was put off by the strangeness of the language, and at the same time the shortness of life.'[62] A difficult language at the best of times, one can only gnash one's teeth at the challenge that faced the Christian Humanists and the Renaissance Hebraists at the end of the fifteenth century. The very first Hebrew grammar written by a Christian was the work of Conrad Pellican (1478–1556), the Swiss Protestant scholar, twenty quarto leaves, printed from woodcut blocks at Strasburg. It was an extract from a larger work, and was more an account of how Pellican divined the rules of Hebrew grammar on his own. The little grammar itself is a mere nineteen pages, followed by a sampler of texts from Isaiah and Psalms (five pages), and a short list of Hebrew words, with their Latin and Greek equivalents.[63]

Johannes Reuchlin produced his more substantial *De Rudimentis Linguae Hebraicae*, published in 1506 and printed back to front like a Hebrew book. Reuchlin had to pay Jews to teach him the language, and this first proper grammar in Latin of the Old Testament language was pathbreaking, not least because, as Reuchlin lamented, 'before me among the Latins no one appears to have done this.' Reuchlin's book was part grammar (very briefly done), part dictionary, and part primer: a description of the Hebrew alphabet for absolute beginners.[64] But it was at least a beginning, and his lead would be followed by others, especially Wolfgang Fabricius Capito (1478–1541) and Sebastian Münster (1489–1552).

Ultimately, there were three so-called Jewish sources that entered the occult tradition and remained an influential part of it. The first was the *Picatrix*, the most important textbook of magic, perhaps the largest and most comprehensive of the *grimoires*, the magical handbooks. It was originally written in Arabic in the twelfth century, although the Latin translation is somewhat shorter. The *Picatrix* was widely circulated during the Renaissance period – Pico had a copy – but none of the existing manuscripts dates before the fifteenth century, and it was not printed until much later.

The next text was the *Sefer Raziel*, attributed to King Solomon. There is no mention of this work in a Jewish source before Pico's Rabbi Yohanan Isaac Allemanno. The book itself is a collection of mystical and magical Hebrew excerpts, and it was first published in Amsterdam in 1701, reprinted many times, in large part because of the belief that mere possession of the book protected the owner from fire. Sixteenth-century manuscripts of the *Sefer Raziel* have survived, including matter from *Sefer haRazim*, a collection of magical formulas and angel lore from Talmudic times.[65]

The final source was the *Sefer Maftayach Shlomo* ('the book of the key of Solomon'), a famous book known to Christian intellectuals as *Liber Clavicula Salomonis*. As it happens, most of the book is a translation of material on magic from Christian sources, but the connection to the builder of the temple in Jerusalem gave it a certain Jewish verisimilitude.

V

This was the structure of the occult universe, then, a place of microcosm vs. macrocosm, a single organism that could be controlled from the inside by someone who understood its inner workings, a *magus*. The theory was very largely worked out before 1600, and even groups and individuals operating within that tradition today base their ideas substantially on the same principles. The Renaissance universe of cosmic living creatures seems strange to us, not only for its conception of an existence based on intelligences rather than impersonal laws of nature, but also for the confidence with which it explained the inner workings of God's Creation. This cosmological world would soon collapse, and would become what we would call an occult outlook, inhabited by people who more often than not are thought to have a tenuous hold on sanity. This process was not immediate, however, but developed over the seventeenth century as Descartes and mechanistic explanation seemed to sweep two and a half millennia of natural philosophy and science into the underground of intellectual history.

TWO

Conspiracy and Enlightenment from the Rosicrucians to Isaac Newton

I

The occult tradition is esoteric by definition, and therefore inevitably became bound up with conspiracies both real and imagined, a theme that is at the heart of the subject even in our own day. Of all the various tales of secret societies, the one that had the greatest influence and most widespread purveyance was that of the Rosicrucians.

According to the myth, there once lived a man named Christian Rosencreutz, who was born in 1378 and lived to be 106, dying in 1484. Following instructions left by the dead man, the followers of Christian Rosencreutz opened his tomb in 1604, on the 120th anniversary of his death.[1] They were said to have discovered his uncorrupted body, various artefacts, and texts that summarised his teachings. Rosencreutz was reported to have amassed a lifetime of amazing experiences while travelling around Spain, Morocco, Egypt and the Holy Land. He became adept in mystical lore, mastering alchemy, Kabbalah, Gnosticism, Hermeticism and Paracelsian medicine. On his return to Europe, Rosencreutz was said to have founded with three companions the Society of the Rose Cross, whose members were to have no other profession than attending the sick for free, in the manner of Paracelsus. They were enjoined to travel the world in search of knowledge, and to report annually in person or by letter to the Home of the Holy Spirit, the new centre established by their founder. Members of the Society of the Rose Cross were ordered not to wear any distinctive clothing, but to employ the rose cross as their symbol, and to seek out like-minded people to join the fellowship.

Everything we know about the Rosicrucians comes from three documents that appeared in Germany and Bohemia at the beginning of the seventeenth century. The first was called *Fama Fraternitatis*, published in German at Cassel in 1614, being an invitation to join the order founded by 'Father C.R.C.'. The next text was written in Latin, and published in the same place the following year as the *Confessio Fraternitatis*, telling the stirring life story of Christian Rosencreutz and the order he founded.[2]

The final document was much longer, really a small book, in German, entitled the *Chymische Hochzeit Christiani Rosencreutz* and published in 1616 at Strasburg. The story of the 'chemical wedding' is obviously allegorical, although many of the details were taken from the actual wedding on 14 February 1613 of Frederick V, Elector Palatine of the Rhine, and Princess Elizabeth, daughter of James I, King of England and Scotland. We are told of Christian Rosencreutz and his participation in the royal nuptials, being summoned on Easter Eve, called away from his preparations for communion to journey to a magical castle full of wonders. During his time there as a member of the wedding party, Christian Rosencreutz is initiated into the chivalric order as a Knight of the Rose Cross and witnesses many marvels. At one level, this is the tale of Frederick V's own initiation into the English Order of the Garter, whose symbol is the red cross of St George. But it is also an obvious alchemical allegory, with the bride and bridegroom as a metaphor for portraying elemental fusion, the mystical marriage of the soul, transmutation of the elements, and so on.

Intellectuals all over Europe heard about the Rosicrucians, read their little books, and wanted to join up, if only they knew where. The Rosicrucian craze spread rapidly, typically with the appearance of posters and pamphlets claiming to be from people trying to get in touch with these elusive mystics. According to the philosopher Gabriel Naudé (1600–53), there was an assembly of Invisible Ones dispersed throughout the world in groups of six, who held a meeting at Lyons that involved devil worship and magical transport. These were precisely the characteristics of a contemporary witches' sabbath, and these were exactly the years of the 'witch craze' of early modern Europe. No one could have failed to notice the connection that Naudé was making. Nevertheless, for many people of an occult bent, the exciting combination of esoteric lore, religion and the new experimental science seemed to promise a Rosicrucian enlightenment in an era of general reformation.

At the same time, however, all of this business about a secret society of Rosicrucian adepts was also an elaborate hoax. Behind some of it was Johann Valentin Andreae (1586–1654), the Lutheran theologian and mystic from Württemberg. Some scholars argue that he was the real author of both the *Fama* and the *Confessio*; most believe that he wrote the *Chemical Wedding*; still others note his proclaimed opposition to Rosicrucianism and take it at face value.[3] In any case, he declared that the entire Rosicrucian phenomenon was a '*ludibrium*', a fiction, a joke.[4] Andreae called instead for a '*societas christiana*', real organisations that would become vehicles for the advancement of learning. Some of this comes out in his most famous work, a description of a utopian city he called 'Christianopolis', which Andreae published at Strasburg in 1619. Although he seems to be saying that instead of searching for fictitious Rosicrucians we can establish actual learned societies, there are a number of ambiguous elements in the text, which may or may not indicate his secret sympathy with the entire Rosicrucian enterprise.[5]

The modern historian who rekindled academic interest in the entire phenomenon was Frances A. Yates (1899–1981). While a good deal was known about the Rosicrucians even before she began her investigations, Yates was really the first scholar who plucked them out of the byways of esoteric lore and gave the movement a central role in early modern European intellectual history. Like many others who were interested in the Rosicrucians, Yates also became obsessed with conspiracies and conundrums, and there is no doubt that her critics were justified in saying that in the end she simply went too far.[6] But she was not entirely wrong, either, and it is her narrative that remains the most convincing way of putting the mass of historical details together.

Yates argued that the Rosicrucian writings were not merely an academic in-joke, but were part of a planned propaganda campaign for the political ambitions of Frederick V (1596–1632), a Calvinist prince who hoped to become Holy Roman Emperor. Seven 'electors', each one a sovereign ruler, determined who would serve in that lofty post, and, even if the emperor had always been a Hapsburg since the late thirteenth century, it was never a sure thing. One of Frederick's main campaign promises was that he would support and usher in a new dawn of occult knowledge. If we want to find the true origins of the Scientific Revolution, Yates insisted, it is not enough to look for thinkers in the past who got the science 'right'. We need to study the period when alchemy was evolving into chemistry, and astrology into astronomy. This was the Rosicrucian Enlightenment, and Frederick V was one of its chief publicists.

Let us look at the Rosicrucians in large part through her eyes, and try to keep the factoids in focus. It was exactly during the years between the wedding of imperial hopeful Frederick V to Princess Elizabeth (1613) and the election of the new emperor (1619) that the Rosicrucian documents made their sudden appearance in Europe. Prague was a perfect place to launch a political campaign backed by the occult tradition, but Frederick knew that in 1547 the Bohemian crown was declared hereditary in the house of Hapsburg, so making any claims on that title was a declaration of war against the man who had the best chance of being elected emperor. A previous emperor, Rudolf II (1576–1612), had earlier moved the imperial court from Vienna to Prague and had himself been very interested in occult studies, drawing to the city people like Giordano Bruno (1548–1600), Johannes Kepler (1571–1630) and Tycho Brahe (1546–1601). He also tolerated the Bohemian church, which had remained very independent since the days of Jan Hus in the fifteenth century. Rudolf's successor was his elderly brother Matthias, who died on 20 March 1619.

Matthias died childless, but he had the foresight to fix up the election of his rather distant but very Roman Catholic cousin as Ferdinand II. On 26 August 1619, the Bohemians broke with tradition and offered the crown to Frederick V, Elector Palatine, whose candidacy was supported by many fellow Protestants, including the poet John Donne (1573–1631). On 28 September 1619, Frederick agreed to take the job, already on the road to Prague, where he was soon crowned (4 November 1619) in the cathedral by radical Protestant Hussite clergy. While his illegal rule in Prague lasted, Frederick's supporters promoted him as a sort of occult messianic figure in the epicentre of a spiritual regeneration that would soon spread throughout Europe. But it was a foolhardy adventure, and once the new emperor got organised he sent his forces to crush Frederick's Bohemian army at the Battle of White Mountain (8 November 1620), earning him a dubious place in history as the luckless 'Winter King'.[7] Even worse, the emperor dispatched imperial Spanish troops to occupy the Palatinate, Frederick's home state, forcing him to flee to The Hague where the deposed prince and his family kept their impoverished (but highly intellectual) court. Frederick died of the plague in November 1632 while visiting his ruined Palatinate.[8]

Where did the authors of the Rosicrucian texts get the idea of presenting Frederick as an occult impresario in a campaign to garner support for his imperial claim? One possible source of inspiration was John Dee (1527–1608), an English mathematician and astrologer who in 1555 had been charged and acquitted in Star Chamber of practising sorcery against Queen Mary. When her half-sister Elizabeth came to the throne three years later, Dee found himself much in demand, especially drawing up geographical accounts of the New World.[9] For several years, Dee worked with Edward Kelley (1555–95), another famous occultist, and seems to have met the occult master Guillaume Postel (1510–81) at the University of Paris. Dee and Kelley were in Prague in 1583, trying to have an influence on Rudolf II. Dee travelled through Germany in 1589 and, on 27 June, he was visited by Dr Heinrich Khunrath (1560–1605) of Hamburg, who would write the famous occult text *Amphitheatrum Sapientiae Aeternae* ('Amphitheatre of Eternal Wisdom'), probably published in Hamburg in 1595. Dee's standing was very high in Germany, to the extent that Frances Yates sees the entire Rosicrucian phenomenon as the 'delayed result of Dee's mission'.[10]

Dee's writings are still authoritative if highly obscure texts.[11] He wrote Latin treatises on logic, mathematics, navigation and alchemy, but his most enigmatic work was the *Monas Hieroglyphica* (1564), published abroad in many editions, and dedicated to the Emperor Maximilian II.[12] In fact, the mystical symbol that forms the centre of Dee's work actually appears in the *Chemical Wedding.*[13]

Another important figure who helped spread the Rosicrucian myth throughout intellectual Europe was Michael Maier (1568–1622) of Bohemia, both a devout Lutheran and a scholar of Hermeticism. Maier was invited to Prague by Rudolf II, but eventually made his way to England and joined forces with Robert Fludd (1574–1637), the Anglican physician who was also an occult adept.[14] Maier produced a number of interesting texts, including the 'Secret of Secrets', which interpreted mythology through the symbols of alchemy.[15] Maier also wrote 'Atalanta Fleeing', a description of the art of alchemy with engravings and poetry. The mythological reference was to the race between Hippomenes and his rival Atalanta, in which she lost the contest by stopping to collect the golden apples that he had strewn in her path. Maier interpreted this story as an alchemical allegory regarding mercury and gold.[16] He also defended the Rosicrucians in 1617 with his *Silentium Post Clamores* ('the silence after the shouting'). Maier drifted back to Germany, and disappeared at Magdeburg during the Thirty Years' War (1618–48), which punished central Europe.

While it is not surprising that anyone with intellectual interests should be drawn to the Rosicrucian excitement, there are some unexpected and still unexplained connections. Take René Descartes, for example, who is often credited with being the key figure who moved early modern philosophy from a magical world view to one that was purely mechanical – in other words, abandoning the occult (and ancient) belief that the universe is alive, and replacing it with the modern picture of a world based on scientific causality.[17] Descartes's great friend Marin Mersenne was convinced that the Rosicrucians were real and needed to be opposed, prompting him in 1623 to write a book attacking the entire system of Renaissance magic and Kabbalah, singling out Ficino, Pico and especially Fludd.

Yet the really odd thing is that Descartes himself was no stranger to the Rosicrucian enlightenment. In 1619, he went to Germany and joined the army of the Duke of Bavaria, who was marching against the upstart Frederick in Prague. It was as his soldier that Descartes spent an entire day shut up in an airless room heated by a stove and had the daydream that led him to postulate, 'I think, therefore I am.' Descartes entered Prague with the victors on 9 November 1620, and was well aware of the Rosicrucian excitement, especially when he returned to Paris in 1623 just as his friend Mersenne was denouncing the (imaginary) movement.

Many years later, however, in 1644, he moved near Leiden, largely in order to be close to his great follower Princess Elizabeth of the Palatinate, the eldest daughter of the ill-fated Winter King and Queen. It was to her that Descartes dedicated his *Principia*, in which he describes her as the daughter of the 'king of Bohemia'. In 1649, the Lower Palatinate was restored to Charles Louis, the eldest surviving son of the exiled rulers, and Princess Elizabeth suggested to Descartes that he come with them, but he chose instead a position as philosophy tutor to Queen Christina of Sweden (reg. 1644–54), in whose service he died in 1650.[18] From all of this, one would think that Descartes was deeply involved in the Rosicrucian movement, despite championing philosophical views that deeply damaged the occult world view. Even if this claim is largely unsubstantiated, it is odd that Descartes's life should be so connected to the nobleman who [may have?] inspired the entire Rosicrucian corpus.[19]

Another unexpected possible fellow traveller was Francis Bacon (1561–1626), one of the so-called fathers of the Scientific Revolution. If you are looking for evidence of Rosicrucian leanings, you can find them in his utopian fable *New Atlantis* (1627). Bacon writes of travellers who are given a scroll graced with a stamp depicting a cross and cherubim wings, and describes an official sporting a white turban with a red cross. Although the Rosicrucians are never mentioned by name in Bacon's story, the connection would have been clear to anyone who knew of the occult craze sweeping learned Europe. Bacon is sometimes denied his full marks in the history of science because he rejected both Copernicanism and the theory of the magnet promulgated by William Gilbert (1544–1603). It may be, however, that Bacon carefully avoided those subjects precisely because they were far too much associated with the dangerous areas of magic and witchcraft, and with occult philosophers like Giordano Bruno and John Dee.[20]

A serious proponent of the Rosicrucian conspiracy theory could point to the official history published in 1667 of the Royal Society, England's premier scientific organisation. A striking engraving appears there as the frontispiece, designed by the diarist John Evelyn (1620–1706) and executed by a Bohemian exile named Wenceslas Hollar (1607–77). If we look closely at the figure of Francis Bacon depicted there as one of the forefathers of the Royal Society, we notice that he is shown under an angel's wing, which puts us in mind of the closing words of the *Fama*, '*sub umbra alarum tuarum Jehova*' ('under the shadow of thy wings Jehovah').[21] It is not impossible that the founders of the Royal Society were trying to disassociate themselves from the earlier magical tradition, and built up Bacon as their inspiration, while at the same time giving an esoteric hint about the occult tradition that formed part of their background.[22]

In the official history, the Royal Society is said to grow out of quiet meetings at Wadham College from about 1648. Yet John Wallis (1616–1703), an early founder, claimed that the origins of the Royal Society were to be found in meetings organised at London in 1645, which included Theodore Haak (1605–90), a German refugee from the Palatinate, and John Wilkins (1614–72), then chaplain to the eldest son of the Winter King. Also involved with this group was Samuel Hartlib (1600–62), another German, who settled in England in 1628 after the Roman Catholic conquest of his city of Elbing in Polish Prussia, and who in 1641 sent the Long Parliament a utopia he had written.[23] Even more striking was the participation of Jan Amos Comenius (1592–1670), a Bohemian Brethren (Hussite) pastor who was present in Prague Cathedral when the Winter King was crowned emperor. Comenius fled to Poland (1628) and then England (1641) when imperial forces burned his house, books and manuscripts; he also lost his wife and a child. Comenius also wrote a utopia in which the Rosicrucians appear, but it is a dark work, depicting a labyrinth in which everything is wrong and all efforts lead to nothing.[24]

In the end, groups calling themselves Rosicrucian were actually organised, but only in the nineteenth century. The first of these was probably the 'Societas Rosicruciana in Anglia' (S.R.I.A.), set up in 1866 by Robert Wentworth Little (1840–78) as a Masonic study group with nine grades and special rituals. The renewed Rosicrucians had greater success in America, where two major societies can be found: the Societas Rosicruciana (Society of Rosicrucians), with headquarters in Kingston, New York; and the Ancient and Mystical Order of Rosae Crucis (AMORC) in San José, California.

What are we to make of all this? Perhaps the best thing would be to compare two summations of the Rosicrucian phenomenon. The first comes from a little book entitled, *Bluff Your Way in the Occult*:

> The Order of the Rosy Cross is one of the all-time classic mysterious orders. It was invented as a joke by Johann Valentin Andreae who anonymously published three short books in Germany in the 1610s . . . The place was buzzing with people wanting to lay their hands on this secret knowledge. Later Andreae admitted to the world that it was a gigantic leg-pull but due to the fact that mystics are usually pretty limited in their sense of humour, people have been claiming to have this pool of knowledge in direct succession ever since.[25]

The second, of course, is from Frances Yates:

> 'Rosicrucian' in this purely historical sense represents a phase in the history of European culture which is intermediate between

the Renaissance and the so-called scientific revolution of the seventeenth century. It is a phase in which the Renaissance Hermetic-Cabalist tradition has received the influx of another Hermetic tradition, that of alchemy. The 'Rosicrucian manifestos' are an expression of this phase, representing as they do, the combination of 'Magic, Cabala, and Alchymia' as the influence making for the new enlightenment.[26]

Whether the Rosicrucians represent a phase or a joke gone badly wrong, there is no doubt that our next stage in mapping the development of the occult tradition is the Scientific Revolution, and its most famous exemplar, Isaac Newton (1643–1727).[27]

II

One of the most persuasive myths used to justify the pursuit of science ('natural philosophy') in the seventeenth century was that of the 'two books'. According to this analogy, God in his goodness has provided mankind with two alternate sources of essential information: the written Book of Scripture and the visible Book of Nature. Thus, even someone who is unable to hear or read the Word of God, even a non-Christian, can deduce the basic metaphysical truths by observing the world around him. Such a person should be able to invent for himself at least the 'argument from design', the realisation that the universe is of such complexity that it could only have been *created* by a superhuman intelligence – the story of the '*watch* upon the ground' found in 'crossing a heath', used with such effectiveness in the nineteenth century.[28] The observation of the stars and planets alone should produce the desired realisation that everything has a place and an order in the divine chain of being.

The Newtonian synthesis was predicated on the idea that God had created the universe to operate in accordance with specific *laws*. Certainly, these were laws which He Himself had promulgated in His role as absolute ruler of the universe that He had created. In normal circumstances these laws might be presumed to operate: there was an implicit divine promise involved here. We may never understand the ultimate causes of the laws of nature, as the Aristotelians hoped to discover, but at least the 'efficient causes' might be divined, which would give us power over Nature. Yet at the same time, just as the notion of a 'Book of Nature' derived from the palpable reality of a 'Book of Scripture', so too was the scientific method applicable in reverse to the Bible. Were not both books bodies of divine knowledge to be understood by the same laws of interpretation, just as the same scientific principles were held to apply anywhere in the universe, both in our world and in superlunary realms? Newton saw the Bible, especially the books of prophecy, as a sort of divine puzzle, set for instruction by God Himself, no less than inscrutable Nature around us. Like Nature, the Bible was to be interpreted according to a fixed set of scientific rules, which would prise open the secrets of the Book of Scripture, and reveal to us the past, the present and even the future.

Newton's theological views are so crucial towards understanding his role in the occult tradition that it is worth having a closer look at their antecedents and subsequent developments.[29] As we have already seen, what united the various occult philosophies was the general conception of the universe, of Nature, as an intelligent and living organism. Like the individual human being, there was an organic connection between the different parts of the whole. R.G. Collingwood, in his classic book on the idea of Nature, called this the 'Greek view'.[30] This occult way of looking at the world was replaced, he tells us, by what he called the 'Renaissance view' of Nature, even though we might date the change at a substantially later point. According to this conception, the universe was far from alive: it was a vast machine empty of either intelligence or life, its movements controlled from without. The perceived regularity of this machine, what we would call the 'laws of nature', was likewise imposed by God according to His divine will.

This notion of laws of nature being imposed from without by an omnipotent God was of enormous fertility and importance. It replaced the earlier idea, so powerful in the Renaissance and earlier, that these laws were *immanent* in the structure of reality itself. Everything then was seen as interdependent. If you could fathom the ultimate nature of things, you could figure out their mutual attractions to one another. By this reasoning, what we naively call the 'laws of nature' are really our expressions of the mutual relations between things that we observe around us. The natural world is alive with intelligence, if only we have ears to hear.

This animistic view of the universe is usually thought to have come to an end with René Descartes (1596–1650), who built on earlier foundations laid by the late medieval Nominalists, especially William of Ockham (*c.*1285–*c.*1349). Descartes likened the universe to an efficient machine, instituted and planned by God. He explained that the entire Creation was made up of two components: 1) matter in extension, i.e. in three dimensions; and 2) matter *not* in extension, i.e. God and the human mind, or soul. This distinction was the famous 'Cartesian dualism'. The entire system, Descartes posited, was set in motion by God at Creation and has continued mechanistically ever since, one particle of matter pushing and displacing another. There was literally no place that did not contain matter: the universe is a *plenum.* What looks to us like a *vacuum* is actually filled to the brim by a 'matière subtile', which allows motion to be conducted from A to B and on for ever. There can never be any action at a distance, since any motion must be caused by a mechanistic push. In a very real sense, every breath we take is the latest result of a colossal chain reaction that began with God's divine nudge. Perhaps most important for the future development of physics, Descartes also showed that Aristotle was wrong in having posited two sets of laws, one for earth (sublunary physics) and a rather different one for the heavens (celestial physics). All physical laws, Descartes argued, are universal in God's creation.

Descartes's mechanistic system of physics had the advantage of emphasising God's role as Creator of the universe, and of countering those near-atheists, ancient and modern, who preferred to think that the world and the matter contained therein had existed since time immemorial. The difficulty of Cartesian physics is that a perfect Creator was more than likely to have constructed a perfect temporal machine, which would not require His intervention thereafter. This was the point that Newton's rival G.W. Leibniz (1646–1716) liked to stress. In a sense, Descartes threatened the entire idea of providence, and even the Calvinistic idea of predestination, which obviously was of vastly greater significance in England and in other Protestant countries than it was in France.

By the second half of the seventeenth century, English natural philosophers were already working on a scheme that could save what was good in Cartesian theological physics, without abandoning the world to an eternal doomsday machine. Their brief was to insist that *matter* was created *ex nihilo* as a result of God's will. *Space* and *time*, however, were not created: they are inherent features of God's existence: He is omnipresent (space) and eternal (time). Space and time are the scene of God's creation, which is an act of His will, beginning with the creation of matter. Having created matter as a result of His own volition, it would be inconsistent with His divine character to have simply designed a machine and then let it run eternally on its own steam, as it were. The reason for this is that God is Ruler of the universe, and without having anything to do He would be a ruler in name only, a sort of figurehead. A ruler without a dominion to rule is no ruler at all. God is therefore responsible not only for creating matter and putting it into motion, the two components of all natural phenomena according to mechanical philosophy, but also for preserving the motion in bodies, by constantly intervening in subtle ways to jog things along. Sometimes we call this intervention 'providence'. For seventeenth-century natural philosophers, this was the way the world goes around.

There is a very nice statement of this issue in the Leibniz–Clarke correspondence, where Samuel Clarke (1675–1729) served as the mouthpiece for the publicity-shy Isaac Newton:

> The notion of the world's being a great machine, going on without the interposition of God, as a clock continues to go without the assistance of a clockmaker; is the notion of materialism and fate, and tends, (under pretence of making God a *supra-mundane intelligence*,) to exclude providence and God's government in reality out of the world. And by the same reason that a philosopher can represent all things going on from the beginning of the creation, without any government or interposition of providence; a sceptic will easily argue still farther backwards, and suppose that things have from eternity gone on (as they now do) without any true creation or original author at all, but only what such arguers call all-wise and eternal nature. If a king had a kingdom, wherein all things would continually go on without his government or interposition, or without his attending to and ordering what is done therein; it would be to him, merely a nominal kingdom; nor would he in reality deserve at all the title of king or governor. And as those men, who pretend that in an earthly government things may go on perfectly well without the king himself ordering or disposing of any thing, may reasonably be suspected that they would like very well to set the king aside:

so whosoever contends, that the course of the world can go on without the continual direction of God, the Supreme Governor; his doctrine does in effect tend to exclude God out of the world.[31]

This emphasis on God's divine will as ruler of the universe was not a concept that developed out of a need to Protestantise Descartes. Historians of philosophy recognise this so-called 'voluntarist' position in the writings of Duns Scotus (1265?–1308) and William of Ockham. They too had argued that of God's three fundamental attributes – wisdom, goodness and power – it was the last that was essential for understanding the world that He had created. The English scientists of the later seventeenth century saw that God's will was a force that surpassed the existence of Nature as a mere machine. Without wishing to retreat to the 'intellectualist' position of Aquinas and theologians in the medieval West who spoke of the semi-immanence of natural law, they recognised that there was a greater intelligence at work around us all the time.

This stress on the power of God as an absolute ruler had immediate implications for anyone engaged in the study of the world as we find it. On the one hand, it was true that just because certain phenomena have been observed to occur in the past – such as things tending to fall down rather than up – there was no guarantee that they would continue to do so in the future. God could simply alter the rules of the natural game. On the other hand, God never intended for chaos to be a guiding principle of mundane life. God has established a world of physics within which one may speak of the 'laws of nature', which will continue to apply until the entire framework is altered in a significant way. The stable existence of the natural world is a kind of continuing promise that it would not be destroyed until the End of Days, as God promised Noah after the Flood:

And the bow shall be in the cloud; and I will look upon it, that I may remember the everlasting covenant between God and every living creature of all flesh that *is* upon the earth.[32]

Indeed, God's covenant with Noah, and His other promises throughout the Bible, gave Restoration scientists the assurance that it was worth studying the laws of nature at all, since there is nothing so permanent as temporary, especially when dealing with divine time. While God has it in His omnipotence to turn our physical world upside down without a moment's notice, His commitments in the Book of Scripture put the stamp on what we may observe in the Book of Nature.

The influence of the Bible in Restoration science was therefore paramount: the promises God made in the Book of Scripture reaffirmed the existence of semi-permanent natural laws. On the other hand, what we know of God the absolute ruler of the universe comes from the picture of God we obtain from the Bible. The God of the Old Testament, from Creation, to the Flood, through to Mount Sinai, is a lawgiver. Some of his commandments are not only reasonable but well-nigh universal. But a good number of the 613 biblical injunctions seem to our imperfect human reasoning to be arbitrary and unreasonable, or at least beyond our current capacity to comprehend. Like the laws of nature, we can only hope that, one day, God's divine plan as revealed in the Bible will be somewhat clearer. From our point of view here, what is important is that the Cartesian physics that Newton and his contemporaries like Henry More (1614–87) and Robert Boyle (1627–91) received was crucially modified, not only by means of ideas inherited from the late medieval Nominalists, but more significantly by applying the wisdom of the Bible in the realm of natural philosophy, science. And just as Newton would argue (with Descartes) that there was only one set of rules that applied throughout the universe, both here on earth and beyond the moon, Newton also insisted that the Book of Scripture be opened through the use of a consistent body of rules of interpretation, fixing biblical images with the exactitude of a precision scientific instrument.

III

At this point, it is worth reflecting for a moment on how dangerously close to the history of religion our discussion of Newton's role has come. We recall the inadequate distinction that James Frazer made between magic and science versus religion: the former was about mechanical manipulation while the latter was dependent on the unpredictable will of a divine being. Newton, however, would have brushed that dichotomy aside, arguing that since it was God who determined the rules of that mechanical manipulation, and Himself abided by them (most of the time), then to discuss magic and science without reference to religion was to mistake superficial effects for ultimate causes. For Newton, the divine rule book was the Bible, and he devoted a tremendous amount of time to understanding that supernatural text. Both the Book of Nature and the Book of Scripture were worthy subjects for scholarly research, since both hid esoteric secrets that God had left for humankind to reveal in its growing wisdom.

Ever on the lookout to learn from divine teaching, Newton developed a keen interest in the exact form of the Temple of Solomon. 'The Temple of *Solomon* being destroyed by the *Babylonians*, it may not be amiss here to give a description of that edifice,' Newton explained in his *Chronology*.[33] Newton was taken with the idea that the temple was a building that had God as its architect, and that there were no doubt occult secrets contained in its very proportions and structure. Newton spent a good deal of time trying to determine the exact length of a cubit.[34] He knew that Moses had restored the original religion of Noah, and had also given to the Israelites the basic form of the tabernacle, which would later be recreated by Solomon. Moses installed a perpetual flame in the tabernacle, which itself served as a model of nature with the fire representing the sun in a heliocentric universe:

> Now the rationale of this institution was that the God of Nature should be worshiped in a temple which imitates nature, in a temple which is, as it were, a reflection of God. Everyone agrees that a Sanctum with a fire in the middle was an emblem of the system of the world.[35]

When Solomon built his temple according to the instructions given by God and recorded in the Book of Ezekiel, he also placed a fire in the centre, surrounded by seven lamps representing the seven planets. We were to understand by this that the heavens themselves were God's temple, no less than the building erected by Solomon. When false religion came to dominate the Egyptians, it was similarly reflected in their misunderstanding of nature. The fire in the centre was misconceived, not as the sun, but as some fire in the centre of the earth. The earth was placed in the centre of the planets. It was not by accident that Ptolemy (AD *c.*100-*c.*170) was also an Egyptian, and his false astronomy misled us for over thirteen centuries until the Copernican revolution.

Newton's understanding of science was therefore fundamentally biblical in nature and inspiration. It is not surprising, then, that he should have strong views about the text of the Bible itself, the ultimate esoteric writing. Newton believed that our copy of the Scriptures is defective, not only because of the passage of time, but because various special-interest groups over the centuries had deliberately falsified the original meaning. That being said, Newton still had no doubts that the prophetic portions of the Bible completely reflected God's intentions, and that it was here that the student of His will should direct all attention if he wanted to uncover the secrets of the divine supernatural.

Generally speaking, Newton's attitude to the prophecies was the exact opposite of the esoteric approach to texts that had been so popular during the Renaissance and which would remain an essential tool in biblical interpretation. Whereas the esoteric tradition saw *mystical* truths in even the most commonplace statements in the Bible, Newton's aim was to produce *realistic* interpretations of every supernatural scriptural passage. Newton accepted that the Bible was written in a secret language, so that the text could be seen to be composed of 'hieroglyphs'. But these 'hieroglyphs' could be understood – the code could be cracked – by anyone who took the trouble to learn the key. As Newton himself put it:

> He that would understand a book written in a strange language must first learn the language and if he would understand it well must learn the language perfectly. Such a language was that wherein the Prophets wrote, and the want of sufficient skill in that language is the main reason why they are so little understood . . . they all wrote in one and the same mystical language, as well known without doubt to the sons of the Prophets as the hieroglyphic language of the Egyptians to their Priests, and this language, as far as I can find, was as certain and definite in its signification as is the vulgar language of any nation whatsoever.[36]

Newton went to the trouble of spelling out the rules for the interpretation of prophecy. 'I have thought my self bound to communicate it for the benefit of others,' he explained, 'remembering the judgement of him who hid his talent in a napkin.' This was a matter of great moment, since 'if God was so angry with the Jews for not searching more diligently into the prophesies which he had given them to know Christ by, why should we think he will excuse us for not searching into the prophecies which he hath given to know Antichrist by?' Newton set himself three tasks. The first was to 'lay down certain general rules in interpretation' so as to identify the 'genuine' one. His second task was to 'prepare the reader also for understanding the prophetic language'. The point of this was to make certain that 'the language of the prophets will become certain and the liberty of wresting it to private imaginations be cut of'. His final goal was to compare the different parts of the Apocalypse and reduce its message into 'propositions'.

Newton follows these general remarks with fifteen 'rules for interpreting the words and language in Scripture', set out in almost mathematical form. A number of general points emerge from his analysis. The first almost axiomatic principle is that the reader must 'assign but one meaning to one place of scripture, unless it be by way of conjecture'. In other words, the images of the Bible are so consistent that it is impossible for them to have more than one meaning. In this they are perhaps even less flexible than words in a language. 'Thus,' Newton explains,

> if any man interpret a beast to signify some great vice, this is to be rejected as his private imagination because according to the style and tenor of the Apocalypse and of all other prophetic scriptures a beast signifies a body politic and sometimes a single person which heads that body, and there is no ground in scripture for any other interpretation.

The important thing is to 'keep as close as may be to the same sense of words, especially in the same vision'. That being said, one should 'choose those interpretations which are most according to the literal meaning of the scriptures unless where the tenor and circumstances of the place plainly require an allegory'. There is no necessity to see figurative language in each and every place in the Bible. So, for example,

> if they describe the overthrow of nations by a tempest of hail, thunder, lightning and shaking of the world, the usual signification of this figure is to be esteemed the proper and direct sense of the place as much as if it had been the literal meaning, this

being a language as common amongst them as any national language is amongst the people of that nation.

This last point is crucial: while Newton firmly believed that the Bible was built on allegory, with each figure having one set meaning, which rendered its interpretation similar to learning the vocabulary of a new language, he also warned against the overutilisation of his method:

> He that without better grounds than his private opinion or the opinion of any human authority whatsoever shall turn scripture from the plain meaning to an allegory or to any other less natural sense declares thereby that he reposes more trust in his own imaginations or in that human authority than in the Scripture. And therefore the opinion of such men how numerous so ever they be, is not to be regarded. Hence is it and not from any real uncertainty in the Scripture that commentators have so distorted it; and this hath been the door through which all heresies have crept in and turned out the ancient faith.

Newton followed these general guidelines with more specific 'rules for methodising the Apocalypse'. He insisted that one ought to 'prefer those interpretations which . . . are of the most considerable things. For it was God's design in these prophesies to typify and describe not trifles but the most considerable things in the world during the time, time of the prophesies.' For this reason, Newton thought that when we see references to the whore of Babylon or the woman clothed with the sun, we should prefer an interpretation that relates these figures not to individuals but to 'kingdoms, churches and other great bodies of men', except for a situation where 'perhaps in any case the single person propounded might be of more note and moment than the whole body of men he stands in competition with, or some other material circumstance might make more for a single person than a multitude'. One should also take into account that the Apocalypse was meant to be a continuous narrative 'without any breach or interfering'.

Newton was very concerned that the interpretation of the Apocalypse should not become overly clever: 'Truth is ever to be found in simplicity, and not in the multiplicity and confusion of things.' This, of course, was Newton's belief not only in biblical interpretation, but in his search for general laws of physics, which would be applicable not only in the mundane world, but throughout the known universe:

> It is the perfection of God's works that they are all done with the greatest simplicity. He is the God of order and not of confusion. And therefore as they that would understand the frame of the world must endeavour to reduce their knowledge to all possible simplicity, so it must be in seeking to understand these visions. And they that shall do otherwise do not only make sure never to understand them, but derogate from the perfection of the prophecy; and make it suspicious also that their design is not to understand it but to shuffle it off and confound the understandings of men by making it intricate and confused.

The interpretation of the Apocalypse was in a sense similar to the construction of a mechanical device. One should 'choose those constructions which without straining reduce contemporary visions to the greatest harmony of their parts'. The key is to avoid 'straining':

> For as of an engine made by an excellent artificer a man readily believes that the parts are right set together when he sees them join truly with one another notwithstanding that they may be strained into another posture; and as a man acquiesces in the meaning of an author how intricate so ever when he sees the words construed or set in order according to the laws of grammar, notwithstanding that there may be a possibility of forcing the words to some other harsher construction: so a man ought with equal reason to acquiesce in that construction of these prophecies when he sees their parts set in order according to their suitableness and the characters imprinted in them for that purpose.

But the analogy with machinery should not be carried too far:

> 'Tis true that an artificer may make an engine capable of being with equal congruity set together more ways then one, and that a sentence may be ambiguous: but this objection can have no place in the Apocalypse, because God who knew how to frame it without ambiguity intended it for a rule of faith.

Newton calls on us to keep things simple, and apply a consistent code to the greatest esoteric text of all if we want it to give up its secrets. Only then, he argued, can we hope to understand and even predict the advent of eternity's final supernatural spectacle, the Second Coming of Christ, complete with the raising of the dead and aerial performances by immaterial beings. At the same time, Newton's comparison between biblical code and machine parts turns the mechanistic universe of Descartes on its head. Descartes postulated a fine-tuned world that runs smoothly in accordance with manifest and visible scientific principles. Newton gives us a universe no less orderly, but teeming with esoteric secrets and occult mysteries planted not only in the Book of Nature but also in the Book of Scripture, awaiting the arrival of a textual *magus* who can bring it all to light. We need to give Isaac Newton a much bigger place in the genealogy of the occult, and at the same time to recognise that messianic Christianity, even long before the Fundamentalists, is in a very real and supernatural sense part of the same story.

THREE

Organising the Occult: Freemasons, Swedenborgians and Mormons

I

Freemasonry was the most obvious available model for anyone who wished to organise ancient wisdom into something resembling a practising religion. From its real beginnings in the seventeenth century, Freemasonry provided a new natural religion for people who had become disappointed with conventional Christianity, and sought to place their trust in the world around them. Freemasonry was rich in ceremony and symbolism, and appealed to the scholastic and artistic bent of its educated followers. Its meetings were both secret and social, giving its members the same sort of social community enjoyed by their more conventionally religious brethren in churches and chapels. Far from being radical, the early Freemasons actually promoted a strong constitutional monarchy, moderate social mobility, religious toleration and the importance of Baconian and Newtonian science as tools for making all this happen.[1]

Before they were a semi-secret society dedicated to the occult philosophy, the Freemasons were a professional craft organisation. Trained workmen who understood the art of masonry, of building, were organised like other craftsmen into professional guilds. But masons were often on the move, working on building sites in places far from urban craft organisations. From the fourteenth or fifteenth centuries, a parallel lodge system evolved for these itinerant workers. They made use of secret signs of identification and emphasised internal discipline, promising various kinds of mutual aid. Once the great medieval ecclesiastical building projects came to an end, the Masonic lodges were established on a permanent basis.

From about the middle of the seventeenth century, people who were not and never had been actual masons began applying to lodges for membership. Within a short time, these 'non-working' or 'speculative' masons would found their own lodges without any proper building craftsmen at all. The earliest 'speculative' Freemason seems to have been Sir Robert Moray (1608–73), who joined up in 1641 and eventually became master of his lodge in Edinburgh. The famous occult scholar Elias Ashmole (1617–92) was made a Freemason in 1646 at Warrington in Lancashire.[2] Both Moray and Ashmole were among the founders of the Royal Society and both supported the king in the English Civil War.

On the face of it, this upper-class amateur interest in building-trade organisations seems more than a little odd. The actual working masons, bemused as they may have been by the sight of wealthy learned gentlemen appearing within their midst and pretending to be one of the lads, were no doubt pleased by the sudden influx of cash, which propped up and expanded worthy lodge projects. Curious intellectuals like Elias Ashmole, for their part, sought membership in what purported to be an ancient society going all the way back to the builders of King Solomon's Temple in Jerusalem. Apart from having an inventive and fascinating mythological history, the Freemasons claimed to be in possession of a huge amount of secret lore and esoteric knowledge, much of it based on the Hermetic tradition.

Moreover, the Masonic lodges were fun – good food, plenty to drink and lively company. There was an understanding that all brothers were meeting 'on the level', in an egalitarian atmosphere that may have been nine parts fiction, but was a social fantasy worth promoting. It is hardly surprising, then, that almost from the very beginning there was a strong connection between speculative Freemasonry and the more liberal political party in England, the Whigs. The earliest speculative lodge in London (that we know of) was headed in the 1690s by Sir Robert Clayton (1629–1707), a successful merchant with many radical associates, such as John Wildman (1621–93), the former Leveller; John Toland (1670–1722), the Deist, and a host of less famous Whigs.

At least from the beginning of the eighteenth century, a greater emphasis was placed on the mysterious connection to the temple that Solomon built at Jerusalem. In the Old Testament, the First Book of Kings provides a good deal of basic information:

And king Solomon sent and fetched Hiram out of Tyre. He *was* a widow's son of the tribe of Naphtali, and his father *was* a man of Tyre, a worker in brass: and he was filled with wisdom, and understanding, and cunning to work all works in brass. And he came to King Solomon, and wrought all his work.

One of Hiram's particular works was a pair of pillars, described in somewhat tedious detail as the text continues:

For he cast two pillars of brass, of eighteen cubits high apiece: and a line of twelve cubits did compass either of them about. And he made two chapiters *of* molten brass, to set upon the tops of the pillars: the height of the one chapiter *was* five cubits, and the height of the other chapiter *was* five cubits: *And* nets of checker work, and wreaths of chain work, for the chapiters which *were* upon the top of the pillars; seven for the one chapiter, and seven for the other chapiter. And he made the pillars, and two rows round about upon the one network, to cover the chapiters that *were* upon the top, with pomegranates: and so did he for the other chapiter. And the chapiters that were upon the top of the pillars *were* of lily work in the porch, four cubits. And the chapiters upon the two pillars *had pomegranates* also above, over against the belly which *was* by the network: and the pomegranates *were* two hundred in rows round about upon the other chapiter. And he set up the pillars in the porch of the temple: and he set up the right pillar, and called the name thereof Jachin: and he set up the left pillar, and called the name thereof Boaz. And upon the top of the pillars *was* lily work: so was the work of the pillars finished.[3]

The Hiram described in this text is apparently not to be confused with 'Hiram king of Tyre' who is asked by Solomon to help him build the temple in the first place, and who appears earlier in the First Book of Kings and in 2 Chronicles.[4] In any case, Hiram the architect's stature grew among the Freemasons, who by the 1720s were calling him 'Hiram Abif', using the term that appears in Luther's Old Testament translation of 1532, and which was taken over by Miles Coverdale (*c.*1488–1568) in his early English translation of 1535. The Freemasons now claimed that Hiram Abif was the half-Phoenician craftsman of King Solomon's Temple, who was supposedly murdered after completing his work. The temple in Jerusalem, the only building in the world that boasted God himself as architect, became a central part of Masonic lore and legend, along with metaphors of architectural order, regularity and stability. From this imagery sprang the full-blown myth of the Templars in all its esoteric glory.

The 'Knights Templar' (also known as the 'Poor Knights of Christ and of the Temple of Solomon') was one of the two main crusading military orders, with headquarters successively at Jerusalem, Acre and Cyprus.[5] They were founded in 1118, when a French knight named Hugh de Payens (d.1136) and eight of his companions vowed to protect pilgrims on the road to the Holy Land. Although fighters, the Templars were also monks, pledged to poverty, chastity and obedience. They lived on donations and were quartered in the temple precincts. In 1127, Hugh de Payens returned to Europe in order to seek approval for his experiment, which he received the following year from the Council of Troyes, including *regula* supposedly drawn up by St Bernard of Clairvaux (1091–1153) himself. The fame of the Templars spread rapidly, and they acquired both property and castles, individual poverty being no impediment to collective wealth. But Jerusalem finally fell to the Muslims in 1244, and when Acre was lost in 1291 and their Grand Master killed, the crusading Templars lost their reason for existing. In the meantime, however, an enormous amount of wealth had been accumulated, deposited in their 'temples' at Paris and London, which had evolved to become virtual banking houses.[6] By the beginning of the fourteenth century, the Templars were too ripe a plum to be overlooked.

The French King Philip IV the Fair (1285–1314) decided against resisting temptation and exploited the testimony of a disgruntled ex-Templar to bring charges of sodomy, blasphemy and heresy against the Order. On 14 September 1307, Philip commanded the arrest of all the Templars in France, which was put into effect a month later. According to the Templar legend, two days before Philip issued the warrant, a hay wain drawn by oxen left the temple in Paris, in which was hidden a group of knights led by a certain Aumont. They supposedly escaped to Scotland, bearing a large amount of Templar gold (perhaps created by alchemy), where they were said to have joined a Masonic lodge in Kilwinning. These Scottish Templars recalled the fate of Hiram Abif, who was murdered because he refused to reveal the secrets of the temple, prompting King Solomon to dispatch the *maîtres élus* ('chosen masters') to avenge his death. Now in Edinburgh, this task was given to the new *élus*, to seek the lives of Philip the Fair and his descendants, the kings of France.

Meanwhile, back in Paris, Jacques de Molay (*c.*1243–1314), the last Grand Master of the Templars, on 26 November 1309 retracted his forced confession, and then, two days later, retracted his retraction, effectively confessing his guilt. By April 1310, fifty Templars were condemned to death, and hundreds of others admitted the charges under torture. Pope Clement V accordingly suppressed the Templars at the Council of Vienne in 1312 and gave away their possessions to their rivals the Hospitallers, apart from property in Spain and Portugal where the *Reconquista* against Islam was going strong. The Templars who confessed were pardoned, while the rest were sentenced to life imprisonment.

In the end, Jacques de Molay found his courage. On 19 March 1314, facing his persecutors at Notre Dame, he declared that all of the Templars were innocent of the monstrous charges against them, and that their only crime was to betray the Temple. He was joined in his moment of glory by Geoffroy de Charney, the Templar preceptor of Normandy. Both men were burned at the stake before the day was out. Popular legend has it that, when Louis XVI was executed during the French Revolution, someone jumped on the guillotine platform and declared, 'Jacques de Molay, you are avenged!'

Freemasons in early eighteenth-century England may well have fancied themselves to be descended from the brave Templars whose nocturnal escape in the back of a hay wain facilitated the transmission of secret hermetic and alchemical lore to the British Isles. Yet they were anything but violent or revolutionary. Indeed, the Glorious Revolution of 1688 transformed the Whig grandees who filled the Masonic lodges into national leaders. The highly symbolic rituals of the Freemasons emphasised the orderly Newtonian God, whose universe was an expression of His scientific laws. Even the Whig Prime Minister Robert Walpole (1676–1745) was a Freemason. The ethos of early eighteenth-century Freemasonry emphasised a strong (Hanoverian) monarchy and a liberal Protestant Latitudinarian Church, which would ensure religious peace and Newtonian science, in a social world lubricated by aristocratic patronage.

The expansion of Freemasonry was part of the same development of the public sphere at that time, which included coffee houses, clubs, salons and secret societies. On 24 June 1717, the four London lodges met at the Apple-Tree Tavern and formed themselves into a 'Grand Lodge', and elected their first Grand Master, being Anthony Sayer (1672–1742). The Grand Lodge at first represented only those in London (although the fact that its records date back only to 24 June 1723 makes its early days difficult to document), but by the middle of the 1730s they claimed authority over the entire English movement. Only the first three Grand Masters were commoners, the last being the great John Theophilus Desaguiliers (1688–1744).[7] He was a Huguenot refugee who grew up in England, taking his MA at Oxford and Anglican orders, becoming a fellow of the Royal Society in 1714, and serving as its curator of experiments until his death. He had also been a tutor and chaplain to the Prince of Wales. By all measures, Desaguiliers was a very respectable and learned gentleman, who earned his living by giving courses in Newtonian science. His trademark lectures used machines to demonstrate scientific principles, and under his leadership Masonic lodges became places where English gentlemen would get up-to-date within a context that proclaimed venerable traditions. In 1721, Desaguiliers visited Scotland, and on 15 October 1736 the Grand Lodge of Scotland was founded and a Grand Master elected. The axioms of English Freemasonry as it developed during these years were codified in its 'Constitutions' or 'Old Charges' (1723), largely drafted by Dr James Anderson (1680?–1739), a Church of Scotland minister. Permanent headquarters were acquired in 1776 with the inauguration of Freemasons' Hall. Between the years 1782 and 1843, all of the Grand Masters were members of the Royal Family; between 1767 and 1907, the Freemasons counted among their number sixteen princes of the blood, of whom four became kings. What could be more respectable, even for a society that owed so much to its origins in supernatural speculation?[8]

Certainly in dramatic terms, Freemasonry became much more interesting when it crossed the Channel and came to Europe. 'Anglomania' was a word in use at the beginning of the eighteenth century, at a time when England seemed very much to be a nation of great advance and cultivation. Not only was England already an important political, military and economic power in the 1720s and 1730s, but in philosophy and science the names of Locke and Newton were not to be trifled with.

Strangely, despite the strong Whig connections of English Freemasonry, it was Jacobite exiles after the Glorious Revolution who brought the so-called Craft to France. Many of them were Scottish or Irish and their hostility to the new order in England strained relations with their Masonic brothers in London, despite formal links between the lodges that were established in 1734. At any rate, the key point is that in no place on the Continent did Freemasonry evolve from an operative lodge of genuine working masons; the movement was transplanted fully grown from England.

One of the places to which Freemasonry migrated was Holland. A private lodge was founded at The Hague as early as 1710 consisting largely of publishers and booksellers under the leadership of radical Deist John Toland and including Bernard Picart (1673–1733) and others. But France was the first European country in which Freemasonry became truly popular, from about 1725. By the time of the French Revolution they numbered 20–50,000 in over 600 lodges with perhaps another 50,000 Frenchmen connected to other varieties of the Craft.[9] At some level, Freemasonry appealed to native traditions of *compagnonnage*, rituals and myths used by French craftsmen. But it was also attractive, as in England, to well-educated members of the ruling class: in 1730, Montesquieu (1689–1755) was initiated in London. Unlike its English counterpart, however, French Freemasonry was aristocratic and anti-Newtonian. Its leader in the early years was a Scottish Jacobite exile in France, a Roman Catholic member of the household of the Stuart pretender – Andrew Michael Ramsay (1686–1743).

It would be easy to say that Ramsay's religious philosophy was a mass of contradictions, but it might be more accurate to see him as a very creative syncretist. While he opposed contemporary trends towards natural religion, he was very drawn to Hermeticism. In his important work, *Les voyages de Cyrus* (1727), he made reference to the entire hermetic corpus, although he located its origins not in Egypt but in China. Ramsay rejected the vision of a godless Enlightenment, and fought to ground the new philosophy in France on Christian principles, but true Christianity, which he argued was originally pietist, mystical, mathematical and quietistic.[10] Unlike many of the Stuart supporters, moreover, Ramsay was also in favour of religious toleration and freedom of speech, principles quite useful for what amounted to a political opposition, but which nonetheless made his look like the human face of the Jacobites. John Roberts (1928–2003), the historian of eighteenth-century secret societies, writes that there 'is something of a mystery here: perhaps he was some sort of double agent'.[11] In fact, in 1730 Ramsay was admitted to a lodge in London, which demonstrates that here was one Jacobite whom even the Whigs could tolerate.

Andrew Michael Ramsay was a key figure in the development of esoteric lore because apart from anything else he expanded it into areas where no Freemason had gone before. In 1737, Ramsay delivered a sensational lecture in which he injected a good deal of additional Templar lore into the Masonic mix, just to make matters more interestingly obscure. Thanks to Ramsay, Freemasonry from the 1740s began to develop higher grades beyond the initial three of (1) entered apprentice, (2) fellow craft, (3) master mason. The expanded system was called 'Scottish masonry', even though it had nothing to do with Scotland beyond Ramsay's penchant for constantly bringing that country into the story, and in any case it was invented in France by these Jacobite exiles. It was also at this time that the Freemasons began using painted floor cloths, which depicted the lore of each degree in a symbolic and visual fashion – these later evolved into the famous 'tracing boards' that hang in the lodges.[12]

Ramsay's most fruitful contribution to Masonic lore was the promotion of the 'Royal Arch' theme. The concept itself was not entirely original but seems to have been invented by Christopher Love (1618–51), the Welsh Presbyterian occultist poet who was executed for connections with a Royalist plot against the Puritan government. In his prophecies Love made reference to an engraved pillar of brass erected before the Flood by Adam and Eve's son Seth and the prophet Enoch.[13] The message was millenarian, and fitted very well with the claim by Josephus (AD 37–c.100) that Seth had made pillars of brick or stone to preserve from the elements the knowledge of heavenly bodies and their properties. In Love's day, and long afterwards, Josephus was seen as an authoritative bridge between the two Testaments, which made supernatural tales about Seth and Enoch seem all the more plausible.

In any case, it was from this very fertile material that Ramsay constructed the 'Ancient Rite', whose fourth degree was called 'the Royal Arch', including new Masonic rituals that became increasingly popular, particularly in the United States at the very end of the eighteenth century. The myth in this latest incarnation told the story of

Enoch, who was instructed in a vision to build an underground temple supported by nine arches, and containing a gold plate on which were engraved certain occult characters, also revealed in the dream. Pillars were also erected outside the temple, specifically engineered to withstand the Flood. One was made of marble and engraved with the secrets of the temple. The other was brass and recorded the principles of the liberal arts, with special emphasis on the practice of masonry. Thousands of years later, it was said, the architects of King Solomon's Temple discovered Enoch's arched temple deep underground, and were thus able to regain for humankind the knowledge of these important mysteries.

The story of Enoch was also useful because it emphasised the perfect knowledge of all things enjoyed by Adam in the Garden of Eden, science that was now being passed on via the mysteries of the Freemasons. Adam's good son Seth understood these weighty matters and transmitted them faithfully to the generations that followed. His evil son Cain, however, poisoned the well of knowledge and introduced numerous errors and falsehoods into the mix. It was Seth's descendant Enoch who had the foresight to preserve this knowledge for humankind before the Flood by engraving its principles and building the arched vault. Traces of this body of knowledge were handed down from Noah to his progeny, but only when Solomon's architects uncovered Enoch's buried plates was true wisdom restored. According to the myth of the Royal Arch, this 'primitive' Freemasonry was passed down through medieval guilds until the rise of speculative Freemasonry, through whose society it was once again made available to those who would take the trouble to enter into its mysteries.

Unfortunately, even the Royal Arch theme made little difference to the attitude of the Roman Catholic Church towards the entire phenomenon of Freemasonry. The Pope excommunicated all Freemasons in 1738, but the authority of the Church was so weakened in the blazing sun of the Enlightenment that nobody really paid attention. Since 1738 there have been fifteen separate papal condemnations of Freemasonry and secret societies in general. Roman Catholics were forbidden to become Freemasons and were threatened with excommunication if they did. Freemasonry was condemned by Pius IX (1846–78) in his notorious 'Syllabus of Errors' (1864) and the Catholic Church refused to let go of this particular bone until 1884, when it issued the last encyclical against it.

Nevertheless, it was just this dichotomy between the true ante-diluvian wisdom of Seth and the falsifications of Cain that opened the door to a proliferation of competing Masonic rites and practices in France and Germany as each group claimed to possess the purest variety. An independent 'Grande Loge Nationale de France' was created in 1756, theoretically replaced on 27 December 1773 by the 'Grand Orient de France', but in fact the two organisations existed side by side until the French Revolution put an end to Freemasonry altogether.

The first properly constituted Masonic lodge in America was established in Boston on 30 July 1733, although many Englishmen from the New World had already been admitted to the Craft in London and elsewhere. We know of the increase in Masonic activity during the Revolutionary War, thanks to the efforts of General Charles Rainsford (1728–1809), who was in charge of shipping German troops from Hesse to aid the British war effort. Rainsford was a keen student of hermetic lore and a great promoter of higher-degree Freemasonry.[14]

Curiously, however, there is a crucial bit of evidence about the origins of Freemasonry in North America, which has been entirely ignored by historians of the Craft, perhaps a bit unhappy with the consequences of admitting its authenticity. There is a document from Newport, Rhode Island, which reads as follows:

Th^s y^e [day and month obliterated] 165[6 or 8, not certain which, as the place was stained and broken; the first three figures were plain] W^{ce} mett att y House off Mordecai Campunall and affter Synagog W^{ce} gave Ab^m Moses the degrees of Maconrie

The original paper itself now appears to be lost, or at least hidden. N.H. Gould of Newport, sometime Master of St John's Lodge, Newport, and then member of the Grand Lodge of Rhode Island, holder of the 33rd Masonic degree, found the document in 1839 (when he was not yet a Mason) among some old papers in a chest that had belonged to a deceased relative, who was a great-great-granddaughter of John Wanton (1672–1740), the governor of Rhode Island, 1734–40. When the Grand Lodge of Massachusetts requested in 1870 to see the document, Gould refused to show it, but gave the text that was printed in the Lodge's *Proceedings* for that year.[15] Two years later, however, the Revd. Jacques Judah Lyons (1813–77) seems to have been allowed to see the paper, although the text as he copied it is somewhat different, while retaining the essential information and the date 1658.[16]

A good claim for the authenticity of this document can easily be made. Samuel Oppenheim (1859–1928), in his article on the early connections between Jews and Masons in the United States, suggested that the author of the text was Moses Pacheco, one of the grantees of the deed for a Jewish cemetery at Newport dated 1677.[17] Oppenheim notes that the administration of Moses Pacheco's estate was granted in 1688 to Caleb Carr (1616–95), whose son's widow was the sister-in-law of John Wanton, the eighteenth-century governor of Rhode Island who seems to be the link between Gould and the seventeenth-century Jews and Masons of Newport. Caleb Carr was himself made governor of Rhode Island just before his death, and Pacheco is mentioned in his will. Indeed, the cemetery deed itself was found in the same group of papers by N.H. Gould, whose son, at the suggestion of Samuel Oppenheim, presented the document to the American Jewish Historical Society at the beginning of the twentieth century.[18]

As might be expected, this Masonic document has placed historians of both Freemasonry and American Jewry in an unenviable position. Instead of jumping at a credible piece of evidence for the existence of speculative Freemasonry in the New World as early as 1656 or 1658, long before the formal establishment of Masonic lodges there, Masonic historians have instead chosen to ignore the possibility, no doubt reluctant to claim Jews as the first-known Masons in America. Such early connections between Jews and Masons would hardly be surprising, given the strong mystical, hermetic and even kabbalistical associations of the movement in the seventeenth century, and the many later Jews who became Freemasons.[19]

So too do Jewish historians shy away from accepting this Masonic document, no doubt because of an unwillingness to confirm that the first Jews in English America were Freemasons, so shortly after the establishment in 1654 of the first enduring Jewish community in the New World at Dutch New Amsterdam.[20] On the other hand, the temptation of finding such early evidence of Jewish residence in New England has been too strong to resist, and one finds Morris Gutstein, the historian of Newport's Jews, falling back on the argument that 'all authorities on the subject agree that 1658 is the date the Jews first came to the shores of Rhode Island as a group'.[21] Even Samuel Oppenheim, who believed that the document was genuine, ultimately relies on the fact that 'families long resident in that town, whose ancestors were in the colony from almost its foundation, and in a position to give them correct information regarding the date of the first arrival of the Jews there, fix the date as 1657 or 1658.' Oppenheim goes on to say that the 'general trend of knowledge on the subject of the early settlement of the Jews in the United States goes to confirm that date', even though he admits that 'contemporary record proof is lacking aside from the document quoted by Gould and the information derived from the cemetery deed just referred to, and also the date in Gould's possession, upon which he based his statements regarding the early arrivals'.[22] In Oppenheim's view, this 'lack of contemporary proof arises from the loss of many of the records of Newport and the colony prior to 1700'.[23]

Certainly by the late eighteenth century, it was undeniable that an increasing number of Jews were becoming involved in Freemasonry: from 1793 there was a 'Jewish' lodge in London, although since anyone who believes in a Supreme Being can become a mason, the lodge has never been officially recognised as such.[24] Jews were very active in French lodges after the Revolution, although in Germany a specifically Jewish lodge, 'L'Aurore Naissante', was founded in Frankfurt in 1808 under the Grand Orient in Paris, which only hardened the hearts of the native German lodges against them, although the situation had its ups and downs there in the nineteenth century.[25]

A number of very colourful branches of Freemasonry developed in the eighteenth century. Antoine Joseph Pernetty (1716–1800), a former Benedictine monk who had already passed through Swedenborgianism, in 1779 formed an extremely mystical and millenarian group in Berlin, which became known as the 'Avignon Society' after being transported to France six years later. Another Masonic group on the fringes followed the philosophy of Louis Claude de Saint-Martin (1743–1803), who organised his people in southern France as the 'juges ecossais' in the 1750s. When these Martinists spread to Paris ten years later, they were known as the '*élus cohens*', preaching a Swedenborgian doctrine in which special rituals could conjure up spirits carrying messages from the non-material world, and holding out the promise that we might rejoin that ghostly dimension of which we had once been a part. The Martinists were more than a branch of Freemasonry; they were almost a religious sect, a universal religion whose tenets were supposedly passed down in history through the biblical heroes Enoch, Melchizedek and

Eli. The Martinists were enlightened – *illuminés* – a term that came to be applied to many others who found their place in the occult tradition.[26]

The Martinists in many ways were an emblematic occult group because they demonstrate the special symbiotic relationship that existed between these newly invented mystical movements and mainstream Freemasonry. The very respectability of Freemasonry in the mid eighteenth century dulled its attraction for many people of an occultist turn of mind; they were drawn instead to groups like the Avignon Society or the Martinists. On the other hand, the fraternal organisation of Freemasonry provided an administrative model that could hardly be improved upon, with its lodges and oaths of eternal secrecy. The price the Freemasons paid for this marriage of inconvenience was that the link between Freemasonry and the occult was strengthened, and the boundaries between different groups were blurred in a most confusing way. Furthermore, it is interesting that a number of new occultist sects – such as the Avignon Society – tended to originate in Germany (or Switzerland) and then migrate to France, which made them seem like a sinister foreign invasion.

Sometimes the tracks went both ways, as in the case of Karl Gotthelf, Baron von Hund (1722–76), who in 1755 introduced the new 'Scottish' rite to Germany. Within a decade it came to be known as the 'Strict Observance', supposedly older than the English system and going all the way back to the Templars (of course). Hund's leadership was challenged by Johann August Starck (1741–1816), who took the Strict Observance even deeper into occult philosophy, a process continued by the key French representative of the school, Jean Baptiste Willermoz (1730–1824).

But undoubtedly the two most notorious eighteenth-century occultists were Saint-Germain and Cagliostro. In a famous exchange, Voltaire (1694–1778) wrote to Frederick the Great of Prussia (1740–86): '*C'est un homme qui ne meurt jamais et qui sais tout.*' He received the clever reply, '*C'est un comte pour rire.*' Claude-Louis, Comte de Saint-Germain (1707?–1784?) appeared in Paris in about 1743; he was arrested in London in December 1745, where he was celebrated as a musician, giving recitals on the violin and the harpsichord. His luck improved in about 1758, when he offered his services to King Louis XV (1715–74) in Paris as an expert in dying, claiming also to possess more occult chemical skills, including the ability to produce the elixir of life and manufacture the philosopher's stone. In the early 1760s, Saint-Germain was sent on various diplomatic missions for Louis XV, travelling to Holland (where he got into some kind of trouble and had to flee to London), then to Russia and Belgium, where he met the Italian adventurer Giovanni Casanova (1725–98) and turned a coin into gold for his edification. He spent more time in Germany in the 1770s, staying at the court of Frederick the Great in 1776 under the name of Count Welldone, proposing various chemical projects. Saint-Germain died in 1784 at Schleswig, at the court of the landgrave of Hesse, where he was manufacturing paints.[27]

Saint-Germain's career, however, only really began to take off after his death. Over the centuries, people claimed to run into him in the most unlikely places. Madame Blavatsky (1831–91) revealed to her followers at the end of the nineteenth century that the count of Saint-Germain was in fact only a single incarnation of the soul that had various identities including Proclus, Roger Bacon, Christian Rosencreutz, Francis Bacon, and many others.[28]

A more accomplished occult imposter was known by the name of Count Alessandro di Cagliostro (1743–95).[29] He was born Giuseppe Balsamo in Palermo and worked as an assistant to an apothecary in a monastery, where he acquired knowledge of chemistry and medicine, which would be essential in his later career. He also seems to have travelled extensively in the Mediterranean. In 1768, he married a woman named Lorenza Feliciani, and together they toured Europe, where Balsamo posed as an alchemist, physician and necromancer, selling love potions and elixirs of youth. Most interestingly, Balsamo exploited the late-eighteenth-century fad for all things Egyptian, and claimed to be the purveyor of an even more esoteric brand of 'Egyptian Freemasonry'. By the summer of 1771, he was in London, living at New Compton Street; then back in Paris; and then in 1776 once again in London. It was at that moment in England that he brought together the experience of a lifetime and reinvented himself as Count Cagliostro, the founder of a new and improved variety of Freemasonry, although he himself never learned English. Cagliostro billed himself as the 'Grand Cophta' of the Egyptian system.[30]

Even more wonderfully, Cagliostro was a key player in the 'Affair of the Diamond Necklace' (1784–6) through his friendship with the Cardinal de Rohan (1734–1803), ambassador to Vienna and archbishop of Strasburg. Rohan was the victim of a confidence trick put in motion by the Comtesse de la Motte,[31] who told him that she had been asked by Marie Antoinette (1755–93) to get the cardinal to purchase a diamond necklace for the queen, to be delivered to the comtesse. A woman purporting to be Marie Antoinette came to Rohan secretly after dark and silently gave him a rose as a token of their arrangement. The diamonds having been procured and delivered, Rohan told the tale to his friend Cagliostro, who noticed something very odd about the queen's receipt of delivery. It was signed 'Marie Antoinette de France', whereas the queen herself always thought that to sign anything more than her name was pointlessly redundant. The receipt was a forgery, and the jewellers were unable to collect the bill.

Marie Antoinette herself – the real one – was furious when she found out that her name had been used in a diamond scam that exploited her well-known obsession with jewels. She had everyone involved arrested – la Motte, Rohan and even Cagliostro, who had been seen wearing diamonds around town. The girl who had impersonated the queen was soon found, but Cagliostro convinced the authorities that his were old jewels unconnected with the heist. Rohan himself was arrested, tried and finally acquitted in 1786, whereas the comtesse was condemned to be whipped, branded and imprisoned, but managed to escape. Cagliostro fled to London, and Rohan was exiled from France. The 'Affair of the Diamond Necklace' was of great use to the opponents of Louis XVI (1774–92), since it showed his queen to be spending huge sums of money on jewels while her people went hungry.[32]

Cagliostro was arrested by the Inquisition in Rome on 27 December 1789, rightly accused of being a notorious Freemason. He was imprisoned in the Castel Sant'Angelo and tried to talk his way to freedom by offering his interrogators juicy gobbets of information about his Masonic past. He spoke of the Templars, the Strict Observance and the Freemasons, claiming to be privy to a secret plan to accumulate funds and use them first to overthrow the French monarchy and then the papacy.[33] Cagliostro's confessions hardly improved matters: on 7 April 1791 he was condemned to death for heresy, but a compassionate pope imprisoned him for life in the fortress of San Leo (Montefeltro) in the Apennines. Cagliostro spent his remaining years until his death on 26 August 1795 in a cell without a door, entered by an opening in the ceiling.[34]

In the year before the French Revolution and immediately afterwards, there was a widespread rumour that people of occult persuasions were meeting secretly in clandestine organisations and plotting to overthrow the existing order of things.[35] This belief was not entirely a fabrication, but fear of rather harmless groups like the Freemasons was blown out of all proportion by the scandal over the Illuminati of Bavaria. The elements in this episode would provide the basis for an avalanche of writings down to our own day purporting to unmask the conspiracies and secret connections of shadowy figures who control the governments of Europe.[36]

The Illuminati began with a professor of canon law at the University of Ingolstadt in Roman Catholic Bavaria, named Adam Weishaupt (1748–1830). Like many professors then and now, Weishaupt was a keen academic intriguer, and would eventually be sacked from his post not for his occult activities but in a dispute over selecting books for the library. Weishaupt had the idea of forming a group of fellow academics who could do battle against the Jesuits and Freemasons in the university. The new group was founded on the basis of an existing student society on 1 May 1776, devoted to the idea that they could study and eradicate false opinions through a graduated reading programme, and then obtain positions of power. They called themselves the 'Order of Illuminati', and Weishaupt took the code name of 'Spartacus'. A wider organisational base being required, the Illuminati decided to infiltrate the local Masonic lodge. As historian John Roberts explains, 'The Illuminati were the first society to use for political subversion the machinery of secret organisation offered by Freemasonry and through the Craft they began again to spread.'[37]

The first lodge 'conquered' by the Illuminati was at Munich in 1779, and from that centre they set up fake daughter lodges that purported to be Masonic. The Illuminati spread to Italy, France, Bohemia and Hungary; by 1782 they had almost three hundred members, many of them rich and famous. By the early 1780s, the secret was out, and government reaction was to throw the baby out with the bath water. In 1784, and again the following year, the Bavarian Elector forbade his subjects to become members of any secret society at all, which should have spelled the end of the original Illuminati, except for the fact that some lodges reorganised as 'reading societies'. In 1786, a raid on the house of a member uncovered a good number of Illuminati documents, including some written by Adam Weishaupt himself. Selections were published in 1787 and reprints followed.[38]

By the time the French Revolution began in 1789, then, not only was there a myth of conspiratorial secret societies, but a reality as well, as life imitated art. More importantly, the Freemasons were now hopelessly implicated, having in their history gone the entire gamut from staunch advocates of a Whig constitutional monarchy to being fellow travellers of esoteric political revolution. Current eighteenth-century elements were melded together into a mixture of Templar, Masonic and occult lore, supposedly directed at the subversion of conventional society. All that was required was for someone to write it up.

The man who accepted the challenge was Augustin, abbé de Barruel (1741–1820), in his *Abrégé des mémoires pour servir à l'histoire du jacobinisme*, published in French at London in 1797–8, with an English translation immediately following.[39] The abbé Barruel returned to France after 1802 when Napoleon came to power and his book was already a sensation. What Barruel did was to put all of the plots and programmes of esoteric Europe together into a single thesis, showing that the Jacobins were part of a united great scheme to overthrow not only the French monarchy but all of religion and society. The first volume was an account of the various philosophies, followed by Volume Two, being a detailed study of Freemasonry, arguing that the French Revolution originated in a conspiracy of the Freemason Duke of Orléans (1747–93) to seize the French throne. Volume Three was an introduction to the Illuminati, amplified by Volumes Four and Five, which detailed their infiltration of Freemasonry, and included accounts of Saint-Germain, Cagliostro and, finally, Immanuel Kant (1724–1804), whose philosophy was said to be identical to that of Weishaupt.

Another key text was written by Johann August Starck (1741–1816), who published an account of the *Triumph der Philosophie im 18. Jahrhundert* (Frankfurt, 1803). Starck's work was on the same massive scale as Barruel's, but quite naturally he laid greater emphasis on the German background to the French Revolution, dwelling on the Illuminati.[40] Finally, there was a book by the notorious Joseph Marie, comte de Maistre (1754–1821) entitled *Quatre chapitres inédits sur la Russie*, written in 1811, but published by his son only in 1859. The last 'chapitre' was 'De l'Illuminisme', and covered the subject in lurid detail.[41]

One bizarre result of all this literary activity about Freemasons, secret societies and plots to overthrow civilisation as they knew it is that some of the readers of these texts became very keen on the violent revolutionary ideas condemned by Barruel and the others, and actually wanted to join an insurrectionist secret society or two. The fear of secret societies created some of them where they did not exist, in a sort of reprise of the Rosicrucian excitement of the seventeenth century.

This pattern can be seen quite clearly in the life of Filippo Michele Buonarroti (1761–1837), described by his modern biographer as 'the first professional revolutionist' and by the Russian anarchist Mikhail Bakunin (1814–76) as 'the greatest conspirator of the century', which presumably was meant as a compliment.[42] Buonarroti's career began when the French set up the first Italian civil administration after their invasion, and put him in charge, only eventually to send him back to Paris to sit in prison on a corruption charge. One of his fellow prisoners there was a radical writer named François Noel 'Gracchus' Babeuf (1760–97). Buonarroti taught his prisoner protégé how to turn revolutionary ideas into reality, especially by manipulating the masses into adopting the views imposed on them by a revolutionary élite.

The so-called 'Babeuf Conspiracy' began in October 1795 shortly after leaving prison, when they founded the 'Society of the Panthéon,' in which revolutionary matters were discussed, and under whose auspices insurrectionist material was published, some of it written by their colleague Sylvain Maréchal (1750–1803). On 8 May 1796, the 'comité insurrecteur' of the group met and agreed on a plan to seize certain public buildings and key officials. Two days later, about 200 conspirators were arrested, including Buonarroti and Babeuf. They were put on trial, but in the end only Babeuf and one other were executed.

Undaunted, Buonarroti continued his career as an active revolutionary, in Italy, Switzerland, Belgium and even in Paris, where he died in 1837. But it was his book about the Babeuf Conspiracy, published at Brussels in 1828, that turned the failed insurrectionist into a martyr in the struggle for equality.[43] Buonarroti was really the last living promoter of the myth of the secret societies, and with his death the entire concept was relegated to the world of paranoid fanatics.

That the last representative of this myth should be an Italian with French connections is rather ironic, because it renders Buonarroti so very emblematic. In Italy, secret societies arose against the background of Napoleon's Italian campaign of May 1796, which for most Italians was their first real contact with the French Revolution. Every Italian state was invaded by French soldiers between 1796 and 1799, with some long periods of occupation. The most important secret society in Italy was the Carbonari, originally a confraternity of charcoal-burners as their name implies, which went through a process similar to the history of the Freemasons as speculative amateurs took over an operative organisation. The first Carbonari lodges were set up in Italy about 1808, very similar to the Freemasons but with only two grades, master and apprentice. It is very hard to say if the Carbonari had any particular philosophy at all, but their very existence and the manner of their expansion make them an interesting part of eighteenth-century esoteric history, and an appropriate backdrop to Buonarroti's intrigues. Incomparably more influential, however, were the Swedenborgians, who flourished at exactly the same time, in England.[44]

II

Among the followers of Emanuel Swedenborg (1688–1772) was the poet William Blake (1757–1827), but by 1790 he already had severe doubts. 'Thus Swedenborg boasts that what he writes is new; tho' it is only the Contents or Index of already publish'd books,' Blake complained. He went on:

A man carried a monkey about for a shew, & because he was a little wiser than the monkey, grew vain, and conciev'd himself as much wiser than seven men. It is so with Swedenborg: he shews the folly of churches, & exposes hypocrites, till he imagines that all are religious, & himself the single one on earth that ever broke a net.

Now hear a plain fact: Swedenborg has not written one new truth. Now hear another: he has written all the old falshoods.

Blake was cross partly because in his view Swedenborg's theology was not completely original: 'Thus Swedenborg's writings are a recapitulation of all superficial opinions, and an analysis of the more sublime – but no further.' Indeed, he wrote, 'Any man of mechanical talents may, from the writings of Paracelsus or Jacob Behmen, produce ten thousand volumes of equal value with Swedenborg's, and from those of Dante or Shakespear an infinite number.'[45] Blake was quite correct to point out his lack of originality, but it was precisely Swedenborg's ability to revitalise and summarise the occult tradition that made him so influential.

Swedenborg made at least eleven visits to England, living at Cheapside but avoiding public notoriety, not so much because of his opinions, but because of poor English made even more opaque by a speech impediment. By the time Swedenborg died in London in 1772 and was buried in the Swedish Church, he had delineated an impressive philosophy more suited to an intellectual school than a radical religious sect.

Emanuel Swedenborg was born in Stockholm in 1688, the son of a man distinguished in Swedish theology. His father changed his name from Swedberg when ennobled in 1719, in recognition of a career that would include the post of court chaplain, professor of theology at Uppsala, and bishop of Skara. His son Emanuel studied at Uppsala until 1709, and then spent five years abroad, in England, France and the Netherlands, where his primary aim was to learn of the latest advances in mathematics and natural science. Swedenborg seems already to have come under the strong influence of Eric Benzelius (1675–1743), his brother-in-law. Benzelius was mystically inclined, visiting the great philosopher G.W. Leibniz (1646–1716) at Hanover in 1697, moving on to Francis Mercurius van Helmont (1614?–99) to sort out the Pythagorean Kabbalah, and travelling to London to meet with the members of the Philadelphian Society. Returning to Sweden in 1700, Benzelius turned more seriously to the study of Hebrew, using the services of Moses ben Aaron of Cracow, a converted Jew who now called himself Johann Kemper. The two men talked of founding a pansophic college in Sweden, and worked on a kabbalistic interpretation of the New Testament and on annotations to Philo, the Jewish philosopher of Alexandria in the first century AD. The young Swedenborg lived in Benzelius's house from 1703 and was surrounded by this combination of arcane scholarship and mystical lore.[46]

Swedenborg came to England in 1710, despite the tense political relations between the two countries in the run-up to the Jacobite rebellion, the 'Fifteen. He there came under the wing of the Swedish ambassador and may have been involved in revolutionary Jacobite and Freemason circles. He had the opportunity to meet, and may have met, such luminaries as William Penn (1644–1718) and Lord Bolingbroke (1678–1751). Swedenborg seems to have visited Dr Jean Esdras Edzardi, whose family had converted many Jews in Hamburg by devising a convincing mixture of Kabbalah and New Testament. It has sometimes been claimed that Swedenborg himself joined a Freemasonic lodge, but as its politics would have been Jacobite, all records were destroyed after the failure of the rebellion in 1715.

With perfect hindsight, Emanuel Swedenborg's activities during those years do look like an ideal preparation for the occult views that he would hold in later life. But here too it is possible to exaggerate. When in Hanover shortly thereafter, he attempted to pay a call on Leibniz but found him away in Vienna. In this, Swedenborg was following in the footsteps of his mentor Benzelius, but the discussion that they would have had would not only touch on esoteric matters, it can be sure. Also puzzling are Swedenborg's relations with Rabbi Haim Samuel Jacob Falk (1708–82), the so-called 'Baal Shem of London', a mystical magician whose exploits made him a well-known figure in late-eighteenth-century London. In his common-place book Falk makes a reference to a certain 'Emanuel, a servant of the king of France', which may refer to Swedenborg with his Jacobite leanings.[47]

In any case, it was at Wellclose Square, near Falk's house, that Swedenborg had his first vision of Christ, on 7 April 1744. His life could never be the same again, although it was only a year later that his mission was divinely confirmed. Swedenborg spent his remaining twenty-seven years dedicated to purely religious questions, publishing about thirty books, all in Latin, mostly anonymously. That in itself points to the nature of Swedenborgianism as an esoteric philosophy more than a mass movement, and his theology should be seen in a more serious context than has often been the case. We need first, therefore, to examine his mature philosophy, especially in light of the fact that he claimed to have received his ideas from personal visits to the spiritual world rather than from mere reflection.

Swedenborg's goal was no less than to discover the substance that held the universe together. This task was complicated by his insistence that the world had more than a simple natural or physical aspect. He tinkered with the idea of magnetism, which would later become the preferred medium of Franz Anton Mesmer (1735–1815), but finally settled on the notion that the common bond was some sort of electrical vibration or very fine indestructible substance.[48] This latter object, he believed, was the soul of man, which not only is immortal but has actual dimensions. The spiritual and natural worlds, therefore, were merely different manifestations of the same substance. (Here Swedenborg is revealing himself as a student of Descartes's body/soul/mind debate, and indeed his thought is thoroughgoingly Cartesian.) Influenced by his near-interlocutor Leibniz, Swedenborg elaborated that all life derived from a single source, but it was organised on different levels or *series*: natural/physical, rational/living/intelligent/moral and spiritual. Every particular object in the universe, therefore, had its own place or *degree* in each of these three series. Parallels between the series were called *correspondences*. Swedenborg was also influenced by the platonic idea that none of the series could survive without a constant *influx* or spiritual input from God, the spiritual sun. Each degree or item in each series enjoyed a particular influx, which passed through the spiritual series, down through the rational, and finally the natural series. As a result, each item or degree on the spiritual plane had its exact counterpart with another item on the rational and natural planes, united by the fact that they were each touched by the same influx. These axioms had platonic consequences, so that man's love and wisdom found perfect expression in the essence of God on a higher plane. Swedenborg was also therefore anti-trinitarian: Christ is God in human form, and at the crucifixion God retained some human aspects, which He maintains on His highest plane, making Him a sort of divine human.[49]

Swedenborg saw himself as commissioned to announce the seventh and last revelation to a New Church, the very same body described in the Book of Revelation as the New Jerusalem. This organisation commenced in 1757 when Jesus returned to earth, not as an inferior fleshly messiah, but this time interiorly and spiritually, by opening the eyes of men to the true meaning of the Bible. Swedenborg's Bible was somewhat shorter than usual, as he excluded thirty-seven of its sixty-six books on the grounds that they were bereft of any spiritual meaning. Nevertheless, he had great respect for the surviving scriptures, and his colossal *Arcana Coelestia* was in effect an extended and unfinished commentary on Genesis and Exodus. But it is in his last work, *The True Christian Religion* (1771), that we get the clearest epitome of his thinking on this subject, as on most others, and understand why he was such an important figure for the occult tradition.

Here Swedenborg approaches the difficulties in extracting holy truth from the Bible:

> The natural man, however, cannot thus be persuaded to believe that the Word is divine truth itself, in which are divine wisdom and divine life; for he judges it by its style which reveals no such things. Yet the style of the Word is a truly divine style, with which no other however lofty and excellent can be compared. The style of the Word is such that it is holy in every sentence, in every word, and sometimes in every letter; and therefore the Word unites man to the Lord and opens heaven.

The kabbalistic tincture of this sentiment needs hardly to be spelled out. Indeed, Swedenborg's theory of correspondences, when specifically applied to Scripture, takes on more than a superficial kabbalistic tone:

> That everything in nature and in the human body corresponds to spiritual things is shown in *Heaven and Hell.* But what correspondence is, has been hitherto unknown, although it was perfectly understood in the most ancient times; for to the men of that time the science of correspondence was the science of sciences, and was so universal that all their manuscripts and books were written by correspondences. The book of Job, a book of the ancient church, is full of correspondences. The hieroglyphics of the Egyptians and the myths of antiquity were the same. All the ancient churches were representative of spiritual things; the ceremonial laws of their worship were pure correspondences; so was everything in the Israelitish church. The burnt-offerings, sacrifices, meat-offerings and drink-offerings were correspondences in every detail; so was the tabernacle with everything in it; and also the feasts of unleavened bread, of tabernacles, and of first fruits; also the priesthood of Aaron and the Levites and their holy garments . . . Moreover, all the laws and judgements relating to their worship and life were correspondences. Now, because divine things manifest themselves in the world by correspondences, the Word was written by pure correspondences; and for the same reason, the Lord, because He spoke from the divinity, spoke from correspondences. For everything from the divinity

flows into such natural things as correspond thereto; and these outward things then conceal in their depth the divine things called celestial and spiritual.[50]

Here, in this long extract, we see some of the key elements of Swedenborg's mystical biblical interpretation. Like the Jewish and Christian Kabbalists, he thought that there was another esoteric meaning to the scriptural word. Like the Deists and many others before them, including Maimonides (1135–1204), Swedenborg championed the notion of 'accommodation', arguing that God had adapted His message to the ability of His hearers to comprehend what he was saying, but reserving a deeper meaning for those with greater spiritual insight. Like the radical biblical critics Joseph Mede (1586–1668) and John Hutchinson (1674–1737), Swedenborg advocated a prolonged close reading of the biblical text by the use of techniques that had been vouchsafed to him alone, in order to undermine the surface reading and penetrate to the divine truths lurking below.[51]

According to Swedenborg, he had 'been informed' by the spirit world that 'the men of the most ancient church, which existed before the flood, were of so heavenly a genius that they conversed with the angels of heaven; and that they had the power to do so by correspondences'. As a result, whenever they saw something on earth, they were able to determine its corresponding form on the spiritual plane. Swedenborg also claimed that 'Enoch and his associates (Gen. v 21–4), made a glossary of correspondences from the speech of the angels, and transmitted this knowledge to posterity'. This fact was to have enormous consequences. 'As a result,' Swedenborg explains, 'the science of correspondences flourished in many kingdoms of Asia, particularly in Canaan, Egypt, Assyria, Chaldea, Syria, Arabia, Tyre, Sidon, and Nineveh, and was thence communicated to Greece, where it became mythical, as may be seen from the oldest Greek literature.' We can therefore see, Swedenborg explains, that:

Religion has existed from the most ancient times, and the inhabitants of the earth everywhere have a knowledge of God and some knowledge of life after death; but this is not from themselves or their own intelligence, but from the ancient Word, and afterwards from the Israelitish Word. From these two Words religion spread to India and its islands, through Egypt and Ethiopia to the kingdoms of Africa, from the maritime parts of Asia to Greece, and thence to Italy. But, as the Word could only be written symbolically, that is, by mundane things corresponding to and therefore signifying heavenly things, the religion of the Gentiles became idolatrous, and in Greece mythical; and the divine properties and attributes were looked upon as so many gods, dominated by a supreme deity called Jove, possible from Jehovah. And they had a knowledge of paradise, the flood, the sacred fire, and the four ages, from the golden age to that of iron (Dan. ii 31–5).

In orthodox fashion, if somewhat eccentrically, Swedenborg thereby postulates the Hebrews as the source of eternal wisdom, a little lower than the angels.[52]

Swedenborg also sought to account for the evident degeneration of the Hebrews from purveyors of a divine monopoly to the superstitious Jews with whom his contemporaries were familiar. In his view, in 'the course of time the representative rites of the church, which were correspondences, began to be turned into idolatry and also into magic'. It was not by accident, but by 'the divine providence of the Lord' that the Israelites lost the 'science of correspondences', which was eventually 'amongst the Israelitish and Jewish nation totally obliterated'. Since their worship consisted entirely of correspondences, this was a crucial loss, and what had originally been a symbolic and pure worship gradually became superstitious. Not only the Jews, but other ancient peoples began to confuse the symbol with the thought expressed and, for example, worshipped images of calves and oxen, forgetting that originally they were powerless objects that merely signified 'the affections and powers of the natural man'. Fortunately, the 'knowledge of correspondences remained among many eastern nations, even till the coming of the Lord'. This is why the wise men came from the East, bearing symbolic gifts. Indeed, the 'ancient Word, which existed in Asia before the Israelitish Word, is still preserved among the people of Great Tartary', a fact that was personally confirmed to Swedenborg by 'spirits and angels who came from that country'.[53]

According to Swedenborg, the 'science of correspondences, which is the key to the spiritual sense of the Word, is to-day revealed, because the divine truths of the church are now being brought to light'. He had been taught this fact during his sojourns in the spiritual world, and indeed his description of the role of the Bible there was truly fantastic. In that higher place, he recalled,

> The Word is kept in the shrines of the angelic temples and shines like a great star, sometimes like the sun with a halo of beautiful rainbows; this occurs when the shrine is first opened. All the truths of the Word shine, as I learnt on seeing that, when any verse is written on paper and thrown into the air, the very paper shines in the form in which it has been cut; so that spirits can by the Word produce various shining forms, even those of birds and fishes. But what is still more wonderful, if any person rubs his face, hands, or clothes against the open Word, so as to touch the writing, his face, hands, and clothes shine as if he were standing in the brilliance of a star. This I have often seen with wonder; and it showed me why the face of Moses shone when he brought down the tables of the covenant from Mount Sinai.

On the other hand, sometimes an opposite process occurs in the spiritual world, for:

> if any person obsessed by falsities looks at the Word lying in its sacred place, darkness shrouds his eyes, and the Word appears to him black and sometimes as if covered with soot; while, if he touches the Word, a loud explosion follows, and he is hurled into a corner of the room, where he lies for a time as if dead. If any one obsessed by falsity writes a passage from the Word on a piece of paper and throws it in the air, a similar explosion follows, and the paper is torn to pieces and vanishes; the same thing happens if the paper is thrown into the nearest corner. This I have often seen.

While somewhat kabbalistic in flavour, then, Swedenborg's attitude to the biblical text was, if possible, even more occult, based on what he believed himself to have witnessed in the spiritual world.[54]

Swedenborg's view of the Hebrew language itself is rather original and unique. 'There was once sent down to me from heaven,' he revealed, a piece of paper covered with Hebrew characters; the letters were curved as among the ancients, not straight as they are to-day, and had little extensions at the top. The angels with me said that each letter had a complete meaning which was largely expressed by the curves and their extensions . . . They told me that writing in the third heaven consists of letters variously curved and inflected, each of which has a special meaning; that the vowels I and E are replaced by Y and EU, and that A, O, and U have a specially rich sound; that they do not pronounce consonants roughly, but smoothly, and for this reason some Hebrew letters had dots in them to indicate a soft pronunciation. They added that hard sounds are used in the spiritual heaven because the truth of that heaven admits of hardness, whereas the good of the Lord's celestial kingdom, or third heaven, does not.

Like the Kabbalists, Swedenborg also thought that the very words and letters of the Bible had mystical powers, which awaited deciphering by the *illuminati.*[55]

Certainly, it is very difficult to argue with a man who claimed to 'have been permitted by the Lord to be in the spiritual and natural worlds at one and the same time; thus I have conversed with angels as with men, and have become acquainted with the state of those who after death pass into that hitherto unknown world'. Heaven, he revealed, was constituted as a *homo maximus*, a giant man, with the parts of his body consisting of angels. Swedenborg testified that he had 'conversed with all my relatives and friends, also with departed kings, dukes and men of learning, and this continually for twenty-seven years'.[56] Sometimes entrance was gained by the technique of taking one breath every thirty minutes.

Apart from spirits and angels, some other sources for Swedenborg's interesting biblical theology suggest themselves. Chief among these is Jacob Boehme (1575–1624), the German mystic who became notorious for stressing the dualism of God, which required evil as a complement to His divine goodness. Boehme's most famous disciple in Swedenborg's time was William Law (1686–1762), whose influence on the Methodist Wesley brothers, and whose connection with the Philadelphian Society of Jane Lead (1623–1704) and Francis Lee (1661–1719) is well documented.[57] Law became a fellow of Emmanuel

College, Cambridge, in 1711, but at the death of the last Stuart monarch Queen Anne, he declined to swear allegiance to the new Hanoverian dynasty, and was therefore classified as a 'non-Juror'. Law was disqualified both from a university post and from church livings, and therefore served ten years as a private tutor in the family of the celebrated historian Edward Gibbon (1737–94). Law's books became very influential, emphasising a God of love rather than wrath, and proclaimed that we can be reborn and redeemed through union with God.[58]

The leadership of the English Behmenists fell to Swedenborg after Law's death in 1762. Swedenborg denied having read Boehme, but there were some very obvious similarities with Law's theology. Among these was the notion that God emitted an 'eternal nature', which was His very body and being, and which was in effect the spiritual world. This higher reality had its counterpart in a lower celestial realm made up of the opposing principles to be found in God's nature – fire/light, good/evil, and so on. This was the angelic world. Below this was an even lower existence, the material world, created by the rebellion of the angels, in which the dualities were no longer in balance. Nevertheless, connections and analogies between the three different levels existed and remained in operation. Man himself, originally an angel, was now a denizen of the material world, and was in effect a spirit trapped in a physical body. Jesus, by taking human form, injected a divine element into mankind, providing the hope of his restoration to the spiritual existence. Law, unlike Boehme, was optimistic that this reunion would eventually occur, Hell would be destroyed, and all mankind would be saved. Swedenborg's ideas were so similar that he appealed to many old Behmenists, such as Thomas Hartley (1709–1784), whose influence on Samuel Taylor Coleridge (1772–1834) is well known.[59]

Swedenborgianism thus began as a philosophy and only gradually mutated into a sect, largely through having been picked up by the rector of a Manchester parish named John Clowes (1734–1831), a former member of the Wesleys' 'Holy Club' who had begun with the writings of William Law and chanced upon Swedenborg's Latin works in 1773. Clowes remained within the bosom of the Anglican Church, even refusing a bishopric in 1804, and introducing only as much of Swedenborg's views into his sermons as he thought the market would bear. The new gospel spread throughout Lancashire, at the same time that the Methodists were making important inroads in this area. Both groups began within the Established Church, and only later, and very reluctantly, declared their independence. Furthermore, the Methodists, like the followers of Swedenborg, placed great emphasis on non-rational religious revelation, convulsions rather than visions, but nevertheless part of the same mixture of folk traditions and respectable religion.[60]

John Wesley (1703–91), the founder of Methodism, was himself in two minds about this strange alliance. He wrote about Swedenborg in his journal:

> Any one of his visions puts his real character out of doubt. He is one of the most ingenious, lively, entertaining madmen that ever set pen to paper. But his waking dreams are so wild, so far remote both from Scripture and common sense, that one might as easily swallow the stories of 'Tom Thumb' or 'Jack the Giant-killer'.

Later on, after reading 'that strange book', Swedenborg's *Theologia Coelestis*, Wesley added:

> It surely contains many excellent things. Yet I cannot but think the fever he had twenty years ago, when he supposes he was 'introduced into the society of angels', really introduced him into the society of lunatics; but still there is something noble, even in his ravings.[61]

Similarly, there was a certain amount of migration between the two groups at the popular level, especially as the Methodist chapel became too much of a symbol of respectability for many Lancashire workers to stomach. Swedenborgianism also appealed to groups outside the Methodist sphere of influence, such as those in the Huguenot community, attracted no doubt by Swedenborg's connection with Freemasonry and other European occultists, such as the French Prophets.

Like the Methodists, the Swedenborgians found themselves drawn almost inevitably into institutionalisation, although one group opposed to separation gathered around Jacob Duché (1738–98), Chaplain of the Asylum for Female Orphans in Lambeth. The first step was the foundation in about 1783 of the prophetically named 'Theosophical Society', which read and discussed Swedenborg's works. The great man's manuscripts had been shipped back to Sweden after his death, where they could not be published, but were now beginning to appear in greater numbers, thanks to Clowes's determination and effort. The very word 'theosophical' was redolent of Freemasonry, and promised a combination of biblical study and fashionable Neoplatonism. One prominent member of the Theosophical Society, General Charles Rainsford, was heavily involved with Kabbalah, Freemasonry, alchemy and astrology, as we have already seen.[62] Continental Freemasonic circles were informed, aware and excited by the existence of Swedenborgian reading groups in England, and these contacts were extended during the 1780s. Rainsford was an important link, and he promoted the Swedenborgian visitation at the Congrès du Philalethes, organised by the French speculative Freemasonic lodge of the Amis Réunis in 1784–5, and again in 1787. Swedenborgian representatives attended the meeting in 1784, which had primarily been called to unite Freemasons on the Continent and to agree on some common elements of doctrine. As a result, some of the leading lights there came to England to see the new philosophy for themselves, including the Marquis de Thomé, Count Tadeusz Grabianka (1740–1807), and even Cagliostro.[63]

This occult tinge was given a somewhat more Christian and less 'pagan' motif in 1785 when, on the advice of the Marquis de Thomé, the Theosophical Society renamed itself the 'Society for Promoting the Heavenly Doctrines of the New Church designed by the New Jerusalem in the Revelation of St John'. One of the virtues of the new name was that it preserved a central element of Swedenborgianism's attraction, its almost Romantic emphasis on the spiritual, as opposed to the arid rationalism of the Enlightenment, which had so influenced the Established Church. Far from being a theological system opposed to empirical science, Swedenborgianism might be seen as a truly pioneering creed, extending the principle of experimentation to the spiritual realm. Most believed that there were spiritual forces at work in our material world; the Swedenborgians were the first to do something about it, and, unlike the Methodists, were not so quick to ascribe these powers to the Devil.[64]

By 1788 it was clear that the followers of Swedenborg would have to open their own chapel, and the Society was renamed the New Church. Ordinations and baptisms soon began, and the group settled into the traditional pattern of English Dissent, without giving up the occult impulses that created it in the first place. Swedenborg's voluminous writings assumed the character of a third testament, and the man himself was increasingly venerated. The New Church underwent a crisis when Swedenborg's *Conjugal Love* was translated into English and published in 1794, for in this book he declared that a man could take a 'concubine' to slake his lust, or even leave his lawful wife if he found a more fitting spiritual partner at a later stage. They were also accused, by the abbé Barruel and others, of being with the Deists one of the illuminist sects that were indirectly responsible for the French Revolution and the political disturbances of the age. In claiming that Christ had already returned, the post-millennial theology of the Swedenborgians was said to alert believers to manifestations of his renewed glory, which most obviously could include revolutionary political change.[65] By the turn of the century, the Swedenborgians were insisting that the Second Coming was spiritual rather than political, and did not involve a restructuring of national governments, but by then their period of dramatic expansion had ended.

The Swedenborgians became more respectable and even more intellectual, especially under the leadership of Samuel Noble (1779–1853), who was chiefly interested in publishing accurate translations of the founder's writings. This more philosophical inclination, which probably would have been blessed by Swedenborg himself, ensured that they would never become a truly popular sect. Not only were the holy books in Latin, but it took a very long time before more simplified versions of Swedenborg's writings appeared. In any case, Swedenborg's theology was contemplative more than congregational or social, and was unsuited for the sort of passionate community that the Methodists engendered. Even if northern congregations attracted a greater number of artisans and people who were locally active, in the south Swedenborgianism would retain a decidedly intellectual tinge.

III

Swedenborgianism was enormously influential in nineteenth-century England and America, and, as we shall see, provided a crucial theological and philosophical underpinning for the later development of spiritualism and psychic research. The issues that Swedenborg raised and brought to the foreground were also crucial in the emergence of the first genuine indigenous American religion, Mormonism, which was a fascinating synthesis of Hermeticism, Gnosticism, popular magic and concepts from the radical Reformation that Luther tried so hard (and so unsuccessfully) to suppress. Despite the efforts of some historians of Mormonism to claim that its origins lie within the opposition to New England Puritanism, it will be perfectly clear that the content of its theology is rooted in the American occult tradition, especially through the medium of Swedenborgianism.[66]

The story of the Mormons, the Church of Jesus Christ of Latter-day Saints, has been told many times. On 22 September 1823, a teenager named Joseph Smith (1805–44) was visited by the angel Moroni, son of Mormon, outside the town of Manchester in New York State. The angel showed him gold plates on which were written the Book of Mormon in the Reformed Egyptian language, but Smith was not allowed to take them away at that time. Exactly four years later, on 22 September 1827, Joseph Smith was presented with the tablets, and given a pair of spectacles fashioned out of the biblical Urim and Thummim set in silver, through which the Reformed Egyptian appeared as American English. Egyptian or not, gold was gold, so Joseph Smith and his wife Emma (1804–79) got out of town with the angel's tablets hidden in a barrel of beans.[67]

The very discovery of these engraved tablets was not thought to be impossible. Joseph Smith and many of his neighbours near and far were active participants in a tradition of divining for buried treasure, and indeed a young man of the same name was said in 1826 to have claimed possession of a 'seer stone', which enabled him to see through the earth.[68] Ancient documents were being discovered all the time, such as the Ethiopic Apocalypse of Enoch (1 Enoch), which was brought to Europe in 1773 and was published in English in 1821, two years before Moroni came to New York State.[69]

Joseph Smith worked three years on the translation of the text, sitting in half of a room divided into two sections by a blanket hung from a rope, with a scribe on the other side taking down dictation. The resulting text was printed in 1830 in Palmyra, New York, 'by E.B. Grandin for the author', under the title of *The Book Of Mormon: An Account Written By The Hand Of Mormon, Upon Plates Taken From The Plates Of Nephi*.[70] Although later editions would be set up typographically like the Bible, in two parallel columns, this first edition looks like an ordinary book, 'By Joseph Smith, Junior, Author and Proprietor'.[71]

The Mormons have been attacked from the very beginning as being the victims of a book club gone spiritual. As early as 1834, Eber D. Howe (1798–1885) argued in a book entitled *Mormonism Unvailed* that Smith plagiarised a science-fiction story written in about 1810 by one Solomon Spaulding (1761–1816). Howe conducted extensive interviews, transcripts of which are published in the book, and came to the conclusion that this document, entitled 'Manuscript Found', ended up in the hands of one of the first Mormons, Sidney Rigdon (1793–1876), who set up a bogus religious sect with the help of Oliver Cowdery (1806–50), a witness and scribe of the Book of Mormon, using Joseph Smith as the front man.[72] The accusation has refused to die, and reverberates in cyberspace with all of the surviving documents. Although Spaulding's original 'Manuscript Found' has never been located, a very similar document turned up in Honolulu in 1884, apparently entitled 'Manuscript Story'. It seems that when Howe sold his business in 1839–40 to a certain L.L. Rice, this 'Manuscript Story' was found among his papers, and was taken by Rice when he moved to Hawaii. In 1884, Rice entertained there James H. Fairchild, the president of Oberlin College in Ohio, who thought that this amusing story was Spaulding's famous work. Rice made a copy for himself, and sent the original to Oberlin, where it remains today. The text of 'Manuscript Story' is not the Book of Mormon by any means, but it is very heavily marked, and is clearly a draft. It may be that 'Manuscript Found' is much closer to the Mormon holy book, but as long as it is lost, it remains rather an insubstantial stick with which to beat the Church of the Latter-day Saints.

A more recent and far more deadly attack on Mormon scripture was the work of a master forger named Mark Hofmann (b.1954), whose counterfeit signatures of Washington, Lincoln, Butch Cassidy, Emily Dickinson, Billy the Kid, Mark Twain, John Brown, Jack London and Al Capone still turn up in auction halls worldwide. Hofmann was born a Mormon, and understood the Church's passion for documentary evidence that might add depth to its history. Hofmann built up a reputation as a document expert and collector of Mormoniana, but in fact he was forging an impressive collection of missing historical texts, such as the 'Anthon Transcript', the 'Blessing of Joseph Smith III', the 'Far West Letter' and the 'Stowell Letter'. His rendition of 'The Oath of a Freeman' almost sold for $1.5 million before doubts were raised about its authenticity.

His most interesting forgery was the 'White Salamander Letter', dated from Palmyra, 23 October 1830, addressed to William W. Phelps (1792–1872), and purported to be written by Martin Harris (1783–1875), who worked as Joseph Smith's first scribe for two months in 1828. Hofmann's work was not only technically superb, but the text itself played on all the old Mormon fears of being connected to folk magic and divining for gold, in the hope that the Church would buy the letter from him and file it away for ever. As it happened, the Mormons faced the challenge, and produced the text with great fanfare at a meeting of the Mormon Historical Association in May 1985.

According to Harris's forged testimony, it was in the summer of 1824 that young Joseph Smith helped build a fence on his land, amazing Harris at how fast he could work. Harris praised the boy to his father Joseph Smith, Senior (1771–1840), who boasted that 'Joseph can see any thing he wishes by looking at a stone Joseph often sees Spirits here with great kettles of coin money'. Harris wrote that 'in the fall of the year 1827 I hear Joseph found a gold bible I take Joseph aside & he says it is true I found it 4 years ago with my stone'. Joseph Smith recounted that 'the spirit transfigured himself from a white salamander in the bottom of the hole & struck me 3 times & held the treasure & would not let me have it'. Eventually,

> on the 22nd day of Sept 1827 they get the gold bible – I give Joseph $50 to move him down to Pa [Pennsylvania] . . . Joseph found some giant silver specticles with the plates he puts them in an old hat & in the darkness reads the words & in this way it is all translated & written down – about the middle of June 1829 Joseph takes me together with Oliver Cowdery & David Whitmer to have a view of the plates our names are appended to the book of Mormon which I had printed with my own money.

This was all very bad news. Not only was Joseph Smith led to the golden plates by his 'seer stone', but the benevolent angel of Mormon historiography turns out to be a nasty spirit who strikes inquirers and likes to take the form of a salamander, a mystical figure from occult lore. In another part of the letter, this spirit even taunts Joseph and says that he can have the plates if he brings his dead brother Alvin with him next time. Joseph, ever naive, replies, 'he is dead shall I bring what remains?' Where was Moroni, the noble son of Mormon, enshrined by the Church of Latter-day Saints?

In retrospect, it is difficult to understand how the White Salamander Letter could have fooled anyone. Photographs show it to be a very convincing forgery, but the text is amazingly similar to one of the testimonies printed in E.D. Howe's *Mormonism Unvailed*. Indeed, it may have been this similarity that gave Hofmann's work a kind of verisimilitude. On 11 December 1833, a certain Willard Chase signed an affidavit before a Justice of the Peace, affirming that it was he who found a curious stone while digging a well with his hired hands, Alvin and Joseph Smith. Chase wanted to keep the stone as a curiosity, but eventually he lent it to Joseph Smith, who refused to return it, claiming in the neighbourhood that it had wondrous powers. In June 1827, Joseph Smith's father told Chase a story similar to the one in Mark Hofmann's forgery, only this time at the bottom of the box in which the gold plates lay, the spirit was 'something like a toad, which soon assumed the appearance of a man, and struck him on the side of his head'. This spirit also demanded that Joseph bring his brother Alvin a year hence, but he was still alive, expiring before the year was out, 'which the old man said was an accidental providence!' Chase had more uncomplimentary things to say about Joseph Smith, and was happy to give Howe his testimony, printed in the book.[73]

In any case, Mark Hofmann was by now an expert at forging Martin Harris's handwriting, and already had a plan to produce the original 116 pages of the first draft of the Book of Mormon, the so-called missing 'Book of Lehi'. These were the pages that Harris recorded when he served as Joseph Smith's first scribe from 12 April to 14 June 1828. Unfortunately, Harris took these 116 transcribed pages home one day and, according to the story, his wife threw them into the fire in disgust at the whole business. Oliver Cowdery arrived in April 1829, and the work of translation and inscribing continued as before. The Mormons always feared that these original pages were hidden somewhere, and if they should come to light, discrepancies with the published Book of Mormon would show that Smith was not reading a set text in Reformed Egyptian but was making it up as he went along. Even if, as alleged, the Devil had meanwhile supernaturally altered the text of the missing Book of Lehi, it would be a problem for interpretation if found.

Encouraged by his success, Hofmann put it about in 1985 that he had uncovered a large number of papers belonging to William McLellin (1806–83), one of the original twelve apostles of 1835, who left the Mormons three years later. This claim was more problematic than the others, for Hofmann had not yet forged any of these documents, which anyway would have been a massive undertaking. Instead, he bluffed his way into borrowing huge sums of money from different people in order to 'buy' the collection. Each of Hofmann's patrons was led to believe himself the sole backer of this major contribution to the Mormon heritage. One of these people, a man named Steven F. Christensen, started pressuring Hofmann to show his cards. On 15 October 1985, Hofmann's home-made bombs killed both Christensen and the wife of his business partner, Kathleen Sheets. The following day, in an attempt to murder Brent Ashworth, another person involved in the purchase, Hofmann blew himself up instead, and, although he survived the blast, he was seriously injured. In February 1986, Hofmann was charged with the murders, and accepted a plea bargain for life imprisonment.[74]

In the end, we are left with the authorised Book of Mormon, consisting of fifteen 'books' of unequal length, totaling 275,000 words. According to this scriptural narrative, after Babel a number of people came to America, where they would become known as the Jaredites. In about 600 BC, before the Babylonian Conquest of the Holy Land, a band of Hebrews – that is, some of the Lost Ten Tribes of Israel – escaped from Jerusalem, and travelled by caravan to the Indian Ocean. There they built boats and sailed to the west coast of America, and lived in peace with the original Jaredites. Eventually, these early inhabitants of America split into two groups: the wicked Lamanites, the ancestors of the American Indians, who were punished with barbarism and the loss of their fair skins; and the righteous Nephites, who were blessed with a manifestation of Jesus Christ after his Resurrection. Joseph Smith further revealed in 1831 that Noah sailed to the Holy Land only after the Flood: he was originally from America. Indeed, we learn, America had been the scene of Christ's work on earth as much as the Holy Land, and would be again when the true church and temple would arise near Independence, Missouri, in Jackson County, the original site of the Garden of Eden. In this way, the true American religion would rise against the apostate churches of old Europe and save the world. Sadly, this path was not straight, for in about AD 421 the good Nephites were exterminated by the evil

Lamanites. Mormon was the father of Moroni, the last prophet of the Nephites, who buried their holy Book of Mormon at the Hill Cumorah in New York State until it was revealed to young Joseph Smith in 1823.

By the time the Book of Mormon was published in 1830, events had moved rather fast. In that year Saints Peter, James and John appeared to Joseph Smith – John the Baptist had already come to him in 1829 – and ordained him priest of the Order of Melchizedek. With the help of Sidney Rigdon, a biblical scholar, Joseph Smith began to elaborate the Mormon theology. He now rejected the traditional Christian dual concept of Heaven and Hell. Instead, he ruled that there were three kingdoms beyond this world, populated by a hierarchical host of gods rather than a single divinity. The highest kingdom was celestial, and included the Melchizedek priests and other Mormons who became gods after their death: in a sense, this was Gnosticism gone individual. Later on, in a sermon on 27 August 1843, Smith distinguished between this higher 'Melchizedek priesthood', which had the power to administer 'endless lives to the sons and daughters of Abraham', and the rather more ordinary 'Aaronic priesthood', which would include nearly every Mormon male.

The middle 'Terrestrial Kingdom' of Heaven is the residence of non-Mormons, good people who did not or were not able to hear the message of Joseph Smith. At the bottom of the afterlife is the 'Telestial Kingdom', where the bad people stay for all eternity. The interesting thing, however, is that they get any kind of heaven at all. Indeed, everyone gets something, except for the 'sons of perdition' who had accepted and then rejected the Mormon gospel. In other words, what the Mormons promised was universal salvation for humanity, and divinity in the part of the afterlife reserved exclusively for Mormons.

By the beginning of 1833, Joseph Smith had refined Mormon doctrine around two key concepts: (1) all things are both spiritual and material; (2) creation was not, as the Hebrew Bible tells us, out of nothing (*creatio ex nihilo*), but instead came out of a pre-existing primal material (*creatio ex materia*), which was very similar to the Hermetic concept of creation from a division of God Himself (*creatio ex deo*). Where Smith obtained such ideas is not clear, but there were plenty of books around that summarised the Hermetic tradition.[75] In any case, in that year 1833, the Mormons abandoned their Missouri Zion, and by July were building a temple in Kirtland, Ohio. Ever eager to deepen Mormon lore, in July 1835 Joseph Smith purchased a number of Egyptian papyrus scrolls, claiming that these were the writings of the patriarchs Abraham and Joseph. When the originals resurfaced in 1967 and were examined by experts, they turned out to be rather ordinary funerary inscriptions written sometime between the first century BC and the first century AD, but in 1835 they created quite a sensation. Joseph Smith translated them as The Book of Abraham, which was proclaimed as an authoritative Mormon scripture in 1842. Essentially, it is another version of Genesis, in which Abraham is instructed by God about the hierarchy of stars, intelligences and divinities in the heavens, who had helped Him mould earth out of *prima materia.*[76] Unfortunately for the later Church of Latter-day Saints, this newly discovered text also specifically excluded black people, the presumed descendants of Ham, from the Mormon priesthood, a ruling that was corrected by later inspiration in 1978.[77]

So too did the Kirtland Seminary in Ohio hire a Jew named Joshua ('James') Seixas (1802–187?) to teach Hebrew to Joseph Smith and the elders of the Church in January 1836. Seixas was a well-known instructor of the language back east, and promised to give his pupils a reading knowledge of Hebrew in just six weeks, meeting with them for one hour each day. He had already done stints in New York, Philadelphia and Washington, and taught students at both Andover and Princeton Theological Seminaries. In 1835 he worked at Oberlin College in Ohio, and came to the attention of the local Mormons, who hired him for a two-month contract from 26 January to 29 March 1836. Seixas thereafter returned to New York, founded the first choir of the famous Spanish and Portuguese Synagogue, and carried on as a Hebrew teacher there.[78]

In 1840, the Mormons established the town of Nauvoo, Illinois, which was their first real attempt to create an independent community for their faith. By August of that year, Joseph Smith announced the doctrine of baptising the dead retroactively, which was codified by a revelation in 1842. The Mormons were not the first to invent the idea – the German Pietist mystics at Ephrata, Pennsylvania, had been doing it since the 1740s – but it is a practice that has turned their Church into the foremost centre of world genealogy today.[79] At the same time, Joseph Smith and his colleagues made the astute political move of giving up their anti-Freemason rhetoric and establishing a new Masonic lodge in Nauvoo, which grew to be larger than all the

other Illinois lodges put together. The new 'temple endowment ceremony', promulgated on 4 May 1842 and still the central Mormon
experience, was clearly Masonic in character, using its symbols of square
and compass, an all-seeing eye, the beehive and distinctive ritual
garments. The Mormons claimed that their inspiration was closer to
the originals of Adam, Seth and Enoch, but like Freemasonry they
also sought secret hermetic knowledge.[80] The 'Articles of Faith', adopted
in 1842, codified their basic theology nicely.

But it was polygamy that really set the Mormons apart. From the
spring of 1843, Joseph Smith began to teach his inner circle about
polygamy, and allowed them to take additional wives. While there
may have been some personal and demographic motivations to this
doctrine, there certainly was a good deal about 'alchemical marriage'
in occult lore, not only in the Rosicrucian 'chemical wedding', but in
the very common trope of a marriage between the elements of mercury
and sulphur as the Sun King and Moon Queen.[81] The Mormon priests
now had a 'sealing ritual', which promised eternal life, in true hermetic
fashion, within the power of humankind to grant. Polygamy was
allowed for all Mormon men in 1852 after the move to Utah, with
three wives being a minimum qualification for higher offices, but it
was abandoned (officially at least) in 1890.

Polygamy may have been Mormonism's most notorious social component, but Joseph Smith's most interesting theological innovation was
revealed in April 1844 at his funeral 'discourse' for a certain King Follet,
which he opened with the following dramatic declaration: 'God Himself
who sits enthroned in yonder heavens is a Man like unto one of your-
selves – that is the great secret!' The same concept was expressed more
succinctly in the famous Mormon proverb, 'As man is now, so once was
God; as God is now, man may become.' This was truly an extraordinary statement. In other words, we are not only the 'children of God'
in the metaphorical pastoral sense, but quite literally His blood relations, and we can aspire to join God the Father on His heavenly plateau
if we become Mormons. It is an enormously optimistic theology, without
original sin, with hope towards eternal life in heaven for (almost) all:
'Adam fell that men might be; and men are that they might have joy.'
In Mormon heaven, the new gods stay married, and have more children, since increase and creation are the prerogatives of the divine. There
is also personal progress, as gods progress up the ladder of divine hierarchy, ruling and creating in the afterlife they inhabit.

In fourteen years, Joseph Smith had been transformed from a local gold-diviner into the leader of a mass movement of hermetic magicians, with a sacred text and holy rites, ruling in this world and in the next. On 27 June 1844, however, Joseph Smith and his brother Hyrum were shot and killed by a mob at Carthage, Illinois, while they were being held in jail under protective custody. According to Mormon lore, his last words were 'O Lord My God', the first part of the Freemason's distress cry. The Mormons continued to live in Illinois until religious disturbance became too troubling for everyone, and a decision was taken to leave. In February 1846, most of the Mormon group crossed the Mississippi into Iowa, and the following July, an advance party led by Orson Pratt (1811–81) went down into the Salt Lake Valley. The acknowledged leader of the Mormons outside Illinois was now Brigham Young (1801–77), and in September 1848 he brought a wagon train of thousands of Mormons into their new home.

The struggle of the Mormons at Salt Lake City is a true American drama. In Weberian terms, they were a 'hydraulic society' with inadequate water resources, and a 'monument-building society' as well. Brigham Young was a dictator, ruling by 'blood atonement', a polite word for execution. Sir Arthur Conan Doyle (1859–1930), who himself was deeply involved in occult studies, wrote his first Sherlock Holmes story, 'A Study in Scarlet' (1887), about Mormon blood atonement.[82] His particular interest was in the 'Danites', a terrorist group established by Sampson Avard (1803–69) in Illinois during the early years, and which remained the basis of numerous legends about secret Mormon bands.[83]

Curiously enough, the Mormon tradition of divining for gold, which was evident from the very earliest days of Joseph Smith, finally paid off on 24 January 1848. On that day, gold was discovered at Sutter's Mill on the Sacramento River in California. Of the ten people present, six were Mormons, from a special Mormon battalion in the US army, which had been raised in the Mexican War to capture California. Hundreds of Mormon soldiers took part in the gold rush that followed, and indeed the majority of those caught up in the frenzy were Mormons during the first few years.

Mormon theology also proved to be dynamic in unexpected ways. Oliver Pratt, the Church's most important theologian, began to argue from about 1853 that if all spirit is matter (as both the Mormons and the Swedenborgians claimed), then the Holy Spirit itself is a kind of fluid deep inside every particle of matter. God is inside us, and everything else, and therefore is more a collection of pure Platonic ideas than a specific Being. Pratt's refinement of Mormon theology was rather awkward, considering the fact that Mormons were promised by Joseph Smith that they could one day in the afterlife become gods, complete with families and the possibility of promotion through a hierarchy of angels.

Brigham Young's contribution to developing Mormon theology was hardly less problematic. He revealed that Adam was in fact a god who with his companion Eve became the progenitor of mankind. Adam was the son of higher gods, especially Elohim (Jehovah), who himself had many wives or queens. Adam was also the father of Christ, which seems to imply that he was God. Much of this new-fangled doctrine was abandoned after Brigham Young's death.

In any event, Brigham Young was eventually forced to face the challenge of the Federal Government, when newly elected President James Buchanan soon after his inauguration sought to have Utah Territory governed by someone who was not a Mormon. The result was the Utah War (1857–8), which ended when the US army marched through a deserted Salt Lake City on 26 June 1858, the inhabitants having moved fifty miles south to Provo and other towns in that area. The soldiers carried on forty miles south-west, where they built Camp Floyd, the first non-Mormon permanent settlement in Utah. Brigham Young, for his part, resigned his post as governor, and began a surprisingly cooperative relationship with his non-Mormon successor, Alfred Cumming (1802–73).[84]

In 1869 the 'Golden Spike' was driven into the ground at Promontory Summit, eighty miles north-west of Salt Lake City, as the Pacific Railway opened Utah to mining and the rest of America. Utah Territory petitioned for statehood six times until Congress would admit it, the first five petitions rejected over the issue of polygamy, despite the Mormon argument that their practice was protected by the First Amendment. Polygamy was outlawed in 1862 by the federal government, and the Supreme Court upheld this position again in 1879. Fortunately for Utah, Wilford Woodruff (1807–98), president of the Church of Latter-day Saints, declared in 1890 that God had revealed to him that Mormons were also under the jurisdiction of federal law, and polygamy was thereupon abolished (in theory if not always in practice) throughout the territory. In 1896, Utah was admitted to the

Union as the forty-fifth state, as the Mormons began to move away from their occult theological heritage, trying to re-create themselves as a Christian denomination, without too much emphasis on the Freemasons and Swedenborgians who laid the foundations of their faith.

FOUR

Occult Without: Re-enchanting Nature

'It was a dark and stormy night . . .' is probably the most risible opening for a novel that anyone could imagine. The 'anyone' in question, however, was Sir Edward George Earle Bulwer-Lytton (1803–73), whose touch was anything but light, and the novel was *Paul Clifford* (1830). His later description of *The Last Days of Pompeii* (1834), where the night was rather more volcanic than dark and stormy, would make him famous. As we have already seen, the Hermetic universe was alive, a sort of gigantic creature formed of people like us, and anything else that existed in Nature. By the end of the eighteenth century, Nature was not only alive but also moody, and this unpleasant characteristic was clearly demonstrated in a new literary genre that emerged at that time, the Gothic novel.

I

Purists would argue that the Gothic novel was born with Horace Walpole (1717–97), who subtitled his book *The Castle of Otranto*, 'A Gothic Story', at least for the second edition of 1765.[1] Walpole was very keen on the imaginary feudal past, and remodelled his house 'Strawberry Hill' as a Gothic mansion. The story he told in his small and rather hokey book would contain many of the elements that became de rigueur for the genre: an historical setting that promoted the suspension of disbelief; a dark and scary castle with secret underground passageways; a defenceless virgin fleeing for her honour and her life; fearsome monsters, and a just quest for the restoration of usurped ancient rights as unambiguous good triumphs over clearly recognised evil. The necessary suspension of disbelief is achieved partly by placing the action in the distant past, when castles and monsters were more common. Walpole started a fad that peaked in the 1790s, at which time about one-third of all published fiction fell into the Gothic category. Indeed, many of these novels have been lost, since they were typically borrowed rather than purchased, and circulating libraries tended to throw out the old stock to make room for the new. Some of these were mere 'shilling shockers', the 'blue books' that were often simply retellings of longer novels in easily digestible form.

Walpole's novel was scary in its way, probably terrifying for many of his readers. Once the success of such works was demonstrated, it was not long before new thrills were necessary, and from about the middle of the 1790s Gothic novels of terror evolved into Gothic novels of horror. The difference was spelled out by Ann Radcliffe (1764–1823), whose own book, *The Mysteries of Udolpho* (1794), was another important terror text:

> Terror and horror are so far opposite, that the first expands the soul, and awakens the faculties to a high degree of life; the other contracts, freezes, and nearly annihilates them . . . where lies the great difference between terror and horror, but in the uncertainty and obscurity, that accompany the first, respecting the dreaded evil?

Terror novels, in other words, open the mind to the apprehension of the sublime, by suggesting awful possibilities or eventualities that never actually materialise. We get scared, but mostly the fear is in our own minds. Horror novels, however, close the mind as we contemplate the truly repulsive, things that actually happen to the characters depicted. These new Gothic horror stories were more complex than their antecedents in that the hero was often a morally ambiguous figure with a complicated psychological profile. Perhaps the first novel of this type was *Frankenstein* (1818), written by Mary Shelley (1797–1851). The last properly Gothic horror novel is said to be *Melmoth the Wanderer* (1820) by Charles Maturin (1782–1824), who curiously enough was the great-uncle of Oscar Wilde.

Looking at the genre as a whole, we can isolate some common characteristics, and can see how the Gothic novel helped prepare the way for a greater emphasis on the supernatural in the nineteenth century. The setting of the novel in distant time and place freed the reader from the limits of everyday standards of morality or proba- bility, although each story included at least one character whose subjec- tive judgement seemed not to be entirely different from our own. The Gothic novel emphasised the psychological elements in the story, with a concern for the interior processes of the mind, symbolised perhaps by the castle with its secret passages and hidden doorways. The hero of a Gothic novel was also sometimes a bit of a villain, and this confu- sion of good and bad often took on an anti-Christian tone, or at least was anti-Roman Catholic, suggesting that it is not within the reli- gious world that man can find the answers to the burning moral ques- tions with which he is faced, especially when pitted against evil in the most trying of circumstances. Even more apparent was the attempt of the Gothic novelist to involve the reader's emotions in a manner that was much more intense and highly focused, drawing him away from the highly restricted forms of eighteenth-century poetry and prose and towards the wild reaches of Romantic literature, which was about to blossom.

II

The precise role of eighteenth-century German philosophical ideas in the development of Romanticism will always be a subject for disagree- ment. But the philosophers whose names are associated with them became part of the canon of occult thought, and even some potted familiarity with their views is necessary to understand what came after- wards. The essential point of origin must be Immanuel Kant (1724–1804), who gave to the occult philosophy the key notion that the entire world as we experience it (that is, the phenomenal world) is dependent on the nature of our apparatus for experiencing it. As a result, things as they appear to us are not identical with the things as they are in themselves (that is, the noumenal world). Philosophers like to call this position 'transcendental idealism', according to which one rules out any possibility of knowledge about God, souls, life after death, or any religious knowledge at all that goes beyond the bounds of experience. In practical terms, this means that religion can only be about ethics, and nothing more metaphysical.

Taking this argument several steps further, Johann Gottlieb Fichte

(1762–1814) argued that if reality is beyond all possibility of apprehension, as Kant claimed, then in fact we have no grounds for claiming
that there is anything out there at all. The entire phenomenal world
is therefore not an independent reality, but the creation of the individual ego that creates this world for itself. The natural world is the
creation of a self that is outside space and time, and therefore there
is no hidden reality behind the natural world, and at my death, my
world of space and time will cease to exist in me and everywhere else.
I myself, however, am immaterial, and although I shall cease to exist
in the space and time worlds of others, I will continue to exist time-
lessly. In fact, the entire phenomenal world is the creation of selves
like myself, so there is no noumenal reality of which the phenomenal
world is a reflection. Nature, in brief, is our own creation.

Admittedly, many of Fichte's ideas were presented in a popular book
called *The Vocation of Man* (1800), which he wrote after being sacked
from his teaching job, in a period when he thought he would have
to earn his living by writing. Fichte set for himself the most extreme
'idealist' position of any serious philosopher, and many of his argu-
ments would be echoed by New Age populists. But it was a compelling
presentation, and had a kind of arresting logic.

More immediately influential on the early Romantics was F.W.J. von
Schelling (1775–1854), especially in his important work called
Naturphilosophie (1797). His central concept was that the empirical world
is one single ever-evolving entity within which inorganic Nature developed into organic Life and then slowly became plant life, animal life
and, ultimately, human life. Reality is not a static state of affairs but
rather an endlessly dynamic process of change, and human beings emerged
wholly within this process as they are an inherent part of it. People are
spiritualised matter; Nature is materialised Spirit, a huge living organism
always developing, evolving, with us a part of it, not outside in a privileged place or part of a hidden reality. Furthermore, there was a goal to
all of this activity, as Nature strove for self-awareness, which it reached
in the highest levels of mankind, especially in creative art. In this way,
great works of art are incarnations of that part of the total reality of
Nature that reveals to itself the reasons for its own existence.

Schelling became *the* philosopher of the Romantic movement.
Seventeenth- and eighteenth-century philosophy saw the natural world
as something to be colonised and mastered, and glorified the intellect as the way to obtain the knowledge that would enable humankind

to achieve this. Schelling, and after him the Romantics, saw humankind as one with Nature, sharing and deriving its spirituality from Nature. No longer were the intellect and its fruits – mathematics, science, technology – our finest product; our highest endeavour was now Art, and the artist himself acquired some of the attributes of a god.[2]

Fichte and Schelling were two of the greatest living philosophers at the turn of the eighteenth century; the third was G.F.W. Hegel (1770–1831). Like Schelling, Hegel emphasised development, but his reality consisted of a single something he called '*Geist*', which was going through a process of change on the way to self-knowledge, recognising itself as the ultimate reality. This process is not arbitrary but operates according to a specific pattern of development that is 'dialectical' (thesis, antithesis, synthesis) and inherently involving conflict.[3] When Arthur Schopenhauer (1788–1860) went up to the University of Göttingen in 1809 at the age of twenty-one, these three men were the philosophical lions, a situation that pleased him not at all. Even worse, Schopenhauer in the 1820s found himself a professor at the University of Berlin, where Hegel was the star attraction. Not to be outdone, Schopenhauer scheduled his lectures at the same time as Hegel's in order to save Germany's youth from his rival's evil influence. Sadly, no one came to Schopenhauer's class and the course of lectures had to be cancelled.[4]

Schopenhauer's view of the world would ultimately be very influential, especially in nineteenth-century England. In his most famous book, *The World as Will and Representation*, Schopenhauer argued rather mystically that, although we are aware merely of this differentiated phenomenal world of material objects (including ourselves) in time and space, we are in fact part of a larger total reality that is immaterial, timeless and spaceless and of which we can never have direct knowledge. Nevertheless, this ultimate thing can be found deep inside us, and is that will to live, to survive, to be. Our brain, our intellect, is the servant of this will, which is limitless energy, without consciousness, impersonal, purposeless and, most importantly, not alive. Schopenhauer was the first great Western philosopher who was openly atheist; he was also the first philosopher read by both Ludwig Wittgenstein (1889–1951) and Karl Popper (1902–94). The views of Germans like Fichte, Schelling, Hegel and Schopenhauer were interpreted to the English-speaking world especially by Samuel Taylor Coleridge (1772–1834), who stole masses of material from Schelling in particular.[5]

At some point, it is helpful to refer to this intensification of feeling that was exemplified by both the rise of the Gothic novel and the influence of quasi-mystical German philosophy as 'Romanticism'. Its principles are difficult to define, but at the very least it is a useful term to describe a particular style that was at its peak between about 1770 and 1848, a literary, intellectual and religious movement which emphasised passion and the human imagination. Certainly one of Romanticism's most important intellectual forebears was Jean-Jacques Rousseau (1712–1778). Its ancestral origins were in Pietism, that Methodist Great Awakening that conquered the hearts (rather more than the minds) of Germans, English and Americans at the end of the eighteenth century. In a sense, Romanticism was Pietism writ large, emphasising the heart not just in religion, but in all spheres. In any case, it was a mood, a tendency, rather than a school of thought. As for religion, Romanticism stood primarily for a religious interpretation of the cosmos that made man's interests central in the universe. Behind Nature there was some Reality, called God or Providence, who is a Friend who cares. Our ideals are secure because that Power behind Nature is dedicated to humankind and its ideals, and to the individual person and his or her feelings.

The Romantic turn of mind also included a number of more general characteristics, which would be crucial for the development of the occult tradition. First among these was what one might call 'organicism', that is, the belief that the cosmos is a single organic being, a living example of the way in which the divine creative power unfolded in a Great Chain of Being. This unfolding takes place in time, and indeed a second important feature of Romanticism is the emphasis on development, an evolutionary process of change. In a sense, then, the Great Chain of Being was no longer seen as static in its unchanging perfection.[6]

It does absolutely no good at all to describe the Romantic movement as anti-religious. God was a Reality that existed at some level beyond or behind this world, but it was Nature that immediately mattered. Whereas their forefathers relied on revealed religion to provide them with emotional certainty and to guarantee their very existence in this life and the next, the Romantics looked to Nature to give them all of that. Their vehicle was *imagination*, a tool that enabled them to see the world in a more powerful light, to explore the deeper reality that lay before us, waiting to be unfolded through a more profound understanding. By unleashing our imagination we can perceive the hidden connections between all things and invest the world with unity and significance. The Romantics did not deny that their aim was to re-enchant the universe, and to bring back some of the mystery of Creation that was rapidly being dissipated under the pressure of scientific advance. The basic occult concept of correspondences and secret connections was simply too comprehensive to be abandoned without a fight, for it provided a full and wonderful explanation of the events and structures of the external world.

At the same time, one should not see the Romantic conception of the world as being utterly opposed to the scientific frame of reference. Although the word 'scientist' was first coined in 1833, there was nothing like a culture of the professional scientist until much later, certainly not before about 1870. The late Victorian scientist worked in an experimental laboratory, and was a product of the new professionalisation of society, which excluded the amateurs and learned dabblers.[7] At the beginning of the nineteenth century, however, there was no strictly scientific culture for the Romantic natural philosopher to oppose. Everything was much more fluid: the borders between modern disciplines had not yet been drawn.

III

Out of the Romantic turn of mind came Victorian occultism, a concerted attempt to find a common ground between the traditional universe of correspondences and the scientific world of cause and effect. This has not always been understood, in part because of a certain confusion of terminology. E.R. Dodds (1893–1979), the historian of the Greeks and the irrational, wrote in his autobiography:

> The occultist, as his name betokens, values the occult *qua* occult: that is for him its virtue, and the last thing he will thank you for is an explanation. He is an intellectual anarchist, a rebel against the concept of natural law, and his unconfessed aim is a destructive one: he would like, if he could, to undermine the whole arrogant structure of modern science and see it crash about our ears.

Certainly there were many nineteenth-century people who held that view, but they do not represent the occultist attitude towards science. Dodds is closer to the mark when he describes his next ideal type:

> The genuine psychical researcher may feel this fascination, as I have sometimes done, but he has disciplined himself to resist it . . . His long-term objective is not to glorify the 'occult' but to abolish it by bringing its true significance to light and fitting it into its place in a coherent world picture. Far from wishing to pull down the lofty edifice of science, his highest ambition is to construct a modest annexe which will serve, at least provisionally, to house his new facts with the minimum of disturbance to the original plan of the building. His guiding principle is the law of parsimony: he will make only such assumptions as appear to him necessary in order to cover observed facts, and even these he will present only as working hypotheses.[8]

This is precisely the point: it would be almost meaningless to make a sharp distinction between the occultist and the scientist in the early nineteenth century, since both regarded themselves as men of research, patiently collecting the evidence that would provide the groundwork for the construction of explanatory theories. As we shall see, there was a considerable overlap between both groups, as a number of people who would be known chiefly for their scientific discoveries at the same time harboured the hope that their work would contribute to solving problems and mysteries that could only be described as supernatural.

Armed with a far less rigid conception of the boundary between science and occultism, we can appreciate the nineteenth-century fascination with the 'miracles' of modern science, no less than with the evolution of the Gothic novel, as we shall see, into the literature of the fantastic and the supernatural. People wanted the unexplainable to erupt into their world, and were prepared for it when it did.

A number of famous ghosts made their appearance during those years: the Cock Lane Ghost (1762), Lord Lyttelton's Ghost (1779), and the Hammersmith Ghost (1804). Ebenezer Sibly (1751–1800) published a very useful handbook of the occult sciences in 1790, which helped explain apparitions such as these. Sibly's expertise was in astrology, and he made a famous horoscope for the birth of the United States as well.[9] New quasi-occult medical techniques also flourished in this environment. Franz Joseph Gall (1758–1828), the German physician, promoted phrenology, which divided the human brain into different clusters, each functioning as a separate and observable unit.[10] Meanwhile, just as phrenology came to Britain in the 1820s and 1830s, an English doctor to the rich and famous was promoting homeopathy as the cure to all ills. Frederick Hervey Foster Quin (1799–1878) argued that his homeopathic method harnessed the natural cures of the life force itself and restored the patient's total equilibrium.[11] John Elliotson (1791–1868), the physician behind University College Hospital in London, was forced to resign his professorship in 1838 as a consequence of being a pioneer of the therapeutic trance in the treatment of patients. He was also among the first English doctors to use a stethoscope, and to prescribe acupuncture and very large doses of medicine. Elliotson's mistake was in theorising his trance as animal magnetism, mesmerism. Yet only three years later, a Scottish surgeon living in Manchester named James Braid (1795–1860) saw a French showman perform mesmerism, and came up with a neutral physiological explanation for what he observed on the stage, giving it in 1842 a more scientific-sounding name: 'neuro-hypnotism', which he changed to 'hypnotism' the following year 'for the sake of brevity'. Braid, therefore, usually gets the credit for having introduced hypnotism to Britain, rather than the unlucky Elliotson.[12] Meanwhile, in Germany, Baron Karl von Reichenbach (1788–1869) posited the existence of an 'odylic force', another kind of magnetic fluid, which was visible to highly sensitive people.

With the boundaries between the natural and the supernatural so very porous in the first decades of the nineteenth century, virtually anything could happen. Historians of religion usually pinpoint the year 1844 as the great watershed in American Protestantism, and we will return to that moment later on when discussing Fundamentalism. Suffice it to say meanwhile that the man who started it all was William Miller (1782–1849), a farmer and retired soldier who dedicated his life to Christ and began a careful study of the Scriptures with the aim of determining the exact date of the Second Coming. Arithmetical analysis of the books of Ezekiel, Daniel and Revelation revealed that glorious day to be no later than 21 March 1844, later recalibrated to 22 October 1844 – the cosmic non-moment forever to be enshrined as the 'Great Disappointment'. Rather than bringing about a general collapse of messianic fervour, however, the dispersal of the Millerites after 1844 sparked a chain reaction of new religions that sought to interpret what did not happen. Most prominent among these were the Jehovah's Witnesses, and the Seventh-day Adventists.[13]

Yet while there is no doubt that the 1840s was a decade of heightened religious sensibility in New England and thereabouts, not all of the people under its spell were drawn to scripturally based Protestantism of one sect or another. At the same time that William Miller was gathering his followers in upstate New York, a wave of Swedenborgianism swept over intellectual America, attracting people sensitised not only by popular Romanticism but also by a general feeling that their new country was at a kind of a crossroads. The foundation of the United States was in part a utopian exercise, as Abraham Lincoln (1809–65) would say, 'the last best hope of earth'.[14] By the early decades of the nineteenth century, this vision was more than a little tarnished, and the presence of both unfreed slaves and so many Roman Catholics made that abundantly clear.[15]

Out of this frustrated American dynamism came a sort of home-grown Swedenborgian philosophy called Transcendentalism. Its key representative was the poet Ralph Waldo Emerson (1803–82), who himself wrote about Swedenborg.[16] Transcendentalism was all about the correspondences in Nature, and Neoplatonic notions of the human spirit ascending through the heavenly spheres to unite with the 'Over-Soul, within which every man's particular being is contained'. The soul has a destiny distinct from the body, and we can manifest that destiny by diving deeply into our innermost essence and discovering our true natures – or words to that effect. Some scholars have argued that Transcendentalism is a philosophy of *motion*; it was the 'kinetic revolution' of a growing and optimistic society whose spirituality was reaching into the infinite. Motion became a kind of absolute perfection in itself, a part of a process of endless evolution through unknown worlds.[17] All this may be true, but it is also a fact that Transcendentalism flourished against the background of a deep religious and moral crisis in American life.

Another movement that emerged after the 'Great Disappointment' was spiritualism. On 31 March 1848, two sisters living in the small town of Hydesville, New York, found a way to communicate with the spirit residing in their house. Their success promoted a craze for spiritualism throughout America, initially focusing on these Fox sisters – Margaret (1836–93), Kate (1841–92), and later Leah Ann (1814–90).

The girls discovered that the ghost responded to rapping sounds, and supernaturally answered in kind, which was not at all surprising since the Morse Code had been invented only ten years earlier and was already widely in use in this world and (apparently) in the next as well.[18] It has always been a characteristic of the unliving that they take full advantage of the latest scientific technology. The women those girls became would many years later confess to having made spirit noises by cracking their knee joints, but in the meantime they were a sensation, promoted across America by no less than showman P.T. Barnum (1810–91) himself.[19]

The Fox sisters may well have been teenagers whose household prank got very much out of hand, but we need to ask the more serious question of why the American public was so receptive in 1848 to the idea of communicating with the dead. The Shakers had long been adept at this practice, and were graced at their meetings by visitations from biblical figures and, of course, from Mother Ann Lee (1736–84) herself. One could point to the much earlier practice of 'scrying', the crystal-gazing that opened a window to the other world and provided a means of communication with superior beings. According to one recent historian of the phenomenon,

> Spiritualism is Swedenborgian ideology, mixed with an experi-
> mentation with transic states inspired by mesmerism that easily
> led to mediumship of Swedenborg's spirits, and set before the
> backdrop of Native American shamanism.[20]

The conduit for the Swedenborgianism was primarily 'the Poughkeepsie seer', Andrew Jackson Davis (1826–1910), although he insisted on his own originality, and denied ever having read the Swedish master.[21] Davis (like Swedenborg) communicated with spirits, and preceded the Fox sisters in making contact through what came to be known as the 'spiritual telegraph'. His inspired lectures on these important themes were published in 1847, the year before the dramatic events at Hydesville.[22] Swedenborgianism took the Neoplatonic concept of the movable and transient soul and amplified it by describing the afterlife as a place for education and personal growth, not merely a heavenly reward. This view was helpfully confirmed by visitors from the spirit world.

Spiritualism, then, was far from being an anti-scientific movement.

Although based in an esoteric religious philosophy, it was very fundamentally empirical, relying for its validity on visible, demonstrable and repeatable proofs apparently no less reliable than the most rigorous scientific experiments. Like early nineteenth-century natural scientists, the research of spiritualists was open to anyone who had the means and the leisure to try. There were as yet no profession guilds to exclude the gifted amateur who attempted to raise the dead in his sitting room. At least from the days of the Fox sisters, if not before, the role of the 'medium' between this world and the next became more prominent, largely replacing the earlier concept of certain people who were 'clairvoyant'. The rappers soon gave way to the trance-speakers, but mediums were here to stay.[23]

Spiritualism was also part of a general revival of the traditional occult sciences of astrology, magic and alchemy. Popular knowledge in these areas could easily be gleaned from books such as *The Magus* (1801) by Francis Barret (1765–1825). Serious investigative spiritualism in the mid nineteenth century was often in competition with stage conjurors such as the famous Jean-Eugène Robert-Houdin (1805–71), and, like his namesake Erik 'Harry Houdini' Weisz (1874–1926) in the early part of the following century, professional magicians liked nothing better than exposing mediums.[24] The 'planchette' also came into use at roughly the same time as a means of communicating with spirits, being a board with two rolling casters underneath and a pencil at the tip, forming the third leg. When a patent was finally applied for in 1890, it was called a 'Ouija Board', but in the meantime it was anything but a toy.[25]

George Bernard Shaw (1856–1950) described English society in the decades before the First World War as:

> superstitious, and addicted to table-rapping, materialization séances, clairvoyance, palmistry, crystal-gazing and the like to such an extent that it may be doubted whether ever before in the history of the world did soothsayers, astrologers, and unregistered therapeutic specialists of all sorts flourish as they did during this half century of the drift to the abyss.[26]

In retrospect, the watershed years were probably about 1869–71. In November 1869, the scientific periodical *Nature* began publishing. 'Darwin's bulldog', Thomas Henry Huxley (1825–95), in that year coined the term 'agnostic', and in 1870 was elected president of the British Association for the Advancement of Science. Charles Darwin (1809–82) in 1871 published *The Descent of Man*, a book that was even more radical than *On the Origin of Species* (1859). Although the concept of evolution might somehow be accommodated to a grandiose divine plan, now by positing a distant ape-like origin for humankind, Darwin was denying the existence of Adam and Eve, and, by extension, the necessary role of Christ as redeemer for fallen man. In that same fateful year 1871, Edward Burnett Tylor (1832–1917) published his study of *Primitive Culture*, the founding text of anthropology, a new science devoted to gathering clues about less advanced contemporary societies that might help us learn more about our real ancestors.

'It's a very queer world,' says one of George Bernard Shaw's literary characters. 'It used to be so straightforward and simple; and now nobody seems to think and feel as they ought. Nothing has been right since that speech that Professor Tyndall made at Belfast.'[27] The reference, as everyone in Shaw's audience knew, was to the 'Belfast Address' given by John Tyndall (1820–93) on 19 August 1874 upon his election to follow Huxley as president of the British Association for the Advancement of Science.[28] Tyndall was already well-known as a champion of the new and more rigorous experimental science, and against the sort of sloppy thinking that he thought was characteristic of spiritualists:

> When science appeals to uniform experience, the spiritualist will retort, 'How do you know that a uniform experience will continue uniform? You tell me that the sun has risen for six thousand years: that is no proof that it will rise to-morrow; within the next twelve hours it may be puffed out by the Almighty.' Taking this ground, a man may maintain the story of 'Jack and the Beanstalk' in the face of all the science in the world.[29]

Tyndall's speech at Belfast was directed particularly against an even more pervasive supernatural organisation, the Roman Catholic Church, whose Pope Pius IX (1846–78) had recently issued a 'Syllabus of Errors' (1864) condemning virtually everything progressive and modern, including scientific study. 'The impregnable position of science may be described in a few words', Tyndall announced at Belfast:

We claim, and we shall wrest from theology, the entire domain
of cosmological theory. All schemes and systems which thus
infringe upon the domain of science must, in so far as they do
this, submit to its control, and relinquish all thought of controlling it. Acting otherwise proved always disastrous in the past,
and it is simply fatuous to-day.[30]

These were fighting words indeed from the man who symbolised the
godless Victorian scientist in a fearless quest for truth.

Yet at almost the same time that Tyndall was orating in Belfast, a
very different kind of meeting was taking place in the London home
of Erasmus Alvey Darwin (1804–81). Present there on 16 January 1874
were younger brother Charles Darwin; cousins Francis Galton
(1822–1911) and Hensleigh Wedgwood (1803–91); George Eliot
(1819–80) and her partner George Henry Lewes (1817–78), and their
protégé Frederic Myers (1843–1901), about whom much more later.
The purpose of their gathering was to participate in a séance, and
towards that end they hired Charles Williams, an American medium.
Like everyone else in London, they knew that, only two years before,
the more famous American trance-speaker Emma Hardinge Britten
(1823–99) was playing to packed Sunday audiences.[31] The Darwins and
their friends were impressed by what they witnessed at the séance,
and, although the evidence from the spirit world was inconclusive,
they could not figure out how the observed phenomena were produced.
If Charles Darwin, the icon of godless Victorian science himself, was
willing to explore the possibility of making contact with the dead,
what does that say about the so-called watershed of science pinpointed
above?[32]

The same phenomenon of sober intellectuals and men of science
taking an apparently unhealthy interest in the supernatural was repeated
the following year, when two prominent professors of physics published
(albeit at first anonymously) an entire book about what they called
'the unseen universe'. Balfour Stewart (1828–87) and Peter Guthrie
Tait (1831–1901) did not specifically make the case for spiritualism,
but argued that our knowledge of the forces of Nature was as yet so
very incomplete that to exclude arbitrarily any unknown forces was
in itself unscientific. The concepts of force, energy, and electricity were
still mysterious, and it was more than likely that ether served as a
kind of bridge between the seen and unseen worlds. Stewart and Tait

argued for continuity in Nature, the Newtonian principle of laws applicable both in our mundane world and in all others. In many ways, this was a very sound and highly scientific idea.[33]

Stewart and Tait believed that there was an 'invisible realm' that existed as part of the natural world, and that there was communication between it and the visible world. What we called divine providence was in fact the transfer of energy from the invisible to the visible realm. Together they formed the 'Great Whole', which was a self-contained system demonstrating the law of the conservation of energy: 'The Great Whole is infinite in energy, and will last from eternity to eternity.' Even the Creation of the world and the resurrection of Christ were not miraculous, but merely 'the result of a peculiar action of the invisible upon the visible universe'.[34]

That same year, 1875, was also notable for the establishment of two societies, which in retrospect would be seen to prefigure the serious study of life after death. The first was the British National Association of Spiritualists, which promised its members a socialist afterlife from its headquarters at 38 Great Russell Street. The second was the short-lived Psychological Society of Great Britain, founded by Edward Cox (1809–79), who died four years later and took his organisation with him to the afterlife. 'Psychology' was coming to be seen as a science in its own right, pursued on the Continent by important experimental pioneers such as William Wundt (1832–1920). The psychic force would gradually become despiritualised, and Cox was one of the people who helped make it a legitimate subject for scientific study.[35]

All of this organisational activity, however, was merely a prelude to the establishment of the Society for Psychical Research in England in 1882, followed by an American branch two years later. The idea of such a group had been brewing at Cambridge at least since 1874, when a number of prominent academics took an informal decision to investigate key occult phenomena. Chief among these, of course, was the possibility of making contact across time, with the dead (spiritualism). No less important was the suggestion that one might have contact across space, with the living (telepathy). At one level, the SPR in true occultist fashion was trying to turn nineteenth-century positivistic science on itself, and use it as a tool to prove one of the pillars of Victorian religion, the reality of life after death. This too was a re-enchantment of Nature, which was no longer to be seen as a cold and lifeless thing, but as an environment pregnant with the spirits of people no longer living but still very much among us. It was always a purely scientific endeavour as well, recognising that the human mind was much more of a complex site than had ever been imagined before.[36]

The leader of the little group that became the SPR was Henry Sidgwick (1838–1900), professor of moral philosophy at Cambridge.[37] John Maynard Keynes (1883–1946) said of Sidgwick: 'He never did anything but wonder whether Christianity was true and prove that it wasn't and hope that it was.'[38] Sidgwick's sister was married to the Archbishop of Canterbury. He himself married Eleanor Mildred Balfour (1845–1936), a mathematician who was later principal of Newnham College, Cambridge. She confided to a friend that she had chosen mathematics as a career 'because she thought a future life would be much more worth living if it included intellectual pursuits'. Her friend noted that 'the abstract nature of pure mathematics seemed to her specially adapted to a disembodied existence'.[39] Eleanor's brother was Arthur Balfour (1848–1930), who became president of the SPR in 1893, and served as Prime Minister between 1902 and 1905. He it was who issued the Balfour Declaration (1917), which called for the establishment of a Jewish state in Palestine, a messianic hope that historians have failed to connect with Balfour's other supernatural pursuits. Chief among these was his prolific thirty-year correspondence via mediums with his late fiancée Mary Catherine Lyttelton, who died of typhus on Palm Sunday 1875.[40] Another Balfour sister married John William Strutt, Lord Rayleigh (1842–1919), the Cavendish Professor of experimental physics at Cambridge. This was a very well-connected network of people indeed.

The other founding members were colourful but not unrespectable. Frederic W.H. Myers (1843–1901) was rather more religious in orientation. He desperately wanted to find evidence that his lost love was trying to contact him from beyond the grave.[41] Edmund Gurney (1847–88) was the only full-time worker at the SPR, though unpaid.[42] Frank Podmore (1855–1910) was also very active in the left-wing Fabian Society, whose meetings were sometimes held on the same night as those of the SPR, at Podmore's rooms in Dean's Yard, Westminster.[43] Soon allied with the SPR were genuinely celebrated individuals such as William E. Gladstone (1809–98); Alfred, Lord Tennyson (1809–92); John Ruskin (1819–1900); Mark Twain (1835–1910), and Lewis Carroll (1832–98).

An excellent example of the interpenetrability of the SPR with the gelling scientific world can be seen in the work of William Crookes (1832–1919), who was elected a Fellow of the Royal Society at the age of thirty-one for the discovery of thallium by spectroscopic analysis. In the middle of the nineteenth century, the very notion of analysing light in order to study even the stars still seemed like a supernatural miracle. In 1875, the Royal Society awarded a gold medal to Crookes for his radiometer, now a child's toy consisting of four vanes on a spindle in a vacuum that rotate when exposed to light. This simple device marked the beginning of the research that would lead to the discovery of radiation and electrons in the 1890s. Röntgen's demonstration of X-rays in 1896 was also based on Crooke's work.

Nevertheless, despite all of this modern-sounding scientific achievement, Crookes himself was convinced that what he had done was to prove the existence of a 'psychic force' in the universe, and argued that spiritualist phenomena needed to be investigated scientifically rather than being dismissed out of hand on the basis of prejudice rather than scientific experiment. Towards this end, Crookes worked with the two most famous mediums of his day: Daniel Dunglas Home (1833–86)[44] and Florence Cook (1856–1904), whose ghostly partner was a disembodied but highly visible spirit named 'Katie King'.[45] This spiritualist activity, however, had little or no effect on his standing within what we might think of as the normative scientific community. Crookes received grants, sat on committees that gave grants, and was knighted in 1897.

The same pattern repeats itself with other Victorian scientists, who pursued spiritualist scientific research and made genuine scientific discoveries almost as a by-product. John Tyndall's assistant William Barrett (1844–1925) was a member of the SPR, and thought he was on to something related to spirits when he noticed the effect of sound on flames. Even without spiritual help, Barrett later received a knighthood. Oliver Lodge (1851–1940) was another prominent member of the SPR, as well as a pioneer of wireless telegraphy, which he thought erroneously had something to do with ether, the medium through which he attempted to communicate with his son Raymond, who was killed in the First World War.[46] Lodge was also knighted.

The world to come was probably a long way away, if human concepts of distance applied at all. In the more mundane Victorian context, it was cable telegraphy that provided the model for communication across huge spaces. The first transatlantic cable was laid in 1866, followed four years later by the completion of a link from England (via Gibraltar) all the way to India. The last part of the chain was forged in 1903, when cable was laid between Canada and New Zealand. If a message could be sent around the world in an unbelievably short time, why should it have been impossible for connections both telepathic (with the living) and spiritual (with the dead) to be achieved? People were quite used to partial and misinterpreted telegraphic messages, and were prepared for the same kind of variable quality from their mediums. Similar associations between the dead and telegraphy are also explored in 'The Wireless' (1902), a short story by Rudyard Kipling (1865–1936).[47]

The invention of the phonograph in 1877 by Thomas Alva Edison (1847–1931) also provided an important boost to a spiritualist conception of the world. Here was a machine that recorded permanently the most ephemeral human quality, a person's voice. In its early days, the phonograph was seen primarily as a tool for preserving voices rather than recording music, even after it was perfected (1888) and sold commercially in England (1898). The last words of the dying were particularly sought after, so that their voices could continue to be heard from beyond the grave. Edison had made a machine that produced for the first time in history a disembodied voice, and preserved it for ever. From that point onwards, the sound of a voice no longer meant that there was a person to go along with it. It should come as no surprise to learn that Thomas Edison was active in the SPR, American branch.[48]

Photography also quickly became a tool for preserving the images of the dying, and for recording the visits of the already dead. Alexander Graham Bell (1847–1922) was a séance-goer as well: he made a pact to communicate with his brothers after the first one went over the edge. The first words spoken on the telephone were directed to his assistant Thomas Watson (1854–1934), a spare-time medium who believed that the crackling on a dead telephone line originated from some supernatural source.[49] We also need to remember that even electricity was poorly understood in the late nineteenth century. Important experiments in the early 1880s focused on understanding the unexplained tendency of electricity to travel around the wires that carried it – what we know now to be an electromagnetic field.[50] Among the key players here were prominent members of the SPR, including Oliver Lodge, Lord Rayleigh and his successor Joseph John Thomson

(1856–1940), who took over from him as director of the Cavendish Laboratory.[51] Indeed, it was Thomson's position that 'telepathy with the dead would present comparatively little difficulty when it is admitted as regards the living'. It was all happening in late-nineteenth-century physics – black light, radio waves, radioactivity – but it was all grist to the mill for men like Crookes (who explained many physical phenomena as the result of 'psychic force') and Lodge (who thought that 'ether' was the medium that united all aspects of his work).[52]

As Thomson himself said, the critical concept was telepathy, which might explain some mysterious phenomena scientifically, and with any luck provide an insight into the question of life after death. There seemed to be something in telepathy, either as a survival from a pre-human state when humankind had an insect-like ability to communicate or as a jump forward on the evolutionary ladder to a place where psychic forces would become more prominent. Either way, the human mind could be seen as a real place.

Experimentation with telepathy involved a crucial methodological switch as well. Since the early days with the Fox sisters, the mediums tended to be female. This gender preference was not invented by the Victorians, but goes back to the seventeenth-century women prophets, and behind them Joan of Arc (c. 1412–31) and the female sibyls of the ancient world.[53] There was always a feeling that a woman's brain had plenty of room to spare, and could be more easily filled by an external intelligence. Apart from Florence 'Katie King' Cook, there were a number of other celebrated lady mediums. The oldest among them was Eusapia Palladino (1854–1918), an uneducated woman of Naples, whose exotic career continued to thrive even after being caught in the fraudulent act at Frederic Myers's home in 1895.[54] Another was Hélène Smith (1861–1929), not foreign but lower middle class. The last of the group was Mrs Leonora Piper (1859–1950), a Boston invalid discovered by the leading American philosopher of religion, William James (1842–1910).[55] Thousands of pages in the *Proceedings of the Society for Psychical Research* were devoted to her case, especially when she visited England in 1889–90 to be tested by Oliver Lodge and Frederic Myers. She was investigated thoroughly by Richard Hodgson (1855–1905), the man who wrote the report that unmasked Madame Blavatsky as a fake and a fraud.[56] Hodgson worked with Mrs Piper from 1887 to 1905, when he himself died. Hodgson joined forces with Myers (d. 1901) in the Great Beyond, and their reports on life after death were communicated to the living through the good offices of Mrs Piper herself. Investigating female spiritualism often involved fairly intimate contact in a closed and darkened room, giving the enterprise an erotically charged ambiance, especially when the medium was young and safely working class or foreign. The wonderful thing about telepathy, however, is that anyone could play, and inter-gender *frisson* was no longer necessarily part of the game. As Pamela Thurschwell puts it, 'Emphasizing thought transference rather than séances allowed the Society to move from touching (primarily) women to not touching (primarily) men.'[57]

This increasing emphasis on telepathy, we need to remember, took place against the background not only of the growing acceptability of hypnosis, but also a continued fascination with various exemplars of the phenomenon all around. In 1876, the Ring cycle of Richard Wagner (1813–83) opened at Bayreuth, with concert-goers expected to enter into a musical trance state. As Peter Gay explains, like 'other crowds, only more decorously, participants in the Bayreuth ambiance surrendered their individuality for a shared spiritual bath and a collective adoration of the genius who had brought them there.'[58] In fact, the very model of the musical conductor as a performing genius who controls the orchestra through the force of his personality only began at about the same time as the Fox sisters discovered spiritualism, and was heralded by the arrival of the baton. Indeed, new sisters were found for the 1880s, the Creery girls, three teenaged daughters of the Revd A.M. Creery of Buxton, with whom William Barrett made over a thousand supervised trials for telepathy. (The girls later revealed that they had used codes to communicate, and had completely outsmarted the scientists who had interviewed them.) The SPR also studied two telepathists from Brighton, Douglas Blackburn (1857–1929) and George Albert Smith (1864–1959): they also confessed to fraud later on.[59]

For the serious scientists of the SPR, it was clear that, even if a medium was unmasked here and there, a hard kernel of truth must surely be found. Between 1882 and 1883, Frank Podmore's rooms at Dean's Yard were outfitted as a proper research laboratory. It was Frederic Myers who in 1882 actually coined the term 'telepathy', linking the phenomenon with other 'tele-technologies', and also with the traditional supernatural concept of sympathy, and the later notion of 'empathy', a union of minds, even love, if you like.[60]

The question still remained, however, if what they were witnessing had anything to do with the dead. A far less extreme, and perhaps more scientific, position would be to argue that even if it was difficult to find the appropriate theoretical underpinning to explain the presence of the dead among us, we might compromise by admitting the existence of 'phantasms of the living', what might be thought of as hologramatic hallucination. Gurney, Myers and Podmore made a careful study of 702 such cases and decided that there was something to it. Curiously, although they made laboratory scientific investigation the centre of their research, these leading lights of the SPR were willing to take field research on board with the same credulity that contemporaneous anthropologists swallowed the stories that trappers and traders sent to them from distant outposts in Australia. Social status alone was often sufficient proof of veracity.[61]

In any case, by the time their study of the 'phantasms of the living' was published, the entire field of telepathy was fast moving in the direction of psychology, a discipline that only now was beginning to win the respectability that its champions craved. Several of the key players themselves passed over at the turn of the century: Henry Sidgwick died in August 1900, followed by Frederic Myers at Rome in January 1901, with William James at his side. In February 1901, the month after his death, Myers announced from beyond the grave, via Mrs Piper, that he had formed a branch of the SPR in the afterlife, and that the spirit of Henry Sidgwick himself had agreed to accept the presidency. By making his appearance in this way, Myers disproved his own view expressed when living that so-called ghosts were merely telepathic phenomena generated by the living that especially sensitive people were able to detect. He was especially active once dead, and communicated through several mediums at once, including Rudyard Kipling's sister Alice (1868–1948), living in India. Myers also dictated an account of the other world via automatic writing, published in 1932.[62]

IV

Just as the Gothic novel of the late eighteenth century had a period of intense interest and activity, so too was the outpouring of spiritualism reflected in the flowering of supernatural literature in the second half of the nineteenth century.[63] Leading the way was the ponderous Bulwer-Lytton, whose novel *Zanoni* (1842) was a veritable guide book to the occult world.[64] In the United States, Edgar Allan Poe (1809–49) produced a famous, if rather weak, story entitled 'Mesmeric Revelation' (1844), beginning with these words:

> Whatever doubt may still envelop the rationale of mesmerism, its startling facts are now almost universally admitted. Of these latter, those who doubt, are your mere doubters by profession – an unprofitable and disreputable tribe. There can be no more absolute waste of time than the attempt to prove, at the present day, that man, by mere exercise of will, can so impress his fellow, as to cast him into an abnormal condition, of which the phenomena resemble very closely those of death, or at least resemble them more nearly than they do the phenomena of any other normal condition within our cognizance; that, while in this state, the person so impressed employs only with effort, and then feebly, the external organs of sense, yet perceives, with keenly refined perception, and through channels supposed unknown, matters beyond the scope of the physical organs; that, moreover, his intellectual faculties are wonderfully exalted and invigorated; that his sympathies with the person so impressing him are profound; and, finally, that his susceptibility to the impression increases with its frequency, while, in the same proportion, the peculiar phenomena elicited are more extended and more pronounced. I say that these – which are the laws of mesmerism in its general features – it would be supererogation to demonstrate; nor shall I inflict upon my readers so needless a demonstration to-day.

Children's literature also reflected the supernatural, and the promise of another world that would contain elements of our own, but in another form or even reversed. These themes come out clearly in Charles Kingsley (1819–75), *The Water-Babies* (1862/1863), and 'Lewis Carroll' (Charles Lutwidge Dodgson), *Alice's Adventures in Wonderland* (1865) and *Through the Looking Glass* (1871). Bulwer-Lytton returned with a splendid science-fiction fantasy about *The Coming Race* (1871), which lived in a secret underground world, nourished by a mysterious substance called 'vril' – metamorphosed in real life by a Scottish entrepreneur into the eternal 'Bovril'.[65] Sir Henry Rider Haggard (1856–1925) found his mysterious civilisation in Africa, described in his gripping book *She* (1888) and the less gripping sequels and prequels that came afterwards. Robert Louis Stevenson (1850–94) reported on *The Strange Case of Dr Jekyll and Mr Hyde* (1886). *The Picture of Dorian Gray* (1891) by Oscar Wilde (1854–1900) also came out of this same super-natural milieu.

Hypnotism provided a fruitful fictional theme, especially the fear that someone or something might get inside one's mind and seize control. This was the concept behind *Trilby* (1894), the runaway best-seller by George Du Maurier (1834–96), the story of a poor English girl living in France who becomes a celebrated singer once her body comes under the control of the evil German–Jewish genius Svengali. Trilby was modelled on the Swedish soprano Jenny Lind (1820–87), who in 1847 came to live in England. In the United States she was managed by P.T. Barnum, and it was there in 1852 that she married Otto Goldschmidt (1829–1907), a German–Jewish pianist, conductor and composer. As it happened, Jenny Lind met Dr James Braid the pioneer of hypnosis while on tour in England in the 1840s: together they managed to get hypnotised servant girls to do back-up for the great singer.[66]

This same curious combination of the supernatural and the scientific comes out very well in *Dracula*, the novel by Irishman Bram Stoker (1847–1912), which was published in 1897 and became an instant and eternal best-seller. The vampire's rather more human inter-locutors were equipped with the latest gadgets that late nineteenth-century science could provide. When Jonathan Harker first comes to the Transylvanian castle of Count Dracula, he notes in his journal that he has 'taken with my Kodak views of it from various points'. Dr Seward keeps a 'phonography diary', and when on the road notes, 'How I miss my phonograph! To write diary with a pen is irksome to me.' 'I feel so grateful to the man who invented the "Traveller's" typewriter,' notes Mina Harker, 'I should have felt quite astray doing the work if I had to write with a pen.' The case against Dracula is built in the novel by a technique of multi-narration, with each witness telling his or her story, as in a law court . . . or in the pages of the *Journal of the Society for Psychical Research.*[67]

Other supernatural fiction that spoke to the same popular interest included Richard Marsh (1857–1915), *The Beetle* (1897), and the much more famous account of *The War of the Worlds* (1898) by H.G. Wells

(1866–1946). So too did the more specific themes emphasised by the SPR continue to fascinate readers.

The novelist Henry James (1843–1916) knew very well of his philosopher brother's involvement with the SPR, and even consented to be his disembodied voice by reading a paper by William James at a meeting of the Society. Henry James's *Turn of the Screw* (1898) is one of the most famous ghost stories of all time. He also played with the role of the medium in his story 'In the Cage' (1898), which told the tale of a girl who worked in a telegraph office.[68] Henry James himself from 1897 was dictating his literary output to a secretary who then typed his words onto a Remington. From 1907 his secretary was Theodora Bosanquet (1880–1961), who, after her employer's death, got in touch with him through a Ouija Board and continued to take posthumous dictation.[69] Interestingly enough, when she described her work at the keyboard while James was still alive, she wrote that the 'business of acting as a medium between the spoken and the typewritten word was at first as alarming as it was fascinating'. Even then she was 'acting as a medium'.[70]

Perhaps the most intense contemporary exploration of the implications of the disembodied voice is *Heart of Darkness* (1899) by Joseph Conrad (1857–1924). This short novel, less than a hundred pages long, is a tale within a tale within a tale. An unnamed frame narrator recalls a story told by a certain Marlow, who is the only person actually given a proper name, apart from Kurtz, the colonial company agent who in his search for ivory has carved out for himself a brutal and vicious little African empire where he is feared and adored as a white god. This Marlow tells his story on board a ship called the *Nellie*, at anchor in the Thames, mostly in the dark, so that 'he, sitting apart, had been no more to us than a voice'. His listeners felt a 'faint uneasiness inspired by this narrative that seemed to shape itself without human lips in the heavy night-air of the river'. Marlow narrates his journey up river as he 'penetrated deeper and deeper into the heart of darkness'. For him it becomes a quest not only to find Kurtz but moreover to hear his voice: 'The man presented himself as a voice . . . He was very little more than a voice.' Marlow, of course, eventually meets Kurtz; hears his voice, and tries to bring him back from the wilderness, only to have the great man expire en route, whispering his famous last words, 'The horror! The horror!' Marlow has now become a human phonograph, duty bound to bring the record of Kurtz's last words back to his Intended, 'the whisper of a voice speaking from beyond the threshold of an eternal darkness.' Rather than repeating Kurtz's terrible verdict on his life, and ignoring the echo of Kurtz's words in the dusk around them, Marlow lies to her, saying. 'The last word he pronounced was – your name.' To Marlow's astonishment, nothing cosmic occurs when he tells her what she wants to hear and makes up a message from beyond the grave; quite the contrary:

> I heard a light sigh and then my heart stood still, stopped dead short by an exulting and terrible cry, by the cry of inconceivable triumph and of unspeakable pain. 'I knew it – I was sure!' . . . She knew. She was sure. I heard her weeping; she had hidden her face in her hands. It seemed to me that the house would collapse before I could escape, that the heavens would fall upon my head. But nothing happened. The heavens do not fall for such a trifle. Would they have fallen, I wonder, if I had rendered Kurtz that justice which was his due? Hadn't he said he wanted only justice? But I couldn't. I could not tell her. It would have been too dark – too dark altogether . . .

Marlow is a bogus medium, but the perpetrator only of a victimless crime.[71]

The image of those lucky few who had contact with spirits in nineteenth-century England and America – and told people what they wanted to hear – is described very well in a poem entitled 'Mr Sludge, "The Medium"' by Robert Browning (1812–89), published in his book *Dramatis Personae* (1864). The character is quite clearly Daniel Dunglas Home, the famous medium who was just then at the height of his powers. Browning's poem is a dramatic monologue, the story of a confrontation in Boston between Sludge the medium and a gentleman who has caught him cheating. Sludge wards off both a beating and the possibility of being denounced 'to Greeley's newspaper', and settles down with 'a parting egg-nogg and cigar' to ruminate about his profession, declaring that 'England's the place, not Boston – no offence!'

> I've been so happy with you! Nice stuffed chairs,
> And sympathetic sideboards; what an end
> To all the instructive evenings!
> . . .

You see, sir, it's your own fault more than mine;
It's all your fault, you curious gentlefolk!
. . .

For instance, men love money – that, you know
And what men do to gain it: well, suppose
A poor lad, say a help's son in your house,
Listening at keyholes, hears the company
Talk grand of dollars, V-notes, and so forth,
How hard they are to get, how good to hold,
How much they buy, – if, suddenly, in pops he –
'*I*'ve got a V-note!' – what do you say to him?
What's your first word which follows your last kick?
'Where did you steal it, rascal?'
. . .

But let the same lad hear you talk as grand
At the same keyhole, you and company,
Of signs and wonders, the invisible world;
How wisdom scouts our vulgar unbelief
More than our vulgarest credulity;
How good men have desired to see a ghost, . . .
If he break in with, 'Sir, *I* saw a ghost!'
Ah, the ways change! He finds you perched and prim;
It's a conceit of yours that ghosts may be:
There's no talk now of cow-hide. 'Tell it out!
'Don't fear us! Take your time and recollect!
'Sit down first: try a glass of wine, my boy!
'And, David, (is not that your Christian name?)'

Having discovered David the Medium, Sludge continues, gentlemen
can hardly resist the pleasure of showing him around to others:

Why should not you parade your lawful prize?
Who finds a picture, digs a medal up,
Hits on a first edition, – he henceforth
Gives it his name, grows notable: how much more,
Who ferrets out a 'medium'? 'David's yours,
'You highly-favoured man? Then, pity souls
'Less privileged! Allow us share your luck!'
So, David holds the circle, rules the roast,

> Narrates the vision, peeps in the glass ball
> Sets-to the spirit-writing, hears the raps,
> As the case may be.

In any case, are David the Medium's stories any more fantastic than those told by Captain Sparks over the way?

> Have not you hunting-stories, scalping-scenes,
> And Mexican War exploits to swallow plump

As for the gentleman's friends, his very social status guarantees the veracity of the medium's testimony, and indeed an unspoken and often unconscious conspiracy soon grows up between the medium and his patron:

> Sir, where's the scrape you did not help me through,
> You that are wise? And for the fools, the folk
> Who came to see, – the guests, (observe that word!)
> Pray do you find guests criticize your wine,
> Your furniture, your grammar, or your nose?
> Then, why your 'medium'? What's the difference?
> Prove your madeira red-ink and gamboge, –
> Your Sludge, a cheat – then, somebody's a goose
> For vaunting both as genuine. 'Guests!' Don't fear!
> They'll make a wry face, nor too much of that,
> And leave you in your glory.

At the end of the monologue, Sludge leaves Boston and goes off to England, asking: 'Beside, is he the only fool in the world?' Hardly, as we shall see.

FIVE

Occult Within: Psychologising the Esoteric

The early stages of the spiritualist adventure were quite clearly marked by a great emphasis on its compatibility with Science, as it developed during the nineteenth century. Yet by the mid-1880s, concepts such as spiritualism and telepathy were moving away from the physical sciences to the new field of psychology, in part because the border between what was scientific and what was not was far less clearly drawn there. Perhaps the end point of that process should be fixed at 1927, when Dr Joseph Banks Rhine (1895–1980) began conducting studies of psychic phenomena at Duke University. Rhine had first become interested in the subject after hearing a lecture by Arthur Conan Doyle (1859–1930), and with the help of his wife and Dr William McDougall (1871–1938), the chairman of the psychology department, he began to accumulate a huge amount of data, which eventually would lead to the establishment of the Duke University Parapsychology Laboratory in 1935. Parapsychology was a new discipline, and for it Rhine invented a new term: 'extrasensory perception', ESP. This journey from physics to psychology and on to parapsychology is what concerns us here.

I

We have already noted the famous (if inadequate) distinction between magic and religion posited by James George Frazer (1854–1941), but it still left open the question of what to do with people who were simply out of their minds. This was an issue that troubled religious thinkers for centuries, especially in the debate over what was called 'enthusiasm'. An enthusiast was someone who claimed to be *en theos*, to be filled with a deity, specifically God. Such a person was likely to exhibit rather eccentric behaviour such as involuntary bodily movements or spontaneous speech, and to report experiences and feelings beyond the realm of normal human happenings. Enthusiasts understood these phenomena as being religious in origin, although they would not deny that God works through the human body and that at one level at least, a physiological explanation could be found. Their opponents, however, denounced the enthusiasts as deluded fanatics.[1] Indeed, the historian Frank Manuel (1910–2003) argued that the study of psychology itself emerged in England not as a neutral investigation of the human mind, but as a religious tool that could distinguish between genuine divine inspiration and the merely mad.[2]

Speculation on these weighty issues began much earlier. The first key text was *The Anatomy of Melancholy* (1621) by Robert Burton (1577–1640).[3] Slightly later on came a *Treatise Concerning Enthusiasme* (1655) by Meric Casaubon (1599–1671), and *Enthusiasmus Triumphatus* (1656), written by Henry More (1614–87).[4] A case could also be made for Jonathan Edwards (1703–58) as the grandfather of modern psychology. This great American preacher was no stranger to ecstatic religious devotion during the 'Great Awakening' in New England, which he himself sparked in a riveting sermon he gave in 1734 at Northampton, Massachusetts. Edwards was troubled by the fact that the same phenomena associated with extreme religious excitement could arise from both true divine and false Satanic origins. There was always the possibility that the person was simply mad, even without the Devil's intervention. Edwards noted that only God could actually dwell in a person's soul, and thereby cause authentic religious excitement by enlivening his or her imagination; this was His path towards influencing an individual believer. Satan, on the other hand, had no access to the soul, and had to make do with poisoning a person's imagination directly, without passing through the soul. So too was the imagination the site of a madman's delusions. Despite the differing causes of religious excitement, the symptoms were identical, and could be explained in naturalistic terms.[5]

These insights concerning the connections between the human body, the imagination and the eternal soul came to be rather more institutionalised in the development of New Thought, or Harmonial Religion. The key figure here was Phineas Parkhurst Quimby (1802–66), who began as a mesmeric healer but eventually came to the realisation that even if magnetic force was the means of controlling the body, at the root of it all was the human mind. It is a person's beliefs and expectations that regulate the magnetic force, so that ultimately it is possible to cure the body by the power of mind. Quimby's ideas were an interesting synthesis of concepts pioneered by Swedenborg, Andrew Jackson Davis and Emersonian Transcendentalism, especially in his attempt to find a common ground between religious faith and scientific medical practice. Faith-healing flourished as a phenomenon in the 1880s, especially through the movement begun by one of Quimby's students, Mary Baker Eddy (1821–1921), called Christian Science. Although she tried to claim that her doctrine was 'hopelessly original', her major text about *Science and Health* (1875) clearly shows the influence of her mentor.[6] From the sixth edition onwards, she also included a 'Key to the Scripture', which was more than a little reminiscent of Swedenborg.[7]

In the potted history of psychology, one of the key dates is 1879, when Wilhelm Wundt (1832–1920) founded his laboratory at Leipzig for experimental psychological research. One might set this as the point when psychology became emancipated from philosophy, and, even more so, from theology. As we have seen with regard to the study of spiritualism, the laboratory had become the very symbol of proper science in a university setting. To conduct the business of research in a laboratory was to announce that one's discipline was now seated at the high table of Science.

By the 1880s, Pierre Janet (1859–1947) in France was working in the field of experimental psychology and developing an entirely new notion of the subconscious. In his view, earlier experts who used hypnotism, such as his teacher Jean-Martin Charcot (1825–93), were wrong in seeing the results either as purely neurological or as the result of alternating personalities.[8] Janet believed that more than one personality or consciousness could exist within the same mind, although these 'secondary selves' were pathological in nature. Consciousness, according to Janet, was divisible; our selves are constituted by 'chains of memory', which are themselves disassociated from other chains, although new chains can be created or accessed through hypnosis.

As can readily be seen, Janet's theory of a divisible consciousness came at a very pregnant time for the development of spiritualist thought. The man to make the connection was none other than our old friend Frederic W.H. Myers, whom we have already met in his dedicated search for evidence of life after death. Myers made a most important contribution to psychology by inventing the notion of a 'subliminal consciousness and subliminal memory' to refer to all mental action below the threshold of our usual consciousness, a phenomenon present in healthy minds, not only in the realm of the pathological:

> I suggest, then, that the stream of consciousness in which we habitually live is not the only consciousness which exists in connection with our organism. Our habitual or empirical consciousness may consist of a mere selection from a multitude of thoughts and sensations, of which some at least are equally conscious with those that we empirically know. I accord no primacy to my ordinary waking self, except that among my potential selves this one has shown itself the fittest to meet the needs of a common life.

Our minds, therefore, are made up of a 'spectrum of consciousness'.[9]

The wonderful thing about the subliminal is that it provided a space for all sorts of unnatural and supernatural phenomena to occur. It was no longer necessary to discuss the *origin* of these abnormal occurrences – possession, conversion, visions, mysticism – but at least we now had a theoretical site in which they could reside. This neutrality regarding the veracity of ideas in the mind made psychology a useful no man's land in late Victorian England where scientists, clergymen and spiritualists could happily meet. At the same time, the notion that our thoughts and desires could actually have an effect on the material world, other people and the future was the essence of magic. Psychology played a great part in re-enchanting the world of late-nineteenth-century England.

II

Among those who recognised Myers's contribution was a central figure in functionalist psychology and the history of philosophy, William James (1842–1910). He is so pivotal that it will be necessary to quote him somewhat at length. James was not ashamed of his fascination with the occult, and was especially drawn to the religious beliefs of people who testified to supernatural incursions into everyday life. He noted:

I cannot but think that the most important step forward that has occurred in psychology since I have been a student of that science is the discovery, first made in 1886, that, in certain subjects at least, there is not only the consciousness of the ordinary field, with its usual centre and margin, but an addition thereto in the shape of a set of memories, thoughts, and feelings which are extra-marginal and outside of the primary consciousness altogether, but yet must be classed as conscious facts of some sort, able to reveal their presence by unmistakable signs. I call this the most important step forward because, unlike the other advances which psychology has made, this discovery has revealed to us an entirely unsuspected peculiarity in the constitution of human nature. No other step forward which psychology has made can proffer any such claim as this.

More specifically,

In particular this discovery of a consciousness existing beyond the field, or subliminally as Mr Myers terms it, casts light on many phenomena of religious biography . . . Mr Myers for the first time proposed as a general psychological problem the exploration of the subliminal region of consciousness throughout its whole extent, and made the first methodical steps in its topography.[10]

James was particularly interested in Christian Science – or as he still called it in the more generic nineteenth-century terminology, 'New Thought' – a concept in his view that 'has recently poured over America and seems to be gathering force every day . . . and it must now be reckoned with as a genuine religious power'. The proof of this, James noted shrewdly, was that 'New Thought' had reached the stage 'when the demand for its literature is great enough for insincere stuff mechanically produced for the market, to be to a certain extent supplied by publishers, – a phenomenon never observed, I imagine, until a religion has got well past its earliest insecure beginnings.' That being said, James did not make such remarks in order to belittle these ideas; on the contrary, he thought, the 'mind-cure gospel' was not merely a 'silly appeal to imagination to cure disease'. In fact, James insisted, he found 'its method of experimental verification to be not unlike the method of all science'. Once again, the defining feature of the nineteenth-century occult world view was its compatibility with normative science.[11]

But it was Myers's concept of the subliminal that James thought to be the key to explaining a huge range of religious experience and behaviour that in any other context would unashamedly be condemned as pathological. When confronted with such examples, James insisted, we 'must describe and name them just as if they occurred in non-religious men'. If Jonathan Edwards located such extremism in the imagination, James (following Myers) posited the subliminal as the site of such eccentric phenomena:

> The most important consequence of having a strongly developed ultra-marginal life of this sort is that one's ordinary fields of consciousness are liable to incursions from it of which the subject does not guess the source, and which, therefore, take for him the form of unaccountable impulses to act, or inhibitions of action, of obsessive ideas, or even of hallucinations of sight or hearing.

James was well aware that these 'impulses may take the direction of automatic speech or writing', some of the standard features of the spiritualist experience. Without hesitation he looks to his occultist associate to understand what happens, noting that 'generalizing this phenomenon, Mr Myers has given the name of *automatism*, sensory or motor, emotional or intellectual, to this whole sphere of effects due to "uprushes" into the ordinary consciousness of energies originating in the subliminal parts of the mind.'

Like Jonathan Edwards in the eighteenth century, William James also looked for a particular area of consciousness where both religious and purely pathological experience could act upon the human subject. Identifying this experience and the mental space in which it might be located, however, left completely untouched the question of origins, be they divine, satanic or mere mental illness:

> But just as our primary wide-awake consciousness throws open our senses to the touch of things material, so it is logically conceivable that *if there be* higher spiritual agencies that can directly touch us, the psychological condition of their doing so *might be* our possession of a subconscious region which alone should yield

access to them. The hubbub of the waking life might close a door which in the dreamy Subliminal might remain ajar or open.

When God acts upon us, He does so through the subliminal consciousness, since ultimately there must be some bridge between His work above and our mundane bodies below.[12]

William James was well aware 'that feeling is the deeper source of religion, and that philosophic and theological formulas are secondary products, like translations of a text into another tongue'. His use of a new-fangled expression such as 'subliminal' was bound to be misinterpreted as an 'explaining' and thus belittling of religious experience. Nevertheless, he wrote,

we cannot, I think, avoid the conclusion that in religion we have a department of human nature with unusually close relations to the transmarginal or subliminal region. If the word 'subliminal' is offensive to any of you, as smelling too much of psychical research or other aberrations, call it by any other name you please, to distinguish it from the level of full sunlit consciousness . . . In it arise whatever mystical experiences we may have, and our automatisms, sensory or motor; our life in hypnotic and 'hypnoid' conditions, if we are subjects to such conditions; our delusions, fixed ideas, and hysterical accidents, if we are hysteric subjects; our supra-normal cognitions, if such there be, and if we are telepathic subjects. It is also the fountain-head of much that feeds our religion. In persons deep in the religious life, as we have now abundantly seen, – and this is my conclusion, – the door into this region seems unusually wide open; at any rate, experiences making their entrance through that door have had emphatic influence in shaping religious history.

When a person is converted to a more intense religious belief, James explained, he 'becomes conscious that this higher part is conterminous and continuous with a MORE of the same quality, which is operative in the universe outside of him, and which he can keep in working touch with, and in a fashion get on board of and save himself when all his lower being has gone to pieces in the wreck.' As for scholars of religion, James wrote,

We must begin by using less particularized terms; and, since one of the duties of the science of religions is to keep religion in connection with the rest of science, we shall do well to seek first of all a way of describing the 'more,' which psychologists may also recognize as real. The *subconscious self* is nowadays a well-accredited psychological entity; and I believe that in it we have exactly the mediating term required. Apart from all religious considerations, there is actually and literally more life in our total soul than we are at any time aware of. The exploration of the transmarginal field has hardly yet been seriously undertaken, but what Mr. Myers said in 1892 in his essay on the Subliminal Consciousness is as true as when it was first written: 'Each of us is in reality an abiding psychical entity far more extensive than he knows – an individuality which can never express itself completely through any corporeal manifestation. The Self manifests through the organism; but there is always some part of the Self unmanifested; and always, as it seems, some power of organic expression in abeyance or reserve.'

The citation from the work of Frederic Myers, to which William James glowingly refers and without embarrassment, is to the 'Proceedings of the Society for Psychical Research, vol. vii. p. 305'.[13]

William James closed his great work with a confession of his chief 'over-beliefs, buildings-out performed by the intellect into directions of which feeling originally supplied the hint'. His own 'over-belief on which I am ready to make my personal venture', James wrote, is that,

The whole drift of my education goes to persuade me that the world of our present consciousness is only one out of many worlds of consciousness that exist, and that those other worlds must contain experiences which have a meaning for our life also; and that although in the main their experiences and those of this world keep discrete, yet the two become continuous at certain points, and higher energies filter in. By being faithful in my poor measure to this over-belief, I seem to myself to keep more sane and true.[14]

In a sense, *The Varieties of Religious Experience* was the most public face of William James, and is certainly the book for which he is most remembered. Reading his work today, long after psychology has jettisoned its early flirtation with spiritualism and other esoteric practices, it is astonishing how porous were the boundaries he erected between religious passion, mysticism, spiritualism and a downright occult perception of the world.

His clear praise for Frederic Myers and by extension for the efforts of the Society for Psychical Research were clear for all to see. Myers is also cited for his views on 'ordinary planchette writing' – that is, the Ouija Board – in James's classic textbook, *The Principles of Psychology* (1890).[15] Indeed, William James became very active in the SPR itself, serving as a corresponding member (1884–89), a vice-president (1890–1910) and actually as president during 1894 and 1895, a post that he noted upon retirement was characterised by 'the absence of any active duties'.[16] Most importantly, it was William James who discovered Mrs Leonora Piper, the Boston medium with whom he worked from 1885 until his own death in 1910.[17]

William James also had a very close personal relationship with Frederic Myers, whom he admired not only as a scientist, as we have seen, but as a human being as well. One of the most original aspects of Myers's work, in James's view, was his ability to weave

> such an extraordinarily detached and discontinuous series of phenomena together. Unconscious cerebration, dreams, hypnotism, hysteria, inspirations of genius, the willing game, planchette, crystal-gazing, hallucinatory voices, apparitions of the dying, medium-trances, demonical possession, clairvoyance, thought-transference – even ghosts and other facts more doubtful – these things form a chaos at first sight most discouraging. No wonder that scientists can think of no other principle of unity among them than their common appeal to men's perverse propensity to superstition. Yet Myers has actually made a system of them, stringing them continuously upon a perfectly legitimate objective hypothesis, verified in some cases and extended to others by analogy.[18]

Despite his intense involvement in psychical research, however, James always regarded the work of Myers and the others in the SPR with a healthy scepticism, keeping the door open for empirical proof, and reserving final confirmation for when it arrived. The very fact that he could do so as late as the first decade of the twentieth century without any diminution to his scholarly reputation demonstrates that sympathy for the occult world view was not yet thought to be a sign of bad judgement.

III

The place of Frederic Myers in the history of psychology is assured not only because he posited the concept of the subliminal, but also because he was chiefly responsible for the introduction into England of the work of Sigmund Freud (1856–1939), in a paper Myers gave to the Society for Psychical Research in 1897 on 'Hysteria and Genius'. The occult was a very dangerous issue for psychoanalysis, a fact that Freud well knew. Freud's life work was to prove that the dead really do live on with us; they haunt us and affect our daily lives.

Adam Phillips, in his very interesting study of psychoanalytic ideas, has observed that although psychoanalysis as a *treatment* was very keen on reclaiming the marginalised parts of its patients, as a *profession*, however, it has always been committed to demonstrating how mainstream it really is. For this reason, it needed to dismiss and even pathologise the supernatural and the occult. What was beyond our capacity for knowledge, including the strange effects that people have on one another, was redefined and renamed as 'the unconscious' and 'sexuality'. Indeed, Phillips claims, in 'psychoanalysis the supernatural returns as the erotic'. Although Freud himself was concerned to adopt a medical model, in one sense at least, the analyst was a kind of medium, providing expression for thoughts that the patient could neither bear nor fully articulate. One might even argue that 'parapsychological phenomena made crudely vivid, the fact that there was a kind of hidden exchange of psychic states going on between people, a black market of feelings that was not subject to conscious control'.[19]

Furthermore, the SPR's research into telepathy raised some very serious issues about Freud's methodology. The very term 'telepathy' was coined by Myers in 1882 'to cover all cases of impression received at a distance without the normal operation of the recognised sense organs'.[20] The concept of 'transference' was soon recognised in psychoanalysis, the idea that a patient reacts emotionally to the analyst, even if this reaction is only a substitute for a more genuine feeling elsewhere. But what if 'transference' was really 'thought transference', as telepathy was often called? What if the patient was simply receiving signals from the analyst's brain via telepathy, inadvertent hypnotism or simply suggestion? Freud was always careful to situate himself behind and out of the patient's line of sight, but even this precaution would hardly prevent telepathic communication, if such a thing existed.

At various points in Freud's life, he toyed with occult ideas, much as he took on and dropped other somewhat outlandish concepts.[21] He was egged on partly by his connection with Sandor Ferenczi (1873–1933), a Hungarian colleague, whose first paper had been on mediumship. They were very interested in studies such as those by Gustave Le Bon (1841–1931) and Frederick Morgan Davenport (1866–1956), which suggested that individuals could be subsumed into a crowd, which then took on the characteristics of a hypnotised person.[22] In such a situation, they suggested, telepathy might come into play, being an 'original, archaic method of communication between individuals', a residual trait of primitive mankind from an earlier evolutionary state. This notion of a collective pool of genetic resources and shared memories from mankind's common origin held great fascination for Freud.

Clearly, Freud's agenda was substantially different from that of Myers and the SPR. Freud was interested in his patients' past, while Myers looked forward to the possibility of life after death, seeing it as a kind of immortality. Nevertheless, there was a good deal of overlap in their subjects of study. There was a bit about the occult in Freud's seminal examination of the *Psychopathology of Everyday Life* (1904), and much more by the time of the third edition of 1910. Freud was made a Corresponding Member of the SPR (London) in 1911, and four years later became an Honorary Fellow of the American branch. His paper on 'Psycho-Analysis and Telepathy' was written in August 1921, but was so sympathetic to the occult that it was not actually published until after his death, in 1941. Meanwhile, a more moderate version called 'Dreams and Telepathy' appeared in 1922.

All of this occult activity was very worrying to Freud's followers, who were desperate to have psychology and psychoanalysis accepted as legitimate scientific endeavours. Chief among them, of course, was Ernest Jones (1879–1958), a physician who had met Freud in 1906 at Salzburg and thereafter became the great man's chief publicist. Jones spent the years 1908 to 1913 in Canada, after being forced out of his medical post in England for having had sexual discussions with young patients. It was in Toronto that he founded the American Psychoanalytic Association (1911); on his return to London in 1912, he organised the London Psychoanalytical Society, which was formally established on 30 October of the following year. The idea was to inaugurate a fully professional body, which would form a cartel that set the standards and practices of the entire profession. In 1920, Jones became president of the International Psychoanalytical Association (founded 1910) and established their journal.

Jones knew about Freud's occult interests and hoped that he could keep them out of the serious business of psychoanalysis. He also had worked with Ferenczi, an experience that left him deeply suspicious of his Hungarian colleague. When Jones came to write his semi-official biography of Freud, he knew that it was necessary to deal with the thorny question of his hero's tendencies towards the supernatural, and devoted an entire chapter to 'Occultism', which he began with these words:

> Freud's attitude toward occultism is of peculiar interest to his biographer, since it illustrates better than any other theme the explanation of his genius . . . an exquisite oscillation between scepticism and credulity so striking that it is possible to quote just as many pieces of evidence in support of his doubt concerning occult beliefs as his adherence to them . . . To him it may prove to be only one more example of the remarkable fact that highly developed critical powers may co-exist in the same person with an unexpected fund of credulity.[23]

Jones tried anxiously to convince Freud that his support for the study of occultism was inappropriate, and was not afraid to use harsh words in this regard:

> You are doubtless right, as usual, when you say that I am too much oppressed by the telepathy matter, for in time we shall overcome the resistance it evokes just as we do all others. But you are lucky to live in a country where 'Christian Science', all forms of 'psych. research', mingled with hocus-pocus and palmistry do not prevail as they do here to heighten opposition to all psychology. Two books were written here trying to discredit [psychoanalysis] on this ground alone. You also forget

Tu quicunq; es:qui hæc legis:fiue grāma/
ticus:fiue orator:feu philofophus:aut theo/
logus:fcito.MercuriusTrifmegiftus fū:quē
fingulari mea doctria & theologica:ægyptii
prius & barbari:mox Chriftiani antiqui the
ologi:ingēti ftupore attoniti admirati funt.
Quare fi me emes:& leges:hoc tibi erit com
modi:quod paruo ære cōparatus fumma te
legentem uoluptate:& utilitate afficiã. Cū
mea doctrina cuicunq; aut   diocriter eru/
dito:aut doctiffimo placeat.Parce oro:fi ue/
rum dicere non pudet:nec piget.Lege modo
me:& fatebere non mētitum:fed fi femel le
ges:rurfum releges : & cæteris confules: ut
me emant & legant.Bene uale.

FRAH.RHOL.TARVISANVS.
GERAR. DE LISA SCRIPTORI :
    MEI COPIAM FECIT.
    VT IPSE CAETERIS
    MAIOREM COPIAM
        FACERET.
        .TARVISII.
.M.CCCC.LXXI.   NOVEMB.

ARGVMENTVM MARSILII FI/
CINI FLORENTINI IN LIBRũ
MERCVR II TRISMEGISTI AD
COSMVM MEDICEM PATRIAE
    PATREM.

O tēpore:quo Moyfes natus
eft:floruit Athlas aftrologus
Promethei phifici frater. ac
maternus auus maioris Mer/
curii : cuius nepos fuit Mercurius Trifme/
giftus. Hoc autem de illo fcribit Aurelius
Auguftinus.Quãq Cicero:aeq; Lactantius:
Mercurios quinq; per ordinē fuiffe uolūt.
quintumq; fuiffe illum :qui ab ægyptiis
:a grecis autē Trifmegiftus appel/
latus eft.Hunc afferunt occidiffe argū:ægi
ptiis præfuiffe:eifq; leges:ac lfas tradidiffe.
Litterarum uero caracteres in animaliū ar/
borumq; figuris inftituiffe.Hic in tanta ho/
minum ueneratiōe fuit:ut in deoꝗ numerũ
relatus fit.Templa illius numinis cōftructa
ꝗplurima.Nomen eius proprium:ob reuerē
tiam quandam pronūtiare:uulgo ac temere

Pages from the first edition of the *Corpus Hermeticum*. Translated from the Greek into Latin by Marsilio Ficino at the request of Cosimo de Medici, it was published in 1471.

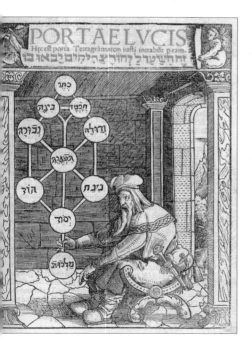

(*Left*) *Portae Lucis*, the Latin translation of the kabbalistic writings of Joseph ben Abraham Gikatilla, 1516.

(*Right*) Page from the *Sefer Raziel*, a collection of kabbalistic texts compiled in the seventeenth century.

Paracelsus (1490–1541).

John Dee (1527–1608).

The Paracelsian cosmos, from Joannes D. Mylius' *Opus Medico-Chymicum, c.* 1618–30.

Joseph Wright of Derby, *The Alchymist in Search of the Philosophers' Stone
Discovers Phosphorus*, 1771.

Johann Valentin Andreae (1586–1654).

Michael Maier (1568–1622).

(*Above*) Francis Bacon (1561–1626) under an
angel's wing: frontispiece of the official history
of the Royal Society, 1667.

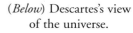

(*Below*) Descartes's view
of the universe.

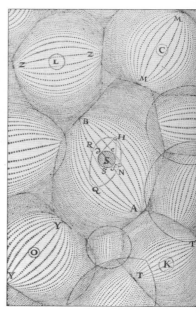

Freemasonry:
the Duke of Montagu
presenting the Roll of
Constitutions to Philip,
Duke of Wharton, 1723.

(*Below left*) The first
degree tracing board.
(*Below right*) The third
degree tracing board.

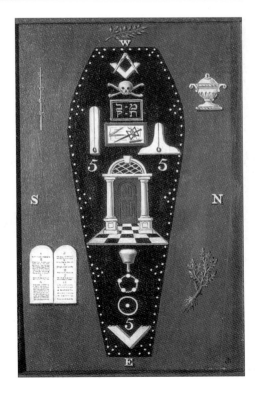

Adam Weishaupt (1748–1830), founder of the Illuminati of Bavaria.

'A Masonic Anecdote' (Alessandro, Count of Cagliostro) by James Gillray, 1786.

The Book of Mormon.

BOOK OF MORMON:

AN ACCOUNT WRITTEN BY THE HAND OF MOR-
MON, UPON PLATES TAKEN FROM
THE PLATES OF NEPHI

Wherefore it is an abridgment of the Record of the People of Nephi; and also of
the Lamanites; written to the Lamanites, which are a remnant of the House of
Israel; and also to Jew and Gentile; written by way of commandment, and also
by the spirit of Prophecy and of Revelation. Written, and sealed up, and hid
up unto the LORD, that they might not be destroyed; to come forth by the gift
and power of GOD unto the interpretation thereof; sealed by the hand of Moroni, and hid up unto the LORD, to come forth in due time by the way of Gentile;
the interpretation thereof by the gift of GOD; an abridgment taken from the
Book of Ether.

Also, which is a Record of the People of Jared, which were scattered at the time
the LORD confounded the language of the people when they were building a
tower to get to Heaven; which is to shew unto the remnant of the House of
Israel how great things the LORD hath done for their fathers; and that they may
know the covenants of the LORD, that they are not cast off forever; and also to
the convincing of the Jew and Gentile that JESUS is the CHRIST, the ETERNAL
GOD, manifesting Himself unto all nations. And now if there be fault, it be the
mistake of men; wherefore condemn not the things of GOD, that ye may be
found spotless at the judgment-seat of CHRIST.

BY JOSEPH SMITH, JUNIOR.

AUTHOR AND PROPRIETOR.

PALMYRA:

PRINTED BY E. B. GRANDIN, FOR THE AUTHOR.

1830.

American outdoor religious meeting, 1839.

(*Left*) Sir William Crookes (1832–1919) with the medium Florence Cook.

(*Right*) Photograph taken by Crookes of Florence Cook using magnesium light.

Madame Blavatsky (1831–91) and Henry Steel Olcott (1832–1907) in London, 1888.

The theologian and dispensationalist John Nelson Darby (1800–82).

sometimes in what a special position you are personally. When so many things pass under the name of [psychoanalysis], our great answer to inquirers is '[psychoanalysis] is Freud', so now the statement that [psychoanalysis] leads logically to telepathy etc. is more difficult to meet. In your private political opinions you might be a Bolshevist, but you would not help the spread of [psychoanalysis] to announce it. So when '*Ru[ü]cksichten der äusseren Politik*' [considerations of external policy] kept you silent before, I do not know how the situation should have changed in this respect.[24]

Freud seems to have regarded Jones's outburst with more humour than anger:

As you remember I already expressed a favourable bias toward telepathy during our trip to the Harz. But there was no need to do so publicly; my conviction was not very strong, and the diplomatic aspect of preventing psychoanalysis from drawing too close to occultism very easily retained the upper hand. Now, the revision of *Traumdeutung* for the collected edition gave me the impetus to reconsider the problem of telepathy. In the meantime, however, my personal experience through tests, which I undertook with Ferenczi and my daughter, have attained such convincing power over me that diplomatic considerations had to be relinquished. Again I was presented with an instance where, on a very much reduced scale, I had to repeat the great experiment of my life; namely, to admit to a conviction without considering the resonance of the world around me. So it was then inevitable. If anyone should bring up my Fall with you, just answer calmly that my acceptance of telepathy is my own affair, like my Judaism and my passion for smoking, etc., and that the subject of telepathy is not related to psychoanalysis.[25]

This spat between Jones and Freud took place in 1926, but Freud's most interesting contribution to the study of the occult was an essay written seven years earlier called '*Das Unheimliche*' ('The Uncanny'). The piece was published at the end of 1919, but in a letter to Ferenczi in May of the same year, Freud remarks that he is rewriting an old paper dug out of a drawer, apparently this one.[26] Freud begins his discussion with a philological discussion of the German words *heim-lich* and *unheimlich*, the positive and negative both of 'canny' and 'homey'. His conclusion is that 'the uncanny is that class of the frightening which leads back to what is known of old and long familiar'. In other words, Freud is arguing that the scariest and strangest phenomena are not those that are exotic, alien and foreign – as in the early Gothic novel – but in fact that which is most 'homey', things so much within us that they have become secret through repression, and are only now coming to light. As Freud himself puts it:

> If psycho-analytic theory is correct in maintaining that every affect belonging to an emotional impulse, whatever its kind, is transformed, if it is repressed, into anxiety, then among instances of frightening things there must be one class in which the frightening element can be shown to be something repressed which *recurs*. This class of frightening things would then constitute the uncanny; and it must be a matter of indifference whether what is uncanny was itself originally frightening or whether it carried some *other* affect.

Freud then provides a literary analysis of 'The Sandman' by E.T.A. Hoffmann (1776–1822), a short tale of madness, automatons and suicide. Then Freud moves on to some general discussion, but also some autobiographical passages concerning his own experiences of the uncanny, such as what occurred during a stroll 'through the deserted streets of a provincial town in Italy', or unexpectedly seeing and not recognising his own reflection in a sleeping-car mirror, or noticing a strange repetition of the number sixty-two. As Freud explains:

> Our analysis of instances of the uncanny has led us back to the old, animistic conception of the universe. This was characterized by the idea that the world was peopled with the spirits of human beings; by the subject's narcissistic overvaluation of his own mental processes; by the belief in the omnipotence of thoughts and the technique of magic based on that belief; by the attribution to various outside persons and things of carefully graded magical powers, or '*mana*'; as well as by all the other creations with the help of which man, in the unrestricted narcissism of that stage of development, strove to fend off the manifest prohibitions of

reality. It seems as if each one of us has been through a phase
of individual development corresponding to this animistic stage
in primitive men, that none of us has passed through it without
preserving certain residues and traces of it which are still capable
of manifesting themselves, and that everything which now strikes
us as 'uncanny' fulfils the condition of touching those residues
of animistic mental activity within us and bringing them to
expression.

As a result, Freud emends his original definition of the uncanny as
based on a repressed feeling that is revived for some reason, now to
include when 'primitive beliefs which have been surmounted seem
once more to be confirmed'.

Not content to leave well enough alone, Freud then launches into
pure speculation of exactly the kind that his minder Ernest Jones
found so objectionable: 'Biology has not yet been able to decide whether
death is the inevitable fate of every living being,' he wrote, 'or whether
it is only a regular but yet perhaps avoidable event in life.' Even more
telling, Freud claimed,

> In our great cities, placards announce lectures that undertake to
> tell us how to get into touch with the souls of the departed; and
> it cannot be denied that not a few of the most able and pene-
> trating minds among our men of science have come to the
> conclusion, especially towards the close of their own lives, that
> a contact of this kind is not impossible. Since almost all of us
> still think as savages do on this topic, it is no matter for surprise
> that the primitive fear of the dead is still so strong within us
> and always ready to come to the surface on any provocation.

Freud understood, moreover, how close his own work came to the
dangerous territory of the occult: 'Indeed,' he wrote, 'I should not be
surprised to hear that psycho-analysis, which is concerned with laying
bare these hidden forces, has itself become uncanny to many people
for that very reason.'

But of course it was Carl Gustav Jung (1875–1961) who amalga-
mated psychoanalysis and the occult to such an extent that it became
impossible to tell where one left off and the other began.[27] Jung was
heavily influenced by William James and by Ernst Haeckel's (1834–1919)

concept of evolutionary monism.[28] Jung even wrote his doctoral thesis (1902) on mediumship. His celebrated theory of 'synchronicity' is clearly a psychological reinterpretation of the classic esoteric notion of correspondences. The problem with Jung, as Freud fully appreciated, was that he insisted on incorporating a huge amount of mythology into his psychology, including a good deal of racist *völkisch* and Aryan material. Jung learned all of the most extreme lessons from the contemporaneous occult fascination with India, inventing a 'cult of the interior sun', which illuminates the individual psyche, a sort of microcosmic version of God's exterior sun. Jung famously developed the notion of the 'collective unconscious' and proved it with the bogus case of the 'Solar Phallus Man' to show that Christianity was no more than an alien mask on the true Aryan God, the pre-Christian Mithras Sun God whose glory has been unjustly obscured. Jung was what Freud could never become: in the words of his recent biographer, an Aryan Christ.[29]

Situating Jung's psychology in the history of the occult tradition is an absorbing subject that would take us well beyond our brief, and it is best merely to mention him here and go no further. For our purposes, Jung stands with one foot in the psychologised esoteric and another in the occult passage to India, which will be the subject of the next chapter in our story.

SIX

The Occult Passage to India

For the earliest scholars of the occult tradition, people like Ficino, the Hermeticists, or even Isaac Newton, the source of all wisdom was located in ancient Egypt. During the nineteenth century, Egypt gradually lost to India its position as ultimate fount of knowledge. In order to trace this important change, one needs to begin with the study of comparative religion.

If the gelling of Victorian science had the effect of experimentalising spiritualism, then the growth of comparative religion and anthropology helped to find a similar common ground between the ghostly and a Protestantism from which everything supernatural but God had been purged. The idea of studying religious beliefs among the non-Christian peoples and looking for shared concepts and categories was certainly on the philosophical agenda by the late eighteenth century. Among the earlier scholars who had gone in this direction were men such as Giambattista Vico (1668–1744), Constantine Francis de Volney (1757–1820), Richard Payne Knight (1750–1824), Godfrey Higgins (1772–1833) and of course Sir William Jones (1746–94), the pioneer of Sanskrit research in the West. The study of Hinduism came into vogue, followed by an examination of Buddhism, and, as we shall see, from the middle of the nineteenth century, India would become an essential component of the European occult tradition.

I

Some scholars explained all religion as a form of sexuality; others emphasised the importance of sun worship. Charles François Dupuis

(1742–1809), who played a key role in the first part of the French Revolution, gave a more specific explanation in the same vein, arguing that religion was a degenerate form of scientific knowledge. The common people were unable to remain at the high level of abstraction that had been achieved by the ancient philosophers, especially the Egyptians, and regressed to worshipping the symbols of the ideas they could no longer understand.[1] Perhaps the most massive study of all was that by Benjamin Constant (1767–1830), a five-volume analysis of religion that showed an evolutionary path between Plato and Protestantism.[2]

For Christians, clearly it was the towering figure of Jesus that needed to be incorporated into any kind of general analysis of comparative religion. The pioneer here was David Friedrich Strauss (1808–74), whose biography of *Das Leben Jesu* (1835) was translated into English by George Eliot in 1846 and remained a central text, leading to his general conclusion that:

> The attempt to retain in combination the ideal in Christ with the historical having failed, these two elements separate themselves: the latter falls as a natural residuum to the ground, and the former rises as a pure sublimate into the ethereal world of ideas.[3]

Although Strauss had an enormous impact in the world of biblical scholarship, even more influential was the work of his French successor Ernest Renan (1823–92). His story of *La Vie de Jésus* (1863) was an attempt to reconstruct the imaginative inner life of Christ, seen as a model for all of humanity, not because of some divine element within, but because somehow, out of the inner recesses of his personality, Jesus came as close to the Godhead as anyone could. Renan saw Jesus as a sort of rustic genius, sitting on his own, gazing at the hills of Galilee, weaving out of his own mind and experience a new and more effective way to approach God. Rather than being the product of a certain cultural milieu – Jewish sectarianism in the first century – Renan's Jesus was a self-made man who found inspiration from within as he communed with Nature, so that even the influence of John the Baptist was ultimately not decisive. The ideal type that Renan portrayed in his biography of Christ was a person who was able to explore his own inner being and, through self-development centring on the imagination, achieve a kind of divinity in this world.[4]

The work of Renan and his followers had the effect of generalising the Christian message and connecting European religion to the beliefs of cultures more physically distant but including ideas that were recognisable even to scholars living in London or Paris. Out of comparative religion evolved the new science of anthropology, and among its founders was Sir Edward Burnett Tylor (1832–1917). One of Tylor's purposes in writing was to draw the boundaries between what might be seen as universal human values, as opposed to simple superstition that should be identified and deleted:

> Beside the question of the absolute truth or falsity of the alleged possessions, manes-oracles, doubles, brain-waves, furniture movings, and the rest, there remains the history of spiritualistic belief as a matter of opinion. Hereby it appears that the received spiritualistic theory of the alleged phenomena belongs to the philosophy of savages. As to such matters as apparitions or possessions this is obvious, and it holds in more extreme cases. Suppose a wild North American Indian looking on at a spirit-séance in London. As to the presence of disembodied spirits, manifesting themselves by raps, noises, voices, and other physical actions, the savage would be perfectly at home in the proceedings, for such things are part and parcel of his recognized system of nature. The part of the affair really strange to him would be the introduction of such arts as spelling and writing, which do belong to a different state of civilization from his.

For Tylor, however, the question at hand was entirely different:

> The issue raised by the comparison of savage, barbaric, and civilized spiritualism, is this: Do the Red Indian medicine-man, the Tartar necromancer, the Highland ghost-seer, and the Boston medium, share the possession of belief and knowledge of the highest truth and import, which, nevertheless, the great intellectual movement of the last two centuries has simply thrown aside as worthless? Is what we are habitually boasting of and calling new enlightenment, then, in fact a decay of knowledge? If so, this is a truly remarkable case of degeneration, and the

savages whom some ethnographers look on as degenerate from a higher civilization, may turn on their accusers and charge them with having fallen from the high level of savage knowledge.

Tylor's answer was emphatic: seen in the comparative and historical perspective, all of this occult mumbo-jumbo was merely a survival of 'savage philosophy and peasant folklore'. As a result, he lamented, the 'world is again swarming with intelligent and powerful disembodied spiritual beings'.

Tylor's argument was that there are 'two great dogmas' that form

> the groundwork of the Philosophy of Religion, from that of savages up to that of civilized men. And although it may at first sight seem to afford but a bare and meager definition of a minimum of religion, it will be found practically sufficient; for, where the root is, the branches will generally be produced.

The first dogma postulated that there are 'souls of individual creatures, capable of continued existence after the death or destruction of the body'. The second principle was that there are 'other spirits, upward to the rank of powerful deities'. These ideas derived from the fact that 'thinking men, as yet at a low level of culture, were deeply impressed by two groups of biological problems'. The first concerned 'the difference between a living body and a dead one; what causes waking, sleep, trance, disease, death?' The second issue was with regard to the transition between sleeping and waking: 'what are those human shapes which appear in dreams and visions?' These ruminations among primitive peoples, Tylor suggested, result in a type of religion he called 'animism', as he explained:

> I purpose [sic] here, under the name of Animism, to investigate the deep-lying doctrine of Spiritual Beings, which embodies the very essence of Spiritualistic as opposed to Materialistic philosophy. Animism is not a new technical term, though now seldom used. From its special relation to the doctrine of the soul, it will be seen to have a peculiar appropriateness to the view here taken of the mode in which theological ideas have been developed among mankind. The word Spiritualism, though it may be, and sometimes is, used in a general sense, has this

obvious defect to us, that it has become the designation of a particular modern sect, who indeed hold extreme spiritualistic views, but cannot be taken as typical representatives of these views in the world at large. The sense of Spiritualism in its wider acceptation, the general doctrine of spiritual beings, is here given to Animism.

Even Tylor had to admit that the concept of 'Spiritualism' had become hopelessly tainted.[5]

In his general book on *Anthropology* (1881), Tylor expanded his views on myth and religion, arguing that both forms came from a common source: the primitive habit of animating nature. The 'savage philosopher', as Tylor called him, knows that the 'anima', the soul, exists, because the dead appear to him in visions and dreams. It was a natural step to extend the privilege of possessing an 'anima' to non-human objects such as animals, plants and stones. Tylor invented the term 'animism' to describe this cultural phenomenon, and called for the study of myths to see what we could learn about mankind's earliest history.[6]

The practitioners of this revitalised discipline of comparative religion looked for knowledge of the Godhead in all higher religions throughout the world, but especially in India. Not only was India quite simply more accessible both in terms of transport and politically, but it was almost part of the European experience by virtue of the Indo-European language group, which was becoming recognised as the ancestor of their own speech. India was injected into the occult tradition through the medium of comparative religion, and took the esoteric into entirely new directions.[7]

Frederick Denison Maurice (1805–72), professor and Christian Socialist, was among the best-known of the men who tried to find the common ground between the great religions of the world.[8] His banner was the 'comparative method' – a term coined by Auguste Comte (1798–1857) – which already had great success in so many fields. Philology, anatomy and zoology had all profited from its application, and it was only natural that it would be implemented at some stage in the history of religions. The comparative method authorised the collection of a limitless amount of ethnographic information from a wide variety of cultures. If a psychic unity existed among mankind, as they believed, then there was nothing wrong with combining ethnographic data from any part of the world. As the early anthropologist Frederick Morgan Davenport (1866–1956) put it:

> We have long grown accustomed to thinking of the body of man as a product of evolution. The structural resemblance to the lower animals, the various rudimentary survivals in the human frame, point unmistakably to a common physical origin for brute and man. But many well-informed persons have perhaps not entirely habituated themselves to the thought of the development of mind by a gradual process. And yet later researches in the psychology of men and animals, in anthropology, in philology, leave little doubt that the mind of man is an evolution as truly as the body.[9]

Just as Darwin posited a slow but progressive evolution of the human body, so too could the human mind be seen to develop from the primitive psyche to its modern form.

F.D. Maurice, indeed, had a number of even more disturbing things to say to those Victorians whose faith rested on the biblical text. He wondered firstly about the paternalistic attitude that Christians often took towards other religions. Before we set forth as missionaries to the so-called heathen, he suggested, we need to ask ourselves some hard questions:

> Was the gift worth bestowing? Were we really carrying truth into the distant parts of the earth when we were carrying our own faith into them? Might not the whole notion be a dream of our vanity? Might not particular soils be adapted to particular religions? And might not the effort to transplant one into another involve the necessity of mischievous forcing, and terminate in inevitable disappointment? Might not a better day be at hand, in which all religions alike should be found to have done their work of partial good, of greater evil, and when something much more comprehensive and satisfactory should supercede them? Were not thick shadows overhanging Christendom itself, which must be scattered before it could be the source of light to the world?

Maurice delivered these statements before a public audience, as one of his Boyle lectures, and implied that the great scientist would have agreed with him.[10]

Maurice's more controversial argument was related to the nature of revelation itself, and, by implication, to the status of the Bible in his more tolerant world:

> Faith it is now admitted has been the most potent instrument of good to the world; has given to it nearly all which it can call precious. But then it is asked, is there not ground for supposing that all the different religious systems, and not one only, may be man's constitution? Are not they manifestly adapted to peculiar times and localities and races? Is it not probable that the theology of all alike is something merely accidental, an imperfect theory about our relations to the universe, which will in due time give place to some other? Have we not reason to suppose that Christianity, instead of being, as we have been taught, a revelation, has its roots in the heart and intellects of man, as much as any other system?

Long before Émile Durkheim (1858–1917), then, Maurice was claiming that society created religion, and not the other way around. With this statement he undercut not only the Christian concept of man's origins, but the authoritative status of the Bible.[11]

F.D. Maurice had opened his Boyle Lectures by praising the work of 'a young German, now in London, whose knowledge of Sanskrit is profound', and who had it in mind to translate and publish all the Vedas.[12] This was Friedrich Max Müller (1823–1900), a German scholar from a distinguished intellectual family, whose work would put flesh on the ideological framework of comparative religion. Max Müller was engaged by the East India Company in 1847 to translate the Rig Veda, which he did from Oxford, living at first near the Press. He soon became an Oxford fixture, elected to a fellowship at All Souls; inviting Jenny Lind to sing at a party there; having Alexander Graham Bell up to his house at 7 Norham Gardens to demonstrate the telephone, the microphone and the phonograph; and entertaining the kings of Sweden and Siam together for tea.[13] He was the favourite for the Boden chair of Sanskrit in 1860, and had the vocal support of many of his colleagues, including the distinguished E.B. Pusey

(1800–82), the Regius Professor of Hebrew and leader of the Oxford Movement.[14] But his German origins and his friendship with 'heretics' worked against him, and it went to [Sir] Monier [Monier-] Williams (1819–99), himself a fine scholar, who would found the Indian Institute at Oxford. Max Müller took his defeat very badly, but eventually began 'to feel that I shall do more, as I am now, than if I were in the easy-chair of Sanskrit'.[15]

Max Müller was correct in the assessment of his own future prospects. In the first place, Oxford was so keen not to lose him that later they created a chair of philology especially for him, Max Müller's name being mentioned in the statute of foundation. As his wife recalled, it was this new chair 'that led him on from the Science of Language to the Sciences of Thought and Religion'.[16] When Max Müller proposed to leave his chair in 1875 and to return to Germany, all forces were mobilised to persuade him to stay, including appointing a deputy to lecture in the professor's stead.[17] More importantly, Max Müller at that time conceived the idea of publishing what would become his eternal monument in fifty volumes, *The Sacred Books of the East*. 'Apart from the interest which the Sacred Books of all religions possess in the eyes of the theologian,' he proclaimed in the prospectus for the project,

> and, more particularly, of the missionary, to whom an accurate knowledge of them is as indispensable as a knowledge of the enemy's country to a general, these works have of late assumed a new importance, as viewed in the character of ancient historical documents.[18]

It was to this need that Max Müller applied himself in his most glorious project.

The first volume of *The Sacred Books of the East Translated by Various Oriental Scholars and Edited by F. Max Müller* was published by the Clarendon Press in 1879. The warning to the reader was published on the very first page. 'Readers who have been led to believe,' he proclaimed, '[that these] are books full of primeval wisdom and religious enthusiasm, or at least of sound and simple moral teaching, will be disappointed on consulting these volumes.' These were different and varied texts from another time and another place, and the labour to understand them is prodigious. But the effort is worth making:

To watch in the Sacred Books of the East the dawn of the religious consciousness of man, must always remain one of the most inspiring and hallowing sights in the whole history of the world; and he whose heart cannot quiver with the first quivering rays of human thought and human faith, as revealed in those ancient documents, is, in his own way, as unfit for these studies as, from another side, the man who shrinks from copying and collating ancient MSS, or toiling through volumes of tedious commentary.

Max Müller swore to tell the whole truth about these documents, even if it meant leaving untranslated 'frequent allusions to the sexual aspects of nature' found therein. 'Scholars also who have devoted their life either to the editing of the original texts or to the careful interpretation of some of the sacred books, are more inclined, after they have disinterred from a heap of rubbish some solitary fragments of pure gold, to exhibit these treasures only than to display all the refuse from which they had to extract them.'[19] This was an academic vice that Max Müller promised to avoid, but his vow did little to prevent him from getting involved in a public dispute with Bishop Reginald S. Copleston of Colombo (Bp. 1875–1902) and others in the Letters column of *The Times* and elsewhere regarding the charge that he was constructing a sanitised picture of Eastern religions and proclivities.[20]

From the strictly religious point of view, the work of Max Müller helped promote Indian wisdom as not a bit inferior to Christian truth, and led men to ponder whether God revealed himself to different peoples in different ways at different times. It might even be argued that the Victorian fascination with things Indian was due primarily to Max Müller, and that without him the occult tradition would never have moved its ancestral roots from Egypt to India. In his own time, he was perhaps even more well-known for his esoteric theory of mythology, which he called 'solarism', arguing that most of the gods and heroes of the Indo-European peoples began life as metaphors for the observed power of the sun. The ancient Aryans proclaimed their deep feelings towards this absolute power in stories we call 'myths' because they were unable to express themselves in straightforward philosophical discourse. The reason for this failure was linguistic: the primitive Aryan spoke a language that was deficient in abstract nouns but plentiful in active verbs, itself a symptom of the fact that primitive man tended to attribute life to inanimate objects. In time, and with concurrent linguistic development, the original meaning of these figurative and metaphorical homilies was no longer remembered or understood, although the stories themselves were preserved, as myths. In Max Müller's famous phrase, myths were therefore a 'disease of language', an artefact created by a linguistic deficiency. It was his emphasis on the primacy of language that prevented Max Müller from accepting Darwin with open arms. His wife recalled that, when the two finally met in 1874 after a long correspondence, the 'conversation turning on apes as the progenitors of man, Max Müller asserted that if speech were left out of consideration, there was a fatal flaw in the line of facts. "You are a dangerous man," said Darwin, laughingly.'[21] Despite its ingenuity, Max Müller's interpretation remained a distinctly minority view, although the so-called 'Nature Mythology School' did include among its adherents the distinguished Semitic scholar Robert Brown (1844–1912).[22]

Max Müller's linguistic sun rose again, oddly enough, in Turkey, thanks to Dr Hermann F. Kvergić of Vienna, who in 1935 sent a typescript in French to Mustafa Kemal Atatürk (1881–1938), which launched the *Güneş-Dil Teorisi* ('Sun-Language Theory'). According to this hypothesis, even if Sanskrit lay behind Indo-European languages, Turkish was even older, being the closest to the original tongue of humankind as spoken in Central Asia. Turkish was therefore the ancestor of *all* modern languages. Language itself began when primitive peoples looked up at the sun and cried 'Aa!', or in modern Turkish spelling, 'Ağ'. It was all uphill after that. Atatürk was entranced by this idea, and ordered the Society for the Study of the Turkish Language to examine it closely. Not surprisingly, the Society adopted the 'Sun-Language Theory' as official gospel in 1936, and compulsory courses about it were instituted at Ankara University. Unfortunately, hardly anyone really was interested in it apart from Atatürk, and when the great man died in 1938, the entire business was quietly dropped. The aptly named İbrahim Necmi Dilmen, the Secretary-General of the Language Society, immediately cancelled the course on the 'Sun-Language Theory' that he was giving at Ankara University. His students wondered why, to which he replied diplomatically, '*Güneş öldükten sonra, onun teorisi mi kalır?*' ('After the sun has died, does its/his theory survive?')[23]

Anyway, back in Victorian England these ghostly themes were taken up and popularised in the rather more journalistic writings of Andrew Lang (1844–1912), the Scottish polymath, who saw Tylor as his mentor. Lang was also a great fan of Rudyard Kipling and Rider Haggard, but he was not happy at all with Max Müller. Lang objected that the same myths that Max Müller had observed in the Indo-European peoples also appeared among other groups outside the Aryan sphere of influence, primitive men who may or may not have had a requisite number of abstract nouns in their quiver. In any case, Lang objected, the solarists never seem to agree on what the underlying fact of the various myths actually was:

> Again, the most illustrious etymologists differ absolutely about the true sense of the names. Kuhn sees fire everywhere, and fire-myths; Mr Müller sees dawn and dawn-myths; Schwartz sees storm and storm-myths, and so on. As the orthodox teachers are thus at variance, so that there is no safety in orthodoxy, we may attempt to use our heterodox method.

Instead, Lang suggested that we should see the myths of primitive people as growing out of a certain set of material, social and psychological conditions. As these were often held in common by primitive· peoples living at the same level of existence, it is no wonder that similar stories evolved.[24] Among these tales were ghost stories, which Lang loved; he published a collection of his essays on this theme, which became among his most famous writings.[25] Eventually, Lang came out against his mentor Tylor's belief that primitive people did not have an idea of a Supreme Being, and argued that the Aborigines' notion of a god who made the world was in itself a theistic belief.[26] In 1911, Andrew Lang accepted the presidency of the Society for Psychical Research, which surprised no one at all.[27]

II

The most unavoidable nineteenth-century figure in the occult world was Madame Helena Petrovna Blavatsky (1831–91). Even the great American philosopher William James could not completely avoid quoting her, but after he did he added the following caveat:

These words, if they do not awaken laughter as you receive them, probably stir chords within you which music and language touch in common. Music gives us ontological messages which non-musical criticism is unable to contradict, though it may laugh at our foolishness in minding them. There is a verge of the mind which these things haunt; and whispers therefrom mingle with the operations of our understanding, even as the waters of the infinite ocean send their waves to break among the pebbles that lie upon our shores.[28]

Some modern readers may find James's remarks even more comical than Blavatsky's, but, in general, there is no denying that her words were harder to swallow. At the same time, if we leave aside for a moment the fakes and the frauds, the bogus séances and the mysterious letters from the Unknown Mahatmas, Madame Blavatsky does deserve a place at the table at the very least for her impressive attempt to synthesise the entire occult tradition into a single esoteric philosophy tinged with an aura of Indian wisdom.

Madame Blavatsky arrived in New York City in July 1874. As she was fond of embroidering her own biography, all we can say for certain is that she was most probably a Russian.[29] Within a few months, in October 1874, she had already met the man who would be her close associate until her death: Henry Steel Olcott (1832–1907), retired colonel, lawyer, and one of the three men who served on the federal committee that investigated the assassination of Abraham Lincoln. The two had met in Chittenden, Vermont, at the home of the Eddy brothers, Horatio (c. 1833–1922) and William (1833–1932), the local spiritualist sensation.[30] By the end of 1875, they were sharing a flat on West 47th Street in New York, and on 17 November of that year the 'Theosophical Society' was launched, with Olcott as President, and Madame Blavatsky serving as 'Corresponding Secretary'.

Their first task was to produce a text. Madame Blavatsky was soon hard at work at what would become *Isis Unveiled* (1877), her initial attempt at an occult synthesis, and about which more later. This weighty tome quite naturally emphasised Egypt as the source of ancient wisdom, conforming to the standard Western esoteric paternity since the Renaissance. But a new contender began to appear over the horizon, especially once the pioneering textual work of Max Müller and others became widely known: India.[31]

Armed with a letter of reference from President Rutherford B. Hayes, Blavatsky and Olcott set out for India at the end of 1878, arriving in Bombay in January. By 1882 they were in Adyar, Madras, which became the centre of Theosophy in India. Among the key players in this period were Dr Anna Kingsford (1846–88), president of the London branch of the Theosophical Society, who was pushed out in 1884 by Alfred Percy Sinnett (1840–1921), the author of a number of important esoteric works.[32] Another central figure joined the Theosophical Society at that time, Charles Webster Leadbeater (1847?–1934), who went out to India as well.

Madame Blavatsky returned to Europe in 1885. One of her first tasks was to deal with the report issued by the Society for Psychical Research in that year, which essentially branded her a conjuror and a fraud. The author of the work was Richard Hodgson (1855–1905), who spent years studying the more convincing Boston medium Mrs Leonora Piper (1859–1950). The report printed letters from Blavatsky's assistant, detailing the fakes at Madras, and included citations to readily available books on the occult that may have provided her with inspiration.

Madame Blavatsky for her part was back at her desk, producing her final and greatest synthesis of the occult tradition, which appeared in 1888 under the title of *The Secret Doctrine*. In theory, this was a commentary on a mysterious 'Book of Dzyan', the 'Stanzas of Dzyan', which she claimed to have seen in a subterranean Himalayan monastery, and whose esoteric doctrines were taught to her by two mahatmas named Morya and Koot Hoomi. Blavatsky opens with a quotation from Swedenborg, which helped put things in perspective:

The ancient Word, which existed in Asia before the Israelitish Word, is still preserved among the people of Great Tartary. In the spiritual world I have conversed with spirits and angels who came from that country. They told me they had possessed from the most ancient times and still possessed a Word; and that they performed their divine worship in accordance with this word which consisted of pure correspondences.[33]

By this time, Blavatsky had quite clearly posited the source of eternal wisdom in India, and revised her synthesis accordingly.

Before dismissing her books outright, it is worth having a closer look at them together, at least in order to understand her rather creative mythology and very interesting ideology.[34] Blavatsky lays the foundations in *Isis Unveiled* and then makes a number of key changes in *The Secret Doctrine*, apart from the replacement of Egypt with India. The underlying concept is that there is an 'ancient wisdom' that has never died out: 'The Gnosis lingers still on earth, and its votaries are many, albeit unknown'. This knowledge has been handed down over the centuries in various secret societies, be they Hermetic, Rosicrucian, Sufi or Druze. Not only that, but we can find echoes of this knowledge in the myths, legends and religious teachings of all peoples, which is why there are so many similar doctrines among different faiths. The goal of theosophy is to put these bits and pieces together into a coherent and comprehensive whole.

Blavatsky tells us that, apart from the forces usually studied by scientists, there is another parallel system that is no less natural, but whose operation is better understood by seers and shamans, who can identify the energy that exists in all things. This energy is called by different names – ether, vril, odic force, animal magnetism, and so on – but in any case it can be channelled by people who can learn its secrets, taking good care to master such sciences as astrology, and techniques such as clairvoyance. Mainstream scientists could do the same work, but they do not yet recognise this very natural force that runs through the cosmos.

The universe itself, according to Blavatsky, is composed of two substances, spirit and matter. Spirit takes precedence in that it is closer to the ultimate source of everything in the universe – the Universal Mind, the Universal Soul, God. Spirit carries the ideas that give form to matter, including thoughts in the material brain, which then send out an aura of subtle waves. What we call consciousness is in fact the union of spirit and matter, and in this sense is a mirror image of God, who is the Unity from which both spirit and matter derive.

Blavatsky argued that the universe – spirit, matter and consciousness – is in a constant process of evolution. She understood this not simply in the Darwinian biological sense, but as a process including the spirit as well, so that human consciousness is seen as undergoing a series of 'initiations' in an ever-improving process of upward movement, leading to a reunion with the divine, or perhaps going on for ever. In classic Gnostic fashion, Blavatsky saw the individual ego or soul as a part of the divine being. As we have seen, the idea of progressive evolution was hardly new in the nineteenth century, even before Darwin. Once Blavatsky discovered India, however, she spiced up this Western idea with the Eastern idea of *karma*, which she defined as 'simply *action*, a concatenation of *causes* and *effects*', that is to say, the force that guides things, although very different from Providence in that it is not based on the divine plan of a personal God. Theosophy would also add the notion of a parallel evolution of quasi-divine figures – the 'devic' – from elves, fairies and gnomes all the way up to powerful demigods.

Christianity was not entirely jettisoned in Blavatsky's cosmos, but was reinterpreted in some interesting ways. She called upon her followers to construe the Bible symbolically, and to understand that the life of Jesus as depicted there did not tell the complete story. Jesus, in fact, was the Egyptian-educated leader of a sect of 'new nazars' on the fringe of Judaism, adepts who practised Chaldean magic and taught Indian Buddhist doctrine. The Christianity that has come down to us is a degenerate form of Christ's original teaching. The good news is that there was no necessity for the vicarious atonement of Christ, and that evil is not part of the divine plan, nor do devils exist. Reincarnation does not appear in *Isis Unveiled*; it is a later addition in *The Secret Doctrine*, in the context of Blavatsky's Swedenborgian affirmation of spiritual progress after death.[35] The spirits that one comes across in séances are not in fact the properly dead, but rather are 'astral shells', psychic corpses as it were.

The most compelling part of her second big book, *The Secret Doctrine*, is the detailed outline of the cyclical process of universal creation. It is a combination of esoteric philosophy and science fiction, and created a lore of its own. The first volume deals with the issue of 'Cosmogenesis', a history of the aforementioned process whereby the original unified primal being emanated and thereby created time, space and matter, causing itself to differentiate into evolving beings that filled the universe. The key elements of this universe are earth, air, fire, water and ether. What one might call the executive officer of this entire process is an electro-spiritual entity called 'Fohat', whom Blavatsky describes as 'a universal agent employed by the Sons of God to create and uphold our world'. Fohat manifests itself as electricity, solar energy and the laws of nature in general.

Volume Two of *The Secret Doctrine* is a more detailed account of what comes after creation, the rise and fall of seven consecutive root races, five past and two future. The first four races were in a process of descent, becoming increasingly enmeshed in the material world. We are currently members of the fifth root race, turning the process around towards a better future. The first and earliest was the 'Astral' race, the 'Moon Ancestors' who lived in an invisible land and without fully developed physical bodies. They eventually became extinct, and were followed by the 'Hyperborean' race: they lived on a vanished polar continent and possessed fluid, watery bodies. After them came the 'Lemurian' race, inhabiting a continent in the Indian Ocean, with bodies that were fully human and sexually differentiated.[36] They were followed by the 'Atlanteans', who largely perished in the Atlantis disaster; and then by the 'Aryan' race, which is the epitome of our own phase of material existence.[37]

This, then, was Blavatsky's mature religious philosophy, if such a phrase can be used in this particular case. In 1889, the year following the publication of *The Secret Doctrine*, Annie Besant (1847–1933) joined the Theosophical Society after reading the book and meeting Madame Blavatsky herself.[38] Besant was separated from her husband, an Anglican vicar, and was a central figure in the National Secular Society, although she later would return to her Christian faith. As we shall see, Annie Besant was crucial for transforming Theosophy into a political movement, which had permanent effects on the political history of India.

By the early 1890s, then, it was clear that India had taken a central place at the bar of antiquity, and was seen as one of the mothers of civilisation. There is no doubt that all of the current India-centred projects played a part in this development: Max Müller in Oxford, Madame Blavatsky in London, and the many writers of contemporary occult texts. Olcott and Blavatsky had begun their work in the United States, and in due course Indomania took root there as well. The watershed was the 'Parliament of Religions', opened on 11 September 1893 as part of the World's Columbia Exhibition, better known as the Chicago World's Fair.[39] One of the minor events of that extravaganza was an associated lecture given the previous July to the American Historical Association by an assistant professor at the University of Wisconsin named Frederick Jackson Turner (1861–1932), entitled 'The Significance of the Frontier in American History', a paper which was to establish the 'Turner Thesis' as a chestnut of American historiography.

Far more celebrated was the appearance at the 'Parliament of

Religions' of an Indian monk named Vivekananda (1863–1902), whose performance was a bombshell.[40] Vivekananda was the monastic name of Narendra Nath Datta, a follower of the celebrated Sri Ramakrishna (1836–86). Swami Vivekananda was in the United States from July 1893 to April 1895; and then again from August 1899 to July 1900, during which time he spent ten weeks at Ridgely Manor, New York, and then began to lecture extensively, especially on the West Coast. It was said that in 1896 he was offered a professorial chair of Eastern philosophy at Harvard University but declined.

Vivekananda was a sensation. William James was taken with him, and noted that 'the paragon of all monistic systems is the Vedânta philosophy of Hindostan, and the paragon of Vedântist missionaries was the late Swami Vivekananda who visited our land some years ago'.[41] Vivekananda wrote what were probably the first books on yoga in the West, now classics.[42] Many of the swami's American followers came to him through Theosophy, but Vivekananda himself had no illusions about Madame Blavatsky and her theories, as useful as she and they were. Privately, he objected to:

> This Indian grafting of American spiritualism – with only a few Sanscrit words taking the place of spiritualistic jargon – Mahâtmâ missiles taking the place of ghostly raps and taps, and Mahatmic inspiration that of obsession by ghosts . . . The Hindus have enough of religious teaching and teachers amidst themselves . . . they do not stand in need of dead ghosts of Russians and Americans.[43]

Despite Vivekananda's disparaging remarks, Blavatsky's theories did very well in the United States, where an independent Theosophical Society was established in 1895.

Back in India, Theosophy continued to thrive, even after the death of Madame Blavatsky in 1891. When Olcott died in 1907, Annie Besant was elected president of the Theosophical Society (Adyar), a post she held until her own demise in 1933. In 1902, she persuaded the Austrian Rudolf Steiner (1861–1925) to form a Germanic section of the Theosophical Society, which he did. The loose cannon in India was Charles Leadbeater, who in 1906 was asked to leave the Theosophical Society after a hotel cleaner discovered a note addressed to a young boy and containing detailed instructions regarding self-abuse. He was allowed to return after a decent interval of two years, and soon after-wards, in 1909, he discovered Jiddu Krishnamurti (1895–1986) on a beach at Adyar and took him in to be educated as an Englishman, although he failed to get him into Oxford. Leadbeater inaugurated the 'Order of the Star in the East' in Krishnamurti's honour in 1911, proclaiming him to be the 'World Teacher'. Rudolf Steiner was so appalled by this turn of events that he refused membership in his German section to anyone who had anything to do with the Krishnamurti cult, and was expelled from the Theosophical Society for his trouble. Steiner founded his own Anthroposophical Society, which continues to thrive from its headquarters in Dorlach, Switzerland.[44]

The later career of Krishnamurti is itself quite fascinating. It was at Ojai, California, that he had the first of a series of mystical experiences – or nervous breakdowns – in August 1922, and exactly seven years later he dissolved the 'Order of the Star in the East' in an appearance before 3,000 members, henceforth speaking only for himself, and not as the head of a religious cult. He had some trouble during the Second World War for his pacifism, but among his followers were numbered famous artistic figures such as Aldous Huxley (1894–1963), Charlie Chaplin (1889–1977), and Greta Garbo (1905–90). Krishnamurti died on 17 February 1985, at his centre in Ojai.[45]

The importance of the Theosophical Society far outstripped the implications of Madame Blavatsky's speculations.[46] One of the key underlying principles of British colonialism was the notion that only a Christian could be a fully functioning and rational human being, while Hindus were incapable of individual development due to their incapacitating fatalistic pantheism, which promoted ascetic with-drawal from an evil world. Theosophists argued in return, and on behalf of the Indians, that it was Christianity that fostered unhealthy individualism, while Hinduism had a more comprehensive view of society, in which people were expected to use their talents for the good of the whole. Even caste was described as social duty, which the British misunderstood as class; karma was seen as a doctrine that provided a rational reason to be a better person, as opposed to Christianity, which allowed last-minute repentance. Freed from the negative influence of British colonialism, the Theosophists argued, the Indians could unite and return to a Golden Age of Hindu glory.

Furthermore, the Theosophical Society (Adyar) provided an all-India organisation in which Hindus could mix freely, not only with their English supporters, but also with local Parsees, Christians, Sikhs and even some Muslims who came along. The English group included some socially prominent liberals who helped promote the Indian cause, such as A.P. Sinnett. Another important figure was Allan Octavian Hume (1829–1912), who joined the Theosophical Society in 1880, and, although he left them three years later, he continued to believe that Unknown Mahatmas were in contact with Madame Blavatsky and calling for an end to British rule. Hume campaigned until he succeeded in establishing the Indian National Congress at the end of 1885, which is something that only a British ex-colonial official could have done. His base of recruitment was the Theosophical Society, and Annie Besant herself became active in the INC from 1914. Finding it too restrained, she founded a rival All-India Home Rule League in 1916, but was elected president of the Indian National Congress the following year, holding the post until 1919, when she was succeeded by Mohandas K. Gandhi (1869–1948), who like Jawaharlal Nehru (1889–1964) was involved with the Theosophical movement. For all her concentration on the world of spirits, Madame Blavatsky left a very real legacy in India, the place from which she claimed wisdom had sprung.

III

Blavatsky was the greatest of what one might call the 'entrepreneurial professional occultists'. Yet there were other esoteric masters who flourished at the end of the nineteenth century. Some were no doubt inspired by her success, and others were independently sensitive to the tenor of the times. Their names have not been completely forgotten, and deserve at least a roll-call here.

The first was 'Allan Kardec', the pseudonym of Léon-Dénizarth-Hippolyte Rivail (1804–69). His famous *Le Livre des esprits* was first published in 1856, and reissued the following year in a revised edition, which served as the basis for many more. This was a record of trance communications received through Mlle Celina Bequet ('Celina Japhet') via a mesmerist named M. Roustan. Kardec was entrusted with the manuscripts and published them himself, following up his initial success with another book called *Le Livre des médiums* (1864). His work was translated and promoted in England by Anna Blackwell, and included esoteric studies of the Christian gospels.[47]

A more dramatic figure was 'Eliphas Lévi', born Alphonse Louis Constant (*c.*1810–75), who had been expelled from a Roman Catholic seminary, although he returned to Catholicism in later life. He wrote a number of studies, especially *Le Dogme et rituel de la haute magie* (1854–6) [translated as 'Transcendental Magic'] and *Histoire de la magie* (1860), and attempted to communicate with the spirit of Apollonius of Tyana, who lived at the time of Jesus and was a famous alternative to Christ.[48]

Encouraged by all of this esoteric activity, a number of English enthusiasts decided to establish the Hermetic Order of the Golden Dawn.[49] The man behind it was Dr William Wynn Westcott (1848–1925), a London coroner interested in Freemasonry and the occult. He came across a manuscript written in a mysterious cipher, which on closer examination proved to be English, being a description of five mystical Masonic-like rituals. Westcott invited his occultist friend Samuel Liddell 'MacGregor' Mathers (1854–1918) to help create a group that might put these rituals into practice.[50] Among the pages of this 'Cypher MS' was the name and address of a certain Anna Sprengel, a German Rosicrucian, who when located authorised Westcott to found an English branch of a German occult order called *'Die Goldene Dämmerung'*, that is, 'The Golden Dawn'. This led to the establishment in 1888 of what was called the 'Isis-Urania Temple of the Hermetic Order of the Golden Dawn' with headquarters in London. Apart from Westcott and Mathers, another early member was Dr William Robert Woodman (1828–91), who was also an occultist and Masonic enthusiast. Other members in the group would include William Butler Yeats (1865–1939)[51], and Arthur Edward Waite (1857–1942)[52] who Christianised many of their rituals. The Golden Dawn collapsed in 1923.

One member who joined in 1898 but soon left after failing to seize control was Edward Alexander 'Aleister' Crowley (1875–1947), the so-called 'wickedest man in the world'. He eventually established the 'Abbey of Thelema' in Cefalu, Sicily, but was expelled by Mussolini. His adventures with his pupil and sexual partner Victor Neuburg (1883–1940) have been often described in sensationalist books about the occult.[53]

Another interesting development of the late nineteenth century was the reinvention of the Tarot. The author of the standard textbooks on the subject was a man known as 'Papus', the occult name of Gérard Encausse (1865–1916). In 1889, he founded the Martinist 'Ordre des Inconnus Silencieux', said to be still active in Paris. He became a medical doctor in 1894, and served on the Western Front during the First World War, dying of tuberculosis in 1916.[54]

Perhaps the last of the nineteenth-century occultists was the inscrutable George Ivanovich Gurdijieff (1877–1949), the Armenian-Greek-Russian founder (in 1922) of the 'Institute for the Harmonious Development of Man' at Fontainebleau. He later worked mostly in the United States and France, and his movement successfully made the transition to what would become New Age religion.[55]

IV

Theosophy was also very influential in Germany and Austria, where it fitted in nicely with *Lebensreform*, the late-Romantic movement that emphasised various alternative lifestyles including vegetarianism, herbal medicine, rural communes and nudism. Despite being rather liberal in orientation, it often overlapped with the nationalistic and racist *völkisch* movement. Blavatsky and Olcott visited Germany in 1884 and established a branch of the Theosophical Society there, which had a very short life, although Theosophical ideas were revived by the influential Franz Hartmann (1838–1912).[56]

The popular writer Guido von List (1848–1919) was the first to combine *völkisch* ideology with occultist and Theosophical concepts, by promoting the notion of 'Wotanism', supposedly an ancient Teutonic Gnostic religion. The set text was the Edda, the old Norse poetry of Iceland, where the Wotanists were said to have fled in the face of persecution by the Christians in early medieval Germany, leaving behind traces in the lore of the Rosicrucians, the Freemasons and in Renaissance Hermeticism. An important part of Wotanism was esoteric knowledge of the *runes*, the archaic Nordic script. Von List also argued that the swastika was a stylised form of the *Feuerquirl* ('fire-whisk') from which the entire cosmos was created, and therefore deserved to be a more widely known symbol. The organisation that was to promote his views was to be a Wotanist priesthood called the *Armanenschaft*, whose highest adepts studied the most esoteric

'Armanist' doctrines.[57] His model was Freemasonry, degrees and all, and the intention was to disseminate the idea that the ancient German-speaking peoples of Europe had originally been part of a superior Teutonic culture that was fatally debilitated by Christianity and was only now being recovered.

In 1893, von List met Jörg Lanz von Liebenfels (1874–1954), who was also very keen on Theosophy. Lanz fine-tuned Blavatsky's narrative of the root races and reported that the Aryans had committed bestiality with pygmies and thereby created the mixed races and the Fall, since Adam was the first pygmy. The 'Theozoa' were the godlike earlier life-forms, while Adam was the first 'Anthropozoa'. Later on down the line came Jesus, whose miracles were in fact electrical phenomena. The Passion narrative is a coded description of the attempted rape of Jesus by pygmies. This science-fiction yarn was detailed in his book *Theozoologie*, published at Vienna in 1905, and subtitled, 'or the Lore of the Sodom-Apelings and the Electron of the Gods'. Lanz published his further research in his magazine *Ostara*, one of whose regular readers was a young Austrian later known as Adolf Hitler (1889–1945), who visited Lanz in 1909. Nevertheless, Lanz was forbidden to publish his work under the Third Reich, and his organisations were forcibly dissolved, by order of the Gestapo.

More immediately influential was Adam Alfred Rudolf Glauer (1875–1945), the son of a train driver who went by the name of 'Rudolf von Sebottendorff' after being adopted by an Austrian of that name. He founded the Thule Society in 1918, and took for its symbol a long dagger with a shining swastika sun wheel. The swastika (*das Hakenkreuz*) had long been a mystical symbol: left-handed (clockwise) was the orientation used by the Theosophists and the secret *Germanenorden* and the Nazis; right-handed (counter-clockwise) was the style preferred by von List and the Thule Society. The Thule Society adopted many of von List's views, especially the notion of Iceland as a haven for German refugees from Christianity. In the summer of 1918, he bought a cheap weekly Munich suburban newspaper called the *Beobachter*, and renamed it the *Münchener Beobachter und Sportblatt* (there were later name changes), publishing a winning combination of anti-Semitic propaganda and racing news, and printing items about the Thule Society and the *Germanenorden*. Curiously, on 31 May 1919, the paper published a twelve-point programme which was very similar indeed to the twenty-five points of the *Nationalsozialistische Deutsche Arbeiterpartei* (NSDAP) that Hitler would proclaim in February the following year. The Thulists founded a workers' ring that became a political party at a tavern meeting on 5 January 1919, the *Deutsche Arbeiterpartei* (DAP). On 12 September 1919, Hitler attended a meeting of the DAP, originally as an army spy, but ended up joining the group and within two months was lecturing in taverns on their behalf. The DAP eventually split from the Thule Society, which in true esoteric fashion remained faithful to its lodge-like origins, like the even more secret *Germanenorden*, with its Masonic-like rituals and ceremonies and its swastika symbol.[58] On 9 November 1919, the Thule Society and the *Germanenorden* held their first joint meeting, at which they heard Sebottendorff's call to take arms against 'Juda'. Sebottendorff himself stopped attending his own Thule Society after 1919, having been accused of letting its enemies get hold of the membership list when the headquarters were finally raided by the Communists on 26 April. On Christmas Day, 1920, a small announcement appeared in the *Beobachter*, announcing that the NSDAP had acquired the paper 'in order to develop it into a relentless weapon for Germanism against any hostile un-German efforts.'[59]

As for Sebottendorff, he spent years wandering around, writing and posing as a baron in spa towns, returning to Munich in 1933 and claiming credit for inventing the Nazis. Sebottendorff published a book entitled *Bevor Hitler kam*, in which he offered the following historical genealogy, which was not entirely fanciful:

Thule members were the people to whom Hitler first turned, and who first allied themselves with Hitler! The armament of the coming Führer consisted – besides the Thule itself – of the Deutscher Arbeiterverein, founded in the Thule by Brother Karl Harrer at Munich, and the Deutsch-Sozialistische Partei, headed there by Hans Georg Grassinger, whose organ was the *Münchener Beobachter*, later *Völkischer Beobachter*. From these three sources Hitler created the Nationalsozialistische Deutsche Arbeiterpartei.[60]

Sebottendorff had become a Turkish citizen in his youth for some reason, so he ended up working for German Intelligence in Istanbul during the Second World War. He committed suicide on 9 May 1945 by drowning himself in the Bosphorus.[61]

Another colourful esoteric theorist of the same inclinations was Rudolf John Gorsleben (1883–1930), who was also very keen on runes and Aryans. Gorsleben placed greater emphasis on crystals (*Kristall*), a word whose etymology he traced back to 'Krist-All', proving that they were at the heart of an ancient Aryan religion with connections to Atlantis that was misconstrued and plagiarised as the new gospel of Jesus Christ. Much of this comes out in his great work, *Hoch-Zeit der Menschheit* ('zenith of humanity'), published at Leipzig in 1930. He founded the 'Edda Society' in 1925, a sort of Aryan Icelandic study group, which became a Nazi organisation in 1933.

Perhaps the most powerful of the Nazi occultists, however, was Karl Maria Wiligut (1866–1946), who was introduced to Heinrich Himmler (1900–45), whose interest in these matters was legendary. Wiligut was made head of the SS prehistory department as an SS officer under the name of 'Weisthor' (1933–9), and designed the *Totenkopfring* ('death's head ring'), which became the symbol of the service. His mythology included the promotion of an ancient Germanic ('Irminist') religion of 'Krist', including giants, dwarves and an earth with a triple sun. By 1935, Wewelsburg Castle near Paderborn had become an SS ceremonial centre and museum, which continued even after Wiligut resigned from the SS in 1939, for reasons unknown.

The late historian George L. Mosse wrote a pioneering article on 'the mystical origins of National Socialism' in 1961, in which he noted that:

> Historians have ignored this stream of thought as too outré to be taken seriously. Who indeed can take seriously an ideology which drew upon the occultism of Madame Blavatski, rejected science in favor of 'seeing with one's soul,' and came dangerously close to sun worship? Yet such ideas made a deep impression upon a whole nation. Historians who have dismissed these aspects of romanticism and mysticism have failed to grasp an essential and important ingredient of modern German history.[62]

Much more needs to be done on this subject, in order to understand the appeal of Nazism to a cultivated people.[63] What is striking, however, is the way in which 'these aspects of romanticism and mysticism' were woven together into what amounted to a kind of occult religion more than a detached body of knowledge. As we shall see, the emphasis on esoteric religious faith in the twentieth century would have enormous consequences on present-day culture, with the evolution of American Fundamentalism.

SEVEN

The Occult (Re-)Turn to Religion: Fundamentalism and New Age

Viewed from the perspective of a more sophisticated and less credulous age, it is rather hard to imagine how anyone could have taken Madame Blavatsky seriously. All of this talk about Unknown Mahatmas 'living in the trans-Himalayan fastnesses of Tibet' began to wear very thin, certainly by the 1920s and '30s, despite the intermittent posthumous success of ideas like hers in Germany and elsewhere. For one thing, Madame Blavatsky was a hard act to follow, and her incorporation of second-hand Indian philosophy and terminology into the Western occult tradition was in its way an act of genius. By the early twentieth century, someone attracted to esoteric teachings and the occult was much more likely to find spiritual satisfaction in movements that looked more like a religion than an eccentric reading group. Indeed, there was a very clear turn – a *return* – to a variety of religion that emphasised the occult, especially in the *Oxford English Dictionary* sense of the 'realm of the unknown; the supernatural world or its influences, manifestations, etc'. This was the world of American Fundamentalism.

I

Fundamentalism is a term more often used than understood, like feudalism or fascism, and it is applied to phenomena in a wide variety of different contexts, so that people frequently even speak of Islamic or Jewish Fundamentalism. If we are intent on seeing American Fundamentalism as part of the occult tradition, then we had better be sure of what we mean. Fortunately, the historical development of a word often reveals how the concept itself evolved. The word 'Fundamentalism' originally referred to a series of a dozen pamphlets entitled *The Fundamentals*, which were distributed free of charge by the American Bible League between 1909 and 1915. The project was funded by two brothers, Lyman and Milton Stewart, who had made their fortunes in the California oil industry, and thought that 250,000 copies of these little books could make a difference.[1]

The Fundamentals emphasised two key points. The first was the truth of the *infallible Bible*, the conviction that the Old and New Testaments represent the complete and exact word of God and are the comprehensive and final authority over faith and practice. The Jews are the recipients and custodians of the Bible and therefore have a special role to play. We can already see how different this original Fundamentalism is from the so-called contemporary Jewish variety, since orthodox Jews see the Old Testament through the Talmud and the Midrash, and are at a considerable distance from the biblical text itself.

The second point stressed the concept of the *born-again* Christian, the conviction that salvation and eternal life are won only as the free gift of God's grace through a radical and sudden commitment to Christ. The conversion of the Jews is a likely precursor to the Second Coming, which is about to occur, these being the Last of Days. Here again, the 'born-again' paradigm is exactly the opposite of conversion within orthodox Judaism, where gradualism is encouraged.

Although we often look back on these pamphlets as a turning point in the history of American Christianity, as it happens, these were hardly new ideas. In fact, these are exactly the key concepts that Martin Luther (1483–1546) emphasised as the basis of Protestant religious revolution in sixteenth-century Europe. Roman Catholicism was and still is based on sacraments that give merit to the practitioner largely irrespective of his or her beliefs or moral stature. Furthermore, the authority of the Church itself, rather than the Bible, is paramount and final. When Luther rebelled against this religious system in 1517 and founded a new school of thought, which would be known later as Protestantism, he rejected the notion of sacraments, and grounded his theology on three doctrines: *sola fide* (by faith alone): it is what you believe in your heart that brings you salvation, not routine actions performed; *sola gratia* (by grace alone): only God's grace can give us salvation and eternal life, since all the good that we do comes from Him; and *sola scriptura* (by Scripture alone): the Bible is the ultimate religious authority in all matters of faith and doctrine. These three *solas* were the principles, or fundamentals, on which Protestantism was based, and even when Luther's school fragmented into hundreds of different sects, these three ideas remained paramount. The basis of modern Christian Fundamentalism is nothing new, merely a clear restatement of the basic tenets of Protestantism, although more extreme elements were added to the Fundamentalist theology and have become more prominent in time, as we shall see.

Even theologians who balk at seeing Fundamentalism as a restatement of Luther's streamlined theology, however, would undoubtedly look back for origins to William Miller (1782–1849), a farmer from upstate New York and retired US army officer who had fought in the War of 1812.[2] Originally a sceptic, Miller had a conversion experience and began to preach as a Baptist, his father's faith.

At an early stage, William Miller was drawn to the prophetic books of Daniel and Revelation, and discovered hidden within the text the actual and hitherto unknown date of the Second Coming, which was to be 21 March 1844, the first day of spring. Miller's reasoning was quite simple. In Daniel 8:14 we read as follows: 'And he said unto me, Unto two thousand and three hundred days; then shall the sanctuary be cleansed.' He kept that figure in mind: 2,300 days. Now, in Ezekiel 4:6 we get another clue: 'I have appointed thee each day for a year.' Therefore, Miller concluded, whenever the Bible talks about 'days', it is really signifying 'years'.[3] Studying his biblical manuals, Miller noted that Ezra was ordered to rebuild the Temple in the year 457 BC. So . . . if we begin with 457 BC and add 2,300 years, we arrive at the year AD 1843. Taking into account that early Christian years were measured from spring to spring, Miller convinced himself that Jesus would return at the conclusion of the year that ran from 21 March 1843 to 21 March 1844, the latter day being the precise moment of the Second Coming.

Miller amassed as many as 100,000 followers, mostly in upstate New York, who awaited patiently the coming of the Lord. Sadly, Jesus did not appear to them on 21 March 1844. Miller did not despair, but instead recalculated the months to 22 October 1844. In what was perhaps the greatest understatement of the millennium, Miller noted in the interval that, 'If Christ does not come within twenty or twenty-five days I shall feel twice the disappointment I did in the spring.'

Christ let Miller down once again, and the date 22 October 1844 became known as 'The Great Disappointment'.[4]

The real tragedy is that Miller and his followers would not have been present to greet Jesus even if he had appeared, since their arithmetical calculations were off by a full year. Historians have only recently come to understand that even literate people in the nineteenth century were barely numerate, and were unable to perform relatively simple calculations.[5] This comes out very well with William Miller: his own arithmetical calculus actually pinpoints 1845 as the date of the Second Coming, because there is no Year Zero. Put quite simply, the third year after 1 BC is not determined by subtracting 1 from 3: if one does that, another year must be added to the final sum. The year AD 3 was the third year after 1 BC: there is no Year Zero. Had Miller understood this, even after the fact, he might have concluded that the Messiah arrived in upstate New York on 21 March *1845*, found no one to welcome him, and returned angrily to heaven.

In any case, after the Great Disappointment, Miller's loyal followers held a Mutual Conference of Adventists to sort it all out. Failing to agree on a common interpretation, they split into different groups. The most important of these was led by James White (1821–81) and his wife Ellen Harmon White (1827–1915), former Methodists, who were said to have received the gift of prophecy. They were called 'Millerites' in the press, and the name was in use for quite a while. Their view was that William Miller had set the right date, but that the events of that day had been wrongly interpreted. The Book of Daniel, after all, says that 'then shall the sanctuary be cleansed'. The Whites argued that this meant that, in 1844, Jesus Christ began an examination of all the names in the Book of Life, and when this is completed, He will return in glory and begin his millennial reign. At that time, Christ's advent will be 'personal, visible, audible, bodily, glorious and premillennial', and, most importantly, it was imminent. That being said, anxious to avoid Disappointment, the Whites were too prudent to set a new date.

What they did do was to tell us how we might help bring forward that wonderful event promised in Scripture. First of all, we should observe the Sabbath on the seventh day, Saturday, as enjoined in the Ten Commandments. Secondly, we should also purify our bodily temples by special diets, supposedly based on the Old Testament. Towards that end, in 1855 they set up their headquarters at Battle

Creek, Michigan, and established a Sanitarium there, which from 1876 was run by John Harvey Kellogg (1852–1943), a surgeon who invented the nearly eponymous breakfast cereal, peanut butter, soya milk, and exercise records for the gramophone, all in the service of the Second Coming. The Seventh-day Adventists became an official denomination in 1863, and Ellen Harmon White travelled and lectured widely in the United States, Europe and Australia, writing prophetically and prolifically. Today there may be as many as thirteen million Seventh-day Adventists worldwide, although only about 800,000 live in the United States, where the movement was born.

Another important movement that grew out of the Great Disappointment was the Jehovah's Witnesses. The founder was Charles Taze Russell (1852–1916) from Pittsburgh, Pennsylvania, who in 1870 fixed the date of the Second Coming as four years thence. Undeterred by this second disappointment, from 1878 Russell began issuing a series of magazines and books, which were sold by his followers. In 1881 he formed the 'Zion's Watch Tower Tract Society', which in 1931 changed its name to the Jehovah's Witnesses.

Russell prophesised the year 1914 as that of the Advent, but when nothing (except the First World War) occurred, like the Whites he explained that it was at that time that the Heavenly Kingdom of God was established, as Jesus invisibly took some of the Annointed Class of 144,000 destined to be saved according to the Book of Revelation.[6] Russell placed himself second in a group of teachers who taught the truths of the Jehovah's Witnesses, the first being the apostle Paul, but including precursors such as John Wyclif (c. 1330–1384) and Martin Luther.[7]

After Russell died in 1916, he was succeeded by 'Judge' Joseph Franklyn Rutherford (1869–1942), who developed the theology of the Jehovah's Witnesses to its present form, including giving them their modern name. He also invented the famous slogan, 'Millions now living will never die', although he himself did, in 1942, which surprised many of his followers who thought that he at least would live to see the millennial kingdom. Jehovah's Witnesses deny allegiance to any political state and reject military service, which led to the murder of as many as 5,000 Witnesses in Nazi concentration camps.

The Jehovah's Witnesses claim an active adult membership of between six and seven million, but, if we include children and others who attend the annual Lord's Supper, this figure is probably much closer to sixteen million followers, with about one million in the United States. They have a 'Beth-Sarim' ('house of princes') in San Diego, California, owned officially by Abraham, Isaac and David, where rooms are booked awaiting their return. Since 1908 their headquarters has been in Brooklyn, in the shadow of the Bridge. The appearance of millennial groups such as the Seventh-day Adventists and the Jehovah's Witnesses helped pave the way for the development of Fundamentalism, which is at the same time a religious movement and a turn of mind that relies heavily on the occult tradition.

II

The Fundamentalist movement includes churches of many sects, but they are primarily Baptist, and it has grown in strength throughout the twentieth century. They first came to public prominence with the 'Monkey Trial' of 1925, over the issue of teaching evolution in the schools instead of the biblical story of Creation as it appears in the Book of Genesis. A number of states passed laws against the teaching of evolution, including Tennessee. In 1925, this statute was challenged in the courts there by the American Civil Liberties Union, in the person of a substitute science teacher named John T. Scopes (1900–70), who was working in Dayton and agreed to serve as defendant in this landmark case. The famous defence attorney Clarence Darrow (1857–1938) and the equally famous assistant prosecuting attorney William Jennings Bryan (1860–1925) fought it out in a battle that left Scopes convicted and fined one hundred dollars. Although this ruling was reversed on technical grounds by the Tennessee Supreme Court, a point had been made, even if it has continually to be made again.[8]

Fundamentalism has thrived in America since the end of the Second World War, usually under the name of 'Evangelical Christianity', which is seen as less pejorative. The success of the movement since 1945 is probably due to a number of factors. The first is the general prosperity of the post-war years, for Fundamentalism is a faith of the well-off, not the economically disadvantaged, and in that it is similar to Calvinism in general. Secondly, there was the religious revival of the 1950s, and Fundamentalism reflected the values of those years. Billy Graham (b. 1918), that era's most prominent preacher, dressed like a successful businessman and used television to convince viewers to make a decision for Christ. His emphasis was not evolution but individual sins, usually related to the family and urban crime. The third issue that aided the expansion of Fundamentalism was the perceived threat of Communism, which came to replace evolution as the chief enemy ideology. Like evolution, Communism came from abroad, it tended to spread subversively and uncontrollably, and it undermined Christianity. Russia was seen as the headquarters of Satan on earth, and this political stance endeared Fundamentalists to American administrations for many decades.

The State of Israel posed a new theological problem for the traditional 'triumphalism' of Evangelical Protestantism, which viewed Zionism as an unscriptural attempt by Jews to jump the messianic gun, failing to realise that their historical role ended with the appearance of their unrecognised messiah. Certainly since the Six Day War of 1967, however, Fundamentalists have taken a much more positive stance towards Israel, supporting its most right-wing governments and opposing the relinquishing of any conquered territory at all to the Palestinians. Support for Israel has been a prominent feature in the missions of many key Fundamentalists, such as Jerry Falwell (b. 1933), head of the Moral Majority; Pat Robertson (b. 1930), who founded the Christian Broadcasting Network, and Hal Lindsey (b. 1929), whose book *The Late Great Planet Earth* (1970) has tens of millions of copies in print. So too was the International Christian Embassy founded in Jerusalem in October 1980, when many foreign embassies decamped to Tel Aviv.

Before we look at some of the more occult views of the Fundamentalist camp, it is worth addressing the question of whether this movement is a fringe group or part of the mainstream, and this is largely a question of numbers. How many Fundamentalists are there in America? This is very difficult to answer, especially when taking into consideration that the United States is the most religious country on planet earth:

95% of Americans believe in God
86% believe in Heaven
78% believe in life after death
73% believe in religious miracles
72% believe in angels
71% believe in Hell

65% believe in the Devil
42% pray every day
34% believe that the Bible is inerrant

Perhaps most intriguing, 40 per cent of the American people claim to have had contact with the dead. Although larger estimates have been made, including by the Gallup poll, we might use as a base line the figures given by the National Survey of Religious Identification (NSRI), according to which 20 per cent of the American population – fifty million people – can be called 'Evangelical Protestants', that is, Fundamentalists.[9]

Approximately the same number of Americans are Roman Catholics. In other words, if we describe the beliefs of Fundamentalists as 'extreme', in the sense of being furthest from the centre, then we need to admit that these opinions are held by a very substantial proportion of Americans, and therefore should more accurately be described as 'mainstream'. 'Mainstream religious extremism' might sound oxymoronic but, for want of a better term, it could be of some use.

What do Fundamentalists believe today, and what constitutes their 'extremism'? Traditionally, they refer to the 'Five Points of Fundamentalism': the inerrant inspiration of the Bible, preserved without error in original manuscripts; the Virgin Birth; the atonement of Christ; his resurrection, and his miracles. They espouse traditional social values: the heterosexual monogamous family couple, the woman in the home, the sanctity of sex and marriage, the Church as the centre of community, and Sabbath observance. There is also an emphasis on economic success: Fundamentalism is a this-worldly religion as well, so joining up is also a financial investment. Patriotism, even xenophobia, is also part of the package, leading in more recent years to intense political action. Fundamentalists have their own version of Scripture, the Scofield Reference Bible, with detailed footnotes and cross-references, which helps make their case. First produced by Cyrus Ingerson Scofield (1843–1921), it is published by Oxford University Press.[10]

But, most importantly, Fundamentalism places a determined emphasis on the 'realm of the unknown; the supernatural world or its influences, manifestations, etc.', which situates it firmly within the occult tradition even by the blandest dictionary definition. Fundamentalists believe in the imminent, visible, sensible and dramatic Second Coming of Christ, according to a plan that they have worked out from encoded references in the Bible, and with supernatural implications for everyone living today on earth.

The Second Coming is often referred to by the Greek word for the arrival of Christ, '*parousia*', and even more often by the Greek for His unveiling or revelation, '*apocalypse*', although there is no phrase in the New Testament that completely corresponds to the idea of a Second Coming. The closest is Hebrews 9:28: 'unto them that look for him shall he appear the second time without sin unto salvation.'

Jesus himself spoke of his Second Coming, and gave a good many hints about the characteristics of the apocalypse, the revelation of Christ. In the twenty-fourth chapter of Matthew, Jesus reveals to his disciples that his return will be preceded by false prophets, wars and rumours of war, nation rising against nation, famine, plague, earthquakes, the darkening of the sun and moon, stars falling from heaven, and an undefined 'sign of the Son of man in heaven'. The 'abomination of desolation' (*sheekootz m'shomaim*) spoken of in Daniel 12:11 will be set up 'in the holy place'. Just when all hope is lost, 'they shall see the Son of man coming in the clouds of heaven with power and great glory'. A trumpet will sound, and angels will 'gather together his elect from the four winds, from one end of heaven to the other'. These are promises for the future: the exact time of their occurrence is as yet unknown to humankind. As Jesus puts it, 'But of that day and hour knoweth no *man*, no, not the angels of heaven, but my Father only . . . Watch therefore: for ye know not what hour your Lord doth come.'

The Revelation of St John the Divine gives further details. He speaks of a 'beast' who rules over mankind for forty-two months, is granted 'great authority' by Satan, and is assisted by a second Beast (later called the 'false prophet'), gaining many followers by performing 'great wonders'. Terrible persecution follows for all who refuse to worship the Beast's image, and they are executed. In order to buy and sell, everyone has to receive 'a mark' either in the right hand or on the forehead, consisting either of the Beast's name or of his number, 666. (These bestial personalities will later fuse in popular lore with Satan and become the 'Antichrist'.)

At a certain point, the kings of the whole world gather at 'a place called in the Hebrew tongue Armageddon' – '*Har Megiddo*', the mountain of Megiddo – followed by natural disasters and ultimately the appearance of the Messiah on a white horse:

> His eyes *were* as a flame of fire, and on his head *were* many crowns; and he had a name written, that no man knew, but he himself. And he *was* clothed with a vesture dipped in blood: and his name is called The Word of God. And the armies *which were* in heaven followed him upon white horses, clothed in fine linen, white and clean. And out of his mouth goeth a sharp sword, that with it he should smite the nations . . . And he hath on *his* vesture and on his thigh a name written, KING OF KINGS, AND LORD OF LORDS.[11]

The Beast and the False Prophet are defeated in battle, and cast 'alive into a lake of fire burning with brimstone', with Satan thrown into a bottomless pit for a thousand years. It is during this millennium that Christ rules on earth with those 'which had not worshipped the beast, neither his image, neither had received *his* mark upon their foreheads, or in their hands; and they lived and reigned with Christ a thousand years.' This is the basis of the idea of a thousand-year rule by Christ and the saints. The text continues to note that this glorious fate is not promised to everyone, 'But the rest of the dead lived not again until the thousand years were finished. This *is* the first resurrection.' After the end of the thousand years, Satan is released for a final battle, again defeated, this time for ever, to join the Beast and False Prophet in the lake of fire. Jesus only then sets up 'a great white throne' for the Last Judgement of all human beings who ever lived, as 'a new heaven and a new earth' descend from above 'for the first heaven and the first earth were passed away'.

Fundamentalists also take great note of the seventh chapter of the Book of Daniel in the Old Testament, with its image of 'four great beasts came up from the sea, diverse one from another'. They argue over the symbolism of these creatures: a lion, a bear, a leopard and a ten-horned monster with 'great iron teeth' on whose head sprouted 'another little horn, before whom there were three of the first horns plucked up by the roots: and, behold, in this horn *were* eyes like the eyes of man, and a mouth speaking great things'. Many people thought these four beasts represented the rise and fall of successive great world empires, perhaps (1) Babylon; (2) the Medes or Persians or Assyrians;

(3) Greece, and finally (4) Rome and the Roman Catholic Church. After the fall of this last beast, a Fifth Monarchy of Saints would arise, which would rule the earth with Christ for a thousand years. By the later medieval period, these obscure phrases in the Old and New Testaments had been woven together into a coherent system. In most respects it remains the same in the theology of modern Fundamentalists.

All well and good, and backed by biblical authority of the highest kind. At the end of the nineteenth century, however, at the other end of the Great Disappointment, a new twist was added to the story, thanks particularly to John Nelson Darby (1800–82), an Irish theologian. His system was known as 'Dispensationalism', and today Evangelical Christians are almost invariably dispensationalist in theology. The term 'dispensation' refers to distinct eras of history, of which the End of Days is the seventh and final one, the others being Edenic, antediluvian, post-diluvian, patriarchal (Abraham to Exodus), legal (Exodus to Christ) and ecclesiastical (Christ until the final days).

Like the Millerites, Darby argued that Christ's kingdom is entirely future and supernatural, and that the divine plan can be worked out by paying careful attention to Daniel 9:24–7, in which a seventy-week programme is described:

> Seventy weeks are determined upon thy people and upon thy holy city, to finish the transgression, and to make an end of sins, and to make reconciliation for iniquity, and to bring in everlasting righteousness, and to seal up the vision and prophecy, and to anoint the most Holy.

'Know therefore and understand,' Daniel goes on, 'that from the going forth of the commandment to restore and to build Jerusalem unto the Messiah the Prince, shall be seven weeks, and threescore and two weeks.' Doing the maths, we add 7 + 60 + 2 and arrive at 69 weeks. The prophet Ezekiel via William Miller already taught us that in the Bible each day stands for a year, so, multiplying 69 × 7, we learn that there is a 483-year period between the rebuilding of the temple during the days of Ezra and Nehemiah to the time of Jesus.

The last and seventieth week, Darby argued, stands for the final seven-year period before the Second Coming, so that the entire history of Christianity was seen to take place in a suspended era between the sixty-ninth week and the seventieth (last) week. The events of this final seven years will include the appearance of the False Prophet, who will lead the apostate churches, and the Beast, a political leader who will rule the ten nations that grew out of the Roman Empire, as predicted in the simile of the ten toes in Nebuchadnezzar's dream from the Book of Daniel.[12] We will also see the return of the Jews to Palestine, the conversion of some of them to Christianity, the persecution of the other Jews, and the appearance of Christ to defeat the Beast, the False Prophet and the renewed Roman Empire, in a great battle to take place in the Holy Land at Armageddon (Megiddo). At this point, the thousand-year rule of Christ on earth will begin, the millennium.

The last seven years of humankind will obviously be very trying. According to most dispensationalists, the saints of the true Church will be spared the tribulations of that time by being taken bodily out of the world in a process called 'the rapture', returning with Christ after seven years. The textual reference for this procedure is 1 Thessalonians 4:16–17:

> For the Lord himself shall descend from heaven with a shout, with the voice of the archangel, and with the trump of God: and the dead in Christ shall rise first: Then we which are alive *and* remain shall be caught up together with them in the clouds, to meet the Lord in the air: and so shall we ever be with the Lord.

Modern Evangelical Christians take the concept of 'the rapture' very literally, and ponder the legal and practical difficulties of people suddenly disappearing from the earth, described very clearly in the *Left Behind* books, a series of religious thrillers, which have sold in tens of millions of copies and are still going strong.[13]

In true modern occult fashion, Evangelical Christians have pondered the scientific process of the End of Days, just as Paracelsus did half a millennium previously. Their imagination has been fired by the testimony in 2 Peter 3:10–12:

> But the day of the Lord will come as a thief in the night; in the which the heavens shall pass away with a great noise, and the elements shall melt with fervent heat, the earth also and the works that are therein shall be burned up. *Seeing* then *that* all these things

shall be dissolved, what manner *of persons* ought ye to be in *all* holy conversation and godliness, Looking for and hasting unto the coming of the day of God, wherein the heavens being on fire shall be dissolved, and the elements shall melt with fervent heat?

Quite obviously, argue the 'Armageddon theologians', the reference here in the New Testament is to nuclear holocaust, which will be God's chosen method for destroying the old world, initiated by humankind itself. When we consider that Evangelical Christianity is a faith that has been embraced by American presidents such as Jimmy Carter, Ronald Reagan and George W. Bush, we might have pause to remember whose finger is on the proverbial button.[14]

Much has been written over the past few years about the increased role that Evangelical Christianity has played in the presidency of George W. Bush. When reporter Bob Woodward asked the president if he consulted with his father about the war in Iraq, the younger Bush replied, 'You know, he is the wrong father to appeal to in terms of strength. There is a higher father that I appeal to.'[15] The popularity of this kind of decision-making process is not universal in the United States, so Bush often resorts to an esoteric code worthy of seventeenth-century Rosicrucians. This came out very forcefully, for example, in his address to the nation on 7 October 2001, only a month after 9/11, announcing air strikes against Afghanistan. He concluded his remarks with the curious phrase, 'May God continue to bless America', the single word 'continue' instantly transforming an anodyne cliché into a genuine religious sentiment. Professor Bruce Lincoln of the University of Chicago submitted that speech to a line-by-line analysis, and found clear references to Isaiah, Job and the Book of Revelation. The image of terrorists who 'may burrow deeper into caves and other entrenched hiding places' sounds merely like awkward writing, Lincoln notes, yet it contains 'biblical allusions plainly audible to portions of his audience who are attentive to such phrasing, but likely to go unheard by those without the requisite textual knowledge'. Lincoln continues:

These allusions are instructive, as is the fact that Bush could only make these points indirectly, through strategies of double coding. Along with Bush's closing benediction, his biblical references acknowledge a serious cleavage within the American public and address those Americans who could be expected to reject the religious minimalism that otherwise characterizes his text. Far from denouncing them as improper Americans, however – the way bin Laden treated his 'hypocrites' as bad Muslims – Bush provided reassurance for those people. Enlisting the specialized reading/listening and hermeneutical skills they cultivate, he encouraged them to probe beneath the surface of his text. There, *sotto voce*, he told them he understands and sympathizes with their views, even if requirements of his office (also, those of practical politics) constrain him from giving full-throated voice not just to the religious values they prefer, but to their maximalist construction of *all* values as religious.[16]

This kind of 'Bible talk' enables George W. Bush to communicate with ordinary people, winking at them conspiratorially as partners in a type of Christianity that is based on the careful reading of an esoteric text.

The Establishment quality of contemporary Evangelical Protestantism should not exclude Fundamentalism from the history of the occult tradition. Fundamentalists predict the future through deciphering a document whose meaning is hidden, occult rather than manifest. God will bring about cosmic destruction and a redeeming millennium through *supernatural* agency. But the Fundamentalist utopia is also *magical*, featuring astonishing creatures doing battle in the skies. 'Magic' and 'millennium' are words that (super)naturally go together.[17]

This comes out very clearly in the development of Pentecostalism alongside the Fundamentalist movement. Pentecostalism, also called the 'Charismatic Movement', is based on the first Christian Pentecost, when the Holy Spirit descended on the Apostles, transforming them into evangelists of the new religion. Some theorists have argued that Pentecostalism is not Protestantism at all, but really a fourth major strand of Christianity. Its main characteristic is 'glossolalia', speaking in tongues, like the first Apostles. Pentecostalists also emphasise healing, miracles and exorcisms from demon possession. Certainly there were antecedents, such as Edward Irving (1792–1834), the Scottish clergyman who built a new church in Regent Square but was forced to retire because of his championship of Pentecostal phenomena. In 1832, he founded the Holy Catholic Apostolic Church, where these practices were part of the ritual, but it was in the United States that this doctrine flourished.

American Pentecostalism began in a non-denominational Bible school in Topeka, Kansas, on 1 January 1901, when a Sunday-school teacher named Agnes Ozman (1870–1937) experienced a powerful internal force and began to speak in an unknown language that she had never learned. Others began to share this experience, and the movement grew, centring from about 1905 on Azusa Street in Los Angeles.[18]

There has been much discussion about whether they speak in a genuine language, or if this is simply a non-conceptual mode of expression. Clearly, the speech is not ecstatic or trance-like. A person undergoing this phenomenon can use the gift at will and calmly, although he or she does not determine what is said, and normally does not understand the utterance itself. If the message is intended for the entire community, someone else with the gift of interpretation may be called upon to translate, although usually what results is rather conventional praise of the Lord.

Today there are about twenty-two million Pentecostalists worldwide, practising a theology that is very much a mixture from other movements, including components such as adult baptism, Adventist eschatology and a strong missionary impulse. Their faith healing is rather more controversial. The main Pentecostalist denominations in the United States are concentrated around Arkansas, in the south, in part because of the high percentage of African-Americans in the movement. Among the largest denominations are the Assemblies of God, the Church of God and the Pentecostal Holiness Church. More colourful groups include the International Church of the Foursquare Gospel, founded by Aimee Semple McPherson (1890–1944); the Christian Catholic Apostolic Church in Zion; the Pentecostal Church of the Nazarene; and the snake-handlers of the Dolley Pond Church of God with Signs Following. The Pentecostalists are particularly strong in Scandinavia, and in Italy they have more adherents than all of the Protestant churches put together. Among the best-known English Pentecostalist churches are the Elim Alliance, the Assemblies of God and the House churches. But the fastest-growing areas are Africa and Latin America, where Pentecostalism is the largest non-Roman Catholic faith.

As with the Fundamentalists, so too with the Pentecostalists: their sheer numbers transform religious extremism into part of society's mainstream. From our point of view, it is clear that just at the moment when the occult tradition entered the twentieth century, there was a clear move to Christianity, forging an alliance with one of the world's greatest supernatural systems, and foreshadowing its current partnership with New Age religion.

III

The occult tradition's turn to religion at the beginning of the twentieth century may signify that this evolving body of knowledge was now about to make an evolutionary jump. We have been looking at the occult tradition as a collection of ideas woven together in creative ways by a number of people and the groups they engendered. From that point of view, our story is concluded, since hardly any really new concepts have been added to the mix in the past hundred years. Certainly there were plenty of theosophical and anthroposophical societies that were very active between the wars, and séances remained ever popular. But New Age religion is today the breeding ground for the occult tradition, and it would be unfair not to pass at least a cursory glance at how it got there, in the expectation that this is the place where any further mutations are likely to spawn.

A few words should be said first about the secrets of the pyramids, because, at least in this area, the ancient Egyptians retained the centrality they acquired in the Renaissance and carried it forward even unto the New Age. This was certainly a well-studied field of interest, and, as we have seen, Isaac Newton himself was very keen. In the inter-war period, it was the British Israelite movement that brought it to the fore, as part of their attempt to demonstrate that the Anglo-Saxons were the literal descendants of the chosen people. The basic idea of pyramidology was that the Great Pyramid is God's original record of revelation, presented in symbols and terms of modern science and preserved in the stones of the pyramid itself. Just as God recorded his revelation in the form of words in the Bible, so too did he give us the same information in stone, which can be deciphered by mathematics, using the measurements of the Great Pyramid.

In practice, what this meant was understanding that there is such a thing as a 'pyramid inch', 1.00106 British inches, exactly one twenty-fifth of the Sacred Cubit (25.0265 British inches), which conveniently

193

is precisely one ten-millionth of the earth's mean polar radius. The builders of the Great Pyramid constructed that massive edifice so that each pyramid inch (especially in the ascending and descending interior chambers) would signify a single year in the history of mankind. Thus in it we can trace the entire history of the world from the beginning of the 'Adamic race', in about 4000 BC, to its conclusion, in about AD 2000, when man will become extinct in the millennial Sabbath. The Great Pyramid documents the dates of the Flood (2352 BC), the Exodus (1513 BC), the life of Christ in great detail, the war between the United States and Mexico (1846), the repeal of the British Corn Laws (also 1846), the First World War, and the abdication of Edward VIII (1936). The Pyramid can also be used to predict future events efficiently. Adam Rutherford, a great pyramidologist of the 1930s, predicted the creation of the State of Israel 'after 1941', and the establishment of Christ's millennial reign on earth at 21 September 1994 on the autumnal equinox.[19] Peter Lemesurier, Rutherford's successor, has since corrected that happy date to 2 July 2989.[20]

Who built the Great Pyramid? It was named for the Pharoah Cheops, but perhaps the builder was Enoch, who led the Shepherd Kings to Egypt and lived for 365 years, symbolically the same number of days in a single year. Perhaps the builder was Melchizedek, who was really Job. But two things are clear, as Rutherford put it: 'That the Great Pyramid in Egypt is a Divinely designed monument and that it is truth in structural form.' In other words, he says, 'the teaching of the Bible and that of the Pyramid are identical in every particular, the one in words, the other in stone'.[21]

Pyramidology is a fascinating subject, and its revival in the period between the two world wars is yet another example of thematic tenacity in the occult tradition. Leaving the Great Pyramid aside, however, it would be hard to pinpoint any twentieth-century occult area of growth before the end of the Second World War, when Fundamentalism began to appeal to an ever-increasing number of people.

Yet, while there were many who did indeed turn to religion in the post-war years, others looked for a different kind of supernatural salvation. One thinks especially of the UFO cults that appeared in the 1950s, which were strongly apocalyptic, made of up of people who passively awaited 'a new heaven and a new earth' to descend from outer space. It is perhaps from this impulse that various alternative, counter-culture communities arose, whose members hoped to create actively a new kind of civilisation. The most famous early group of this variety set up at Findhorn, in Scotland. Already there was talk of an 'Age of Aquarius', or a 'New Age', a term apparently coined by Alice A. Bailey (1880–1949), the founder in 1923 of the Arcane School. Nevertheless, it was only in the late 1970s that people began to talk of a New Age *movement* as such, arguing that there were a number of broad similarities among the huge variety of alternative ideas and practices from California to parts East and West.

Most of the writing about the New Age has been anthropological and sociological, focused on practice rather than belief. More recently, the group of researchers of the occult associated with Antoine Faivre, especially Professor Wouter J. Hanegraaff, have begun to take New Age thinkers seriously, and to classify their ideas.[22] According to Hanegraaff, the philosophy of the New Age movement is based on a common pattern of criticism directed against dominant cultural trends, especially against Christian dogmatic dualism and scientific rationalistic reductionism. The first rejected (religious) category includes such contrasts as Creator vs. created, God vs. man, spirit vs. matter, man vs. nature. The second discarded (scientific) category relates to the tendency towards fragmentation, the kind of science in which organic wholes are seen as mechanisms that can be reduced to their smallest components and then explained in terms of these parts.[23]

New Age philosophy, on the other hand, argues that there is a third option, *holism*, which rejects neither opposite, but instead combines them into a higher synthesis, and thus helps save the world. The term 'holism' is much older than the New Age, having been coined by South African statesman Jan Christian Smuts (1870–1950) in 1926. As Smuts defined it, holism describes what he saw as:

> the ultimate synthetic, ordering, organising, regulative activity in the universe which accounts for all the structural groupings and syntheses in it, from the atom and the physico-chemical structures, through the cell and organisms, through Mind in animals, to Personality in man. The all-pervading and ever-increasing character of synthetic unity or wholeness in these structures leads to the concept of Holism as the fundamental activity underlying and co-ordinating all others, and to the view of the universe as a Holistic Universe.[24]

This is exactly the concept that would become so important fifty years later, especially after the notion of 'holistic medicine' became more common in the 1960s, seeking to look at the entire person and not merely at his or her symptoms.[25]

According to Hanegraaff, the New Age movement is not the product of an Oriental renaissance; Eastern concepts are assimilated only insofar as they are adaptable within already existing Western frameworks, and the Orient mainly functions as a symbol of true spirituality and a source of exotic terminology. New Age philosophy is nothing more than a *réchauffé* version of Western esotericism as it stood *c.*1900. All of the elements of New Age cultural criticism would have been acceptable to nineteenth-century Western esotericists, but, whereas in the earlier period this criticism was formulated against the background of a generally 'enchanted' world, the New Age movement intentionally adopts an 'enchanted' world within a secularised context, which leads Hanegraaff to claim that New Age philosophy is a kind of 'secularised esotericism'. Although New Age philosophy, or religion if you will, takes from traditional Western esotericism the emphasis on the primacy of personal religious experience, it reinterprets esoteric components from a secular perspective, using elements of scientific causality, comparative religion, evolutionism and psychology. In other words, New Age philosophy or religion is not a simple return to the occult tradition of the Renaissance and after, but rather a new syncretism of esoteric and secular elements. As Hanegraaff puts it, the 'New Age movement is characterised by a popular Western culture criticism expressed in terms of a secularised esotericism', and even if different groups *say different things*, what unites them into a single 'New Age movement' is that they are *opposed to the same things*.

Hanegraaff has performed the enormous service of actually reading through mountains of turgid New Age material, stopping only when he began to get rapidly diminishing returns. He found a number of 'major trends' in New Age religion. The first is an emphasis on 'channelling', not of the recent dead (spiritualism), but including trance channelling, automatisms, clairaudient channelling, and open channelling. A key figure here was Edgar Cayce (1877–1945), who was also a conservative Christian. Other major trends are healing and personal growth, including the notion of holistic health, and neopaganism, including ritual magic and the Wicca movement, founded in 1939 by Gerald Gardner (1884–1964).

The most interesting trend is what one might call New Age science, although we might recognise it more as a religious belief system than anything else. The New Age search for a Grand Unified Theory has a very strong religious dimension, and is in essence a modern version of *Naturphilosophie* that we saw at work in the eighteenth century. New Age philosophers look for the Reality underlying phenomenal reality, emphasising internal consistency, philosophical elegance and religious profundity, embracing accepted scientific knowledge as well. Among the central figures here are physicist David Bohm (1917–92), whose 'theory of the implicate order' suggested that since each fragment of a hologram contains information about the entire object, this might be a good model for the universe itself.[26] Another is neurologist Karl H. Pribram (b.1919), who argued that each memory fragment is distributed over the whole of the brain, so that each part of the brain also contains information about the whole.[27] Even though Bohm and Pribram did not work together, potted summaries of their scientific research (such as these lines above) have been invaluable for supporting the holisitic view of reality, and websites about them haunt the internet.

Yet another scientific theory popular with New Age philosophers is that of the 'self-organising universe'. This notion is based on the work of the 1977 Nobel Prize winner in chemistry Ilya Prigogine (1917–2003), as popularised by Erich Jantsch (1929–80).[28] The basic concept is that the universe is evolving in an open-ended process of creative self-organisation. From the New Age point of view, this in itself is proof that the cosmos is alive. This idea is further enhanced by the 'hypothesis of formative causation' championed by biologist Rupert Sheldrake (b. 1942), which postulates the existence of invisible organising fields that operate by 'morphic resonance'.[29] Finally, there is the rather more popular 'Gaia hypothesis' of independent scholar James Lovelock (b.1919), suggesting that Planet Earth is a living organism, if by that we mean a self-regulating system.[30]

Despite the scientific veneer of much New Age writing, it is clearly a belief system much more akin to faith, and therefore should be seen as part of the turn to religion in the occult tradition that has become so apparent in this century. The boundary between religious belief and supernatural faith is so porous that we could continue discussing groups such as the Unification Church, founded by Sun Myung Moon (b. 1920), and popularly known as the 'Moonies'.[31] So too we might include the Nation of Islam (the 'Black Muslims'), founded by Wallace D. Fard (1877–1934?), and afterwards led by Elijah Muhammad (1897–1975), Malcolm X (1925–65), and Louis Farrakhan (b. 1933), which has a strong science-fiction element in its theology.[32] Finally, we might look at Scientology, founded by L. Ron Hubbard (1911–86), which began as a mental health technique in 1950, and was organised as a church three years later.[33] The first two of these groups are religions with creative mythologies; the last is something else, best left to someone else to decipher.

IV

We began with James G. Frazer, and playing the role of straw man he deserves to have the last word. In the course of writing *The Golden Bough*, Frazer had come to the conclusion that 'in the most backward state of human society now known to us we find magic thus conspicuously present and religion conspicuously absent'. He thought that one 'of the great achievements of the nineteenth century was to run shafts down into this low mental stratum in many parts of the world, and thus to discover its substantial identity everywhere.' Indeed, he warned,

> We seem to move on a thin crust which may at any moment be rent by the subterranean forces slumbering below. From time to time a hollow murmur underground or a sudden spirt of flame into the air tells of what is going on beneath our feet. Now and then the polite world is startled by a paragraph in a newspaper which tells how in Scotland an image has been found stuck full of pins for the purpose of killing an obnoxious laird or minister, how a woman has been slowly roasted to death as a witch in Ireland, or how a girl has been murdered and chopped up in Russia to make those candles of human tallow by whose light thieves hope to pursue their midnight trade unseen.

Frazer took hope in the fact that the 'shrewder intelligences must in time have come to perceive that magical ceremonies and incantations did not really effect the results which they were designed to produce'. Such people realised that they 'had been pulling at strings to which nothing was attached'. These 'deeper minds may be conceived to have made the great transition from magic to religion':

> Thus religion, beginning as a slight and partial acknowledgment of powers superior to man, tends with the growth of knowledge to deepen into a confession of man's entire and absolute dependence on the divine; his old free bearing is exchanged for an attitude of lowliest prostration before the mysterious powers of the unseen, and his highest virtue is to submit his will to theirs.

Enlightened man finally understood that he was in the thrall of 'a force stronger than any that he could wield, and in obedience to a destiny which he was powerless to control'. The Age of Magic was thus superceded by the Age of Religion.[34]

Frazer thought that the key moment here was when 'men for the first time recognised their inability to manipulate at pleasure certain natural forces which hitherto they had believed to be completely within their control'.[35] But knowledge itself is also a kind of power, of control, and prophecy a particularly powerful kind of supernatural knowledge. The ability to predict the future can turn mortal men into magicians, into prophets, as Frazer's line between magic and religion is hopelessly blurred. Many of these people preached a kind of magical millenarian religion, for as Frazer said of the magician-scientists:

> They lure the weary enquirer, the footsore seeker, on through the wilderness of disappointment in the present by their endless promises of the future; they take him up to the top of an exceedingly high mountain and show him, beyond the dark clouds and rolling mists at his feet, a vision of the celestial city, far off, it may be, but radiant with unearthly splendour, bathed in the light of dreams.[36]

The growth of 'dispensationalist' American Fundamentalism during Frazer's own lifetime would challenge the academic's tidy boundaries between religion, magic and the occult tradition. How he would have reacted to the burgeoning of the New Age is anyone's prophecy.

NOTES

Introduction

1. We know that Newton was working on the manuscript only a few days before his death. It was published the following year as *The Chronology of Ancient Kingdoms Amended* (London, 1728). The plans of the temple appear as three plates between page 346 and 347. For much more on Isaac Newton and the occult, see chap. 2 below.

2. Theodor W. Adorno, 'The Stars Down to Earth: The *Los Angeles Times* Astrology Column', *Telos*, 19 (1974), 13–90: repr. *Adorno: The Stars Down to Earth and Other Essays on the Irrational in Culture*, ed. Stephen Crook (London, 1994), pp. 34–127, esp. pp. 36, 39.

3. Frances Yates, *Giordano Bruno and the Hermetic Tradition* (London, 1964). German-speaking scholars might prefer to point to the earlier work by Will-Erich Peuckert (1895–1969), *Pansophie: ein Versuch zur Geschichte der Weissen und Schwarzen Magie* (2nd edn, Berlin, 1956); *idem, Gabalia: ein Versuch zur Geschichte der Magia Naturalis im 16. bis 18. Jahrhundert* (Berlin, 1967); and other writings.

4. Keith Thomas, *Religion and the Decline of Magic: Studies in Popular Beliefs in Sixteenth- and Seventeenth-Century England* (London, 1971).

5. H.R. Trevor-Roper, *Religion, the Reformation and Social Change, and Other Essays* (London, 1967), chapter 3, and repr. in many forms, including as a separate volume.

6. The number of recent studies of witchcraft is so large that the reader is left to the open shelves of any university library. Among the key works should be included: E. William Monter, *European Witchcraft* (New York, 1969); Alan Macfarlane, *Witchcraft in Tudor and Stuart England* (London, 1970); *Witchcraft in Europe,*

1100–1700: A Documentary History, ed. Alan C. Kors & Edward Peters (Philadelphia, 1972); Norman Cohn, *Europe's Inner Demons: an Enquiry Inspired by the Great Witch-Hunt* (London, 1975); Carlo Ginzburg, *Ecstasies: Deciphering the Witches' Sabbath* (London, 1990); Robin Briggs, *Witches and Neighbours: the Social and Cultural Context of European Witchcraft* (London, 1996); James Sharpe, *Instruments of Darkness: Witchcraft in England 1550–1750* (London, 1996); Stuart Clark, *Thinking with Demons: the Idea of Witchcraft in Early Modern Europe* (Oxford, 1997); Wolfgang Behringer, *Witches and Witch-Hunts* (London, 2004); Lyndal Roper, *Witch Craze* (London & New Haven, 2004).

7. Arthur O. Lovejoy, *The Great Chain of Being: A Study of the History of an Idea* (Cambridge, USA, 1936), pp. 3, 5, 15, 19, 22. The text was first delivered as the William James Lectures at Harvard University in 1933.

8. Wouter J. Hanegraaff, 'Introduction: The Birth of a Discipline', in *Western Esotericism and the Science of Religion* (Leuven, 1998), ed. Antoine Faivre & Wouter J. Hanegraaff, pp. xii–xiii. Cf. *idem*, 'Some Remarks on the Study of Western Esotericism', *Esoterica*, 1 (1999), 3–19.

9. For a well-known literary exploration of what happens when a sociologist of religious cults goes native, see Alison Lurie, *Imaginary Friends* (New York, 1967).

10. George Orwell, *The Road to Wigan Pier* (London, 1937), chap. 11.

11. Colin Campbell, 'The Cult, the Cultic Milieu and Secularization', *A Sociological Yearbook of Religion in Britain*, 5 (1972), 119–36, esp. pp. 121–3, 135.

12. Adorno, 'Stars', pp. 36–7.

13. Ibid., p. 117.

14. See, for example, Steven Shapin, *A Social History of Truth: Civility and Science in Seventeenth-Century England* (Chicago, 1994).

15. Adorno, 'Stars', pp. 116, 120. Campbell, 'Cultic Milieu', is very fond of the term 'seekers'.

16. Umberto Eco, *Foucault's Pendulum* (London, 1989), p. 276.

1. Religion, Magic and the Occult Tradition

1. J.G. Frazer, *The Golden Bough* (London, 1890¹, 1900², 1911–15³). Quotations here from the new abridgement by Robert Fraser,

published by the Oxford World's Classics (Oxford, 1994), based on the 2nd and 3rd edns: pp. 12, 52, 53.

2. See Frazer's *Totemism* (Edinburgh, 1887); *idem, Totemism and Exogamy: A Treatise on Certain Early Forms of Superstition and Society* (London, 1910). Cf. Sigmund Freud, *Totem und Tabu* (1913). For Frazer's biography, see Robert Ackerman, *J.G. Frazer: His Life and Work* (Cambridge, 1987).
3. Frazer, *Golden Bough*, ed. Fraser, pp. 45, 46, 48, 55.
4. Ackerman, *Frazer*, p. 167.
5. This quotation appears in the preface to the 3rd edn of *Golden Bough*, Part VII, Vol. 1, and therefore is never reprinted in the abridged editions.
6. See generally David S. Katz, *God's Last Words: Reading the English Bible from the Reformation to Fundamentalism* (London & New Haven, 2004), chap. 3.
7. A. Jacques Matter, *Histoire critique du Gnosticisme* (Paris, 1828).
8. Frances A. Yates, *The Occult Philosophy in the Elizabethan Age* (London, 1979), p. 1. See also J.S. Mebane, *Renaissance Magic and the Return of the Golden Age* (London, 1989).
9. See especially Antoine Faivre, *Access to Western Esotericism* (Albany, 1994), pp. 10–15. See also his *Theosophy, Imagination, Tradition* (Albany, 2000). Other general works include Désirée Hirst, *Hidden Riches: Traditional Symbolism from the Renaissance to Blake* (London, 1964); Mircea Eliade, *Occultism, Witchcraft, and Cultural Fashions* (Chicago, 1976); James Webb, *The Occult Underground* (La Salle, IL, 1974): orig. pub. as *The Flight from Reason* (London, 1971); *idem, The Occult Establishment* (La Salle, IL, 1976); *On the Margin of the Visible: Sociology, the Esoteric, and the Occult*, ed. Edward A. Tiryakian (New York, 1974); Ioan P. Couliano, *Eros and Magic in the Renaissance* (Chicago, 1987); Michael Baigent & Richard Leigh, *The Elixir and the Stone: a History of Magic and Alchemy* (London, 1997); B.J. Gibbons, *Spirituality and the Occult: From the Renaissance to the Modern Age* (London, 2001); Anthony Aveni, *Behind the Crystal Ball* (Boulder, 2002). See also the classic R.G. Collingwood, *The Idea of Nature* (Oxford, 1945) [based on lectures given in 1934 and 1937], especially for the earlier period, and Carolyn Merchant, *The Death of Nature* (San Francisco, 1980). A wonderful collection of images can be found in Alexander Roob, *The Hermetic Museum: Alchemy and Mysticism* (Köln, 2001).

The most important library for the study of the occult is the Bibliotheca Philosophica Hermetica, the J.R. Ritman Library, in Amsterdam.

10. 'All that is above is like that which is below, and all that is below is like that which is above': 'Emerald Tablet': see below, n. 18.

11. Cf. Edward Tiryakian, *On the Margin of the Visible: Sociology, the Esoteric, and the Occult* (New York, 1974), p. 267: he uses the term 'esoteric culture' to refer to a style of thought that relies on commonly available religious texts, e.g. the Bible, but insists that meaning is not exhausted by ordinary reading . . . and which claims that an esoteric group has a unique understanding of the secret/real meaning in the text . . . and adopts a parlance that seems obscure to the outside world.

12. Similar to 'panentheism', a term invented by K.C.F. Krause (1781–1832), to describe the force of divinity which 'enlivens' nature. For another look at these concepts, see Lorraine Daston, 'The Nature of Nature in Early Modern Europe', *Configurations*, 6 (1998), 149–72.

13. This was a term invented by Agostino Steuco (1497–1548) with reference to an ancient genealogy of divinely inspired philosopher sages. It was also used in the nineteenth century in the field of comparative religion to show the ultimate unity common to all particular and individual religious traditions, and was employed by the Theosophists, who emphasised primordial but hidden traditional wisdom: see Charles B. Schmitt, 'Perrenial [*sic*] Philosophy: From Agostino Steuco to Leibniz', *Jnl History of Ideas*, 27 (1966), 505–32.

14. Generally see Frances Yates, *Giordano Bruno and the Hermetic Tradition* (London, 1964); Wayne Shumaker, *The Occult Sciences in the Renaissance: a Study in Intellectual Patterns* (Berkeley, 1972); Garth Fowden, *The Egyptian Hermes: a Historical Approach to the Late Pagan Mind* (Cambridge, 1986); *Hermeticism and the Renaissance: Intellectual History and the Occult in Early Modern Europe*, ed. Ingrid Merkel & Allen G. Debus (London, 1988).

15. Although the city of Harran in north-western Mesopotamia fell to Islam in the mid seventh century, its pagan inhabitants resisted conversion, as they had earlier refused Christianity. The Harranis took the name 'Sabi'an' from the Koran as a term for a prophetic religion of the book that might be tolerated by the Muslims, and

for their prophet they chose Hermes Trismegistus, whom they identified with Idris and the biblical Enoch. Although many of the Harranis converted to Islam in the early ninth century, the Hermetic Sabi'ans held out until the middle of the eleventh century: *Hermetica*, ed. B.P. Copenhaver (Cambridge, 1993), xlv-vi; Jonathan Elukin, 'Maimonides and the Rise and Fall of the Sabians: Explaining Mosaic Laws and the Limits of Scholarship', *Jnl History of Ideas*, 63 (2002), 619–37.

16. *Hermetica*, ed. Copenhaver, pp. 67–92. The Latin *Asclepius* was published in 1469.

17. For example, John of Stobi (=Stobaeus) compiled an anthology *c.* AD 500, which has forty excerpts from Hermetic writings, incl. CH 2, 4, 9 and *Asclepius*, but he did not know the *Corpus Hermeticum* as a whole.

18. The Latin text of the Emerald Tablet probably first appeared in Europe in translations by Johannes Hispalensis (*c.* 1140) and by Philip of Tripoli (*c.* 1243) of the Arabic 'Book of Advice to Kings' [Kitab Sirr al-Asar], known as the *Secretum Secretorum*. In 1923, E.J. Holmyard discovered an abridged Arabic text in Abu Musa Jabir ibn Hayyan (*c.* 721–*c.* 815) [known to the West as 'Geber'], 'Second Book of the Element of the Foundation'. This appears to be the oldest copy of the Emerald Tablet, probably translated into Arabic from Syriac, perhaps taken from the Harrani pagans, and based on a Greek original.

19. The manuscript is now in Florence in the Biblioteca Medicea Laurenziana, Plut. 71, 33. Ficino later sold the manuscript to Angelo Poliziano (1454–94), where it was found after his death among his papers.

20. Modern editions include *Corpus Hermeticum*, ed. A.D. Nock, trans. A.-J. Festugiere (Paris, 1945–54) = 4 vols; and the now authoritative *Hermetica*, ed. Copenhaver.

21. Augustine, *City of God*, 18.39.

22. Proclus was the first to make such a list, but he mentioned only Greek philosophers, and did not include Hermes Trismegistus. Plethon thought that Zoroaster was older than Hermes Trismegistus, and eventually convinced even Ficino that Zoroaster was the first of the ancient theologians . . . and, since Ficino decided that there could only be six ancient theologians, when Zoroaster was placed at the head of the list, Philolaus had to be

dropped: see D.P. Walker, *The Ancient Theology: Studies in Christian Platonism from the Fifteenth to the Eighteenth Century* (London, 1972).

23. Ficino's preface to a *Book on the Power and Wisdom of God, Whose Title is Pimaner*, quoted in *Hermetica*, ed. Copenhaver, p. xlviii.

24. Generally, see the classic book, D.P. Walker, *Spiritual and Demonic Magic from Ficino to Campanella* (London, 1958); and his later *Unclean Spirits: Possession and Exorcism in France and England in the Late Sixteenth and Early Seventeenth Centuries* (London, 1981). See also Penelope Gouk, *Music, Science and Natural Magic in Seventeenth-Century England* (London, 1999).

25. See the *Canon Episcopi*, the ninth- and tenth-century compendium, which gives a good picture of the Church's view of demonic magic before the witchcraze of the early modern period.

26. See the classic Mark Pattison, *Isaac Casaubon 1559–1614* (2nd edn, Oxford, 1892): first pub. 1875.

27. Isaac Casaubon, *De rebus sacris et ecclesiasticis exercitationes XVI* (London, 1614), dedicated to King James I of England.

28. See Edward Rosen, 'Was Copernicus a Hermeticist?', in *Historical and Philosophical Perspectives of Science*, ed. R.H. Stuewer (Minneapolis, 1970), pp. 163–71.

29. For a rejection of Yates's view on Bruno, see Hilary Gatti, *Giordano Bruno and Renaissance Science* (Ithaca, 1999).

30. John Emsley, *The Shocking History of Phosphorus* (London, 2000); William R. Newman, *Gehennical Fire: the Lives of George Starkey, an American Alchemist in the Scientific Revolution* (Cambridge, USA, 1994); Lawrence M. Principe, *The Aspiring Adept: Robert Boyle and his Alchemical Quest* (Princeton, 1998); *Secrets of Nature: Astrology and Alchemy in Early Modern Europe*, ed. William R. Newman and Anthony Grafton (Cambridge, USA, 2001); William R. Newman & Lawrence M. Principe, *Alchemy Tried in the Fire: Starkey, Boyle, and the Fate of Helmontian Chymistry* (Chicago, 2002); William R. Newman, *Promethean Ambitions: Alchemy and the Quest to Perfect Nature* (Chicago, 2004). Generally, see *Alchemy: A Bibliography of English-language Writings*, ed. Alan Pritchard (London, 1980). See also Zakiya Hanafi, *The Monster in the Machine: Magic, Medicine, and the Marvelous in the Time of the Scientific Revolution* (Durham, 2000).

31. Zur Shalev, 'Measurer of All Things: John Greaves (1602–1652),

the Great Pyramid and Early Modern Metrology', *Jnl History of Ideas*, 63 (2002), 555–75; and chap. 2 below.

32. Martin Bernal, *Black Athena: The Afroasiatic Roots of Classical Civilization* (London, 1987), followed by Mary R. Lefkowitz, *Not Out of Africa: How Afrocentrism Became an Excuse to Teach Myth as History* (New York, 1996), followed in turn by Martin Bernal, *Black Athena Writes Back* (Durham, NC, 2001).

33. Johan Huizinga, *The Waning of the Middle Ages: A Study of the Forms of Life, Thought, and Art in France and the Netherlands in the Fourteenth and Fifteenth Centuries* (London, 1924): translation by F. Hopman of *Herfstij der middeleeuwen* (Haarlem, 1919). See also the new English translation by R.J. Paton and U. Mammitzsch as *The Autumn of the Middle Ages* (Chicago, 1996).

34. Edward Gibbon, *The Decline and Fall of the Roman Empire* (new Everyman edn, London, 1993–4), vi. 233.

35. Steven Runciman, *The Fall of Constantinople 1453* (Cambridge, 1965), p. 42.

36. Ibid., p. 15.

37. Ibid., p. xi.

38. Ibid., p. 188.

39. See esp. Brian Copenhaver, 'Astrology and Magic', in *The Cambridge History of Renaissance Philosophy*, ed. C.B. Schmitt et al. (Cambridge, 1988), pp. 264–300.

40. Marsilio Ficino, *Three Books on Life*, ed. C.V. Kaske & J.R. Clarke (Binghamton, 1989). See also Wouter J. Hanegraaff, 'Sympathy or the Devil: Renaissance Magic and the Ambivalence of Idols', *Esoterica*, 2 (2000), 1–44.

41. This appears in Ficino's commentary on Plato's *Symposium*.

42. See Armando Maggi, *Satan's Rhetoric: A Study of Renaissance Demonology* (Chicago, 2001).

43. See generally Carl Landauer, 'Erwin Panofsky and the Renascence of the Renaissance', *Renaissance Quarterly*, 47 (1994), 255–281.

44. For more on *View*, see *View: Parade of the Avant-Garde: an Anthology of View Magazine (1940–1947)*, ed. Charles Henri Ford, Catrina Neiman and Paul Nathan (New York, 1991); Dickran Tashjian, *A Boatload of Madmen: Surrealism and the American Avant-Garde, 1920–1950* (New York, 1995); Martica Sawin, *Surrealism in Exile and the Beginning of the New York School* (Cambridge, USA, 1995).

45. The standard English translation used by everyone was made by Elizabeth Livermore Forbes and appears in *The Renaissance Philosophy of Man*, ed. Ernst Cassirer, Paul Oskar Kristeller & John Herman Randall, Jr. (Chicago, 1948), pp. 213–54. Yet there is also a preface to the book (p. iii) dated 'Summer 1945' from Columbia University in which Kristeller and Randall note that 'Most of the treatises included in this volume have never before been published in an English version', and among the exceptions they include 'Pico's *Oration*, of which another translation appeared last year in *View* magazine, long after the present one had been ready for publication'. In fact, Kristeller continues (p. 216n.), 'the present translation has been ready for publication for many years, and several passages from it were published as early as 1942'. As Kristeller points out, the first partial English translation of Pico's 'Oration' did appear in the *Jnl. History of Ideas*, 3 (1942), 347–54, 'taken from an unpublished edition prepared by Elizabeth Livermore Forbes, including the Latin text, an English translation, a critical introduction, and notes.' The first full published translation, however, was made by Charles Glenn Wallis and was printed as 'Pico della Mirandola's Very Elegant Speech on the Dignity of Man', *View*, 4 (1944), 88–90, 100–101, 134–5, 146–51. Alongside Pico were articles by Man Ray (1890–1976) and André Breton (1896–1966). Charles Glenn Wallis's translation appeared later (Indianapolis, 1965) in the classic Bobbs-Merrill series, 'The Library of Liberal Arts', whose yellow paperbacks were the essential companions of generations of philosophy undergraduates. See also my forthcoming article on the circumstances of Pico's first English appearance.

46. Noel L. Brann, *The Abbot Trithemius (1462–1516): The Renaissance of Monastic Humanism* (Leiden, 1981); *idem*, *Trithemius and Magical Theology: A Chapter in the Controversy over Occult Studies in Early Modern Europe* (Albany, 1999).

47. Charles IX was born in 1550, ruled from 1560–74, and gave the (reluctant) order for the Saint Bartholomew's Day massacre of Protestants, which began on 24 August 1572.

48. Ellic Howe, *Nostradamus and the Nazis* (London, 1965). See also his *Astrology and Psychological Warfare During World War II* (New York, 1967) [pub. in the UK as *Urania's Children*].

49. There are many editions of Nostradamus, but a handy one with

the French originals is *The Prophecies of Nostradamus*, trans. &
ed. Erika Cheetham (London, 1974).

50. Anthony Grafton, *Cardano's Cosmos: The Worlds and Works of a
Renaissance Astrologer* (Cambridge, USA, 1999).

51. On Pico generally, with reference to the Kabbalah, see e.g. Ernst
Cassirer, 'Giovanni Pico della Mirandola: A Study in the History
of Renaissance Ideas', *Jnl History of Ideas*, 3 (1942), pp. 123–44,
319–46.

52. On Kabbalah generally, see Gershom Scholem, *Major Trends in
Jewish Mysticism* (Jerusalem, 1941); *idem, Kabbalah* (Jerusalem,
1974). On Christian Kabbalah, see J.L. Blau, *The Christian
Interpretation of the Cabala in the Renaissance* (New York, 1944);
F. Secret, *Les Kabbalistes Chrétiens de la Renaissance* (Paris, 1964);
W.J. Bousma, 'Postel and the Significance of Renaissance
Cabalism', *Jnl Warburg & Crtld Inst.*, 17 (1954), pp. 318–32; Yates,
Occult Philosophy. See the major new reinterpretation in Moshe
Idel, *Kabbalah: New Perspectives* (New Haven, 1988).

53. Jacob Burckhardt, *The Civilization of the Renaissance in Italy*
(Phaidon edn, London, 1960), p. 120, from the 2nd German edn
(1868), trans. S.G.C. Middlemore.

54. Johannes Reuchlin, *De rudimentis Hebraicis* (Pforzheim, 1506);
idem, De verbo mirifico (Basle, 1494); *idem, De arte Cabalistica*
(Haguenau, 1517).

55. Moshe Idel, 'The Magical and Neoplatonic Interpretations of the
Kabbalah in the Renaissance', in *Jewish Thought in the Sixteenth
Century*, ed. B. Cooperman (Cambridge, 1987), p. 212.

56. C. Wirszubski, *A Christian Kabbalist Reads the Law* [Hebrew]
(Jerusalem, 1977); Flavius Mithridates, *Sermo de Passione Domini*,
ed. C. Wirszubski (Jerusalem, 1963); S. Simonsohn, 'Some Well-
Known Jewish Converts During the Renaissance', *Revue des Etudes
Juives*, 148 (1989), 17–52.

57. Idel, 'Magical', p. 187.

58. Moshe Idel, 'Kabbalah and Ancient Theology in R. Isaac and
Judah Abrabanel' [Hebrew], in M. Dorman & Z. Levy, eds, *The
Philosophy of Love of Leone Ebreo* (Haifa, 1985), pp. 73–112. Cf.
idem, 'Kabbalah, Platonism and Prisca Theologia: The Case of R.
Menasseh ben Israel', in Y. Kaplan, M. Mechoulan & R.H. Popkin,
eds, *Menasseh ben Israel and His World* (Leiden, 1989), pp. 207–19.

59. David B. Ruderman, *Kabbalah, Magic, and Science: The Cultural*

Universe of a Sixteenth-Century Jewish Physician (Cambridge, USA, 1988).

60. See also H.H. Ben-Sasson, 'The Reformation in Contemporary Jewish Opinion', *Proc. Israel Academy of Sciences and Humanities*, 4 (1970), pp. 239–326.

61. D.S. Katz, 'The Language of Adam in Seventeenth-Century England', in Hugh Lloyd-Jones, Valerie Pearl, & Blair Worden, eds, *History and Imagination: Essays in Honour of H.R. Trevor-Roper* (London, 1981), pp. 132–45.

62. Erasmus to John Colet, [*c.*Dec.] 1504, from Paris: *The Collected Works of Erasmus*, ed. B.M. Corrigan, et al. (Toronto, 1974–), ii. 87 (letter # 181).

63. [Conrad Pellicanus], *De modo legen. et intelli. hebraevm* (Strassburg, 1504), printed by J. Grüninger. The work was originally leaves F ix-xxviii of Gregorius Reisch, *Margarita philosophica* (Basle, 1535), a famous compendium of useful knowledge. A facsimile is also repr. in pamphlet form by E. Nestle (Tübingen, 1877).

64. Johannes Reuchlin, *De rudimentis Hebraicis.*

65. It was reconstructed from geniza fragments and others: *Sefer haRazim* [Hebrew], ed. Mordecai Margolioth (Jerusalem, 1966).

2. Conspiracy and Enlightenment from the Rosicrucians to Isaac Newton

1. It was also in the year 1604 that new stars appeared in the constellations Serpens and Cygnus, which provided further evidence of the possibility of change in the heavens, and greatly impressed Johannes Kepler and John Donne, among others: Frances Yates, *The Rosicrucian Enlightenment* (London, 1972), pp. 79–81. The first celestial event of this kind had already occurred in 1572, when a supernova was visible in the sky for sixteen months.

2. The *Fama* and the *Confessio* are printed as an appendix to Yates, *Rosicrucian Enlightenment*, and can also be easily found on the internet.

3. J.W. Montgomery, *Cross and Crucible: Johann Valentin Andreae (1586–1654): Phoenix of the Theologians* (The Hague, 1973) argues that Andreae was 'the chief orthodox opponent of the Rosicrucian ideology' and had nothing to do with writing either the *Fama* or the *Confessio*. Other older general studies include A.E. Waite, *Real*

History of the Rosicrucians (London, 1887); *idem, The Brotherhood of the Rosy Cross* (London, 1924); Magus Incognito [Clifford Edward Brooksmith], *The Secret Doctrine of the Rosicrucians* (Chicago, 1918). See also *A Christian Rosenkreutz Anthology*, ed. Paul M. Allen (Blauvelt, NY, 1968).

4. One of his important sources was Simon Studion's unpublished manuscript, 'Naometria' (1604), an enormously long prophetic work based on numerology and discussing Solomon's Temple in great detail. Studion predicted that the reign of the Antichrist would end in 1620 with the fall of the Pope and Islam, leading to the onset of the millennium in 1623: cf. Montgomery, *Cross*, pp. 202–6.

5. J.V. Andreae, *Reipublicae Christianopolitanae Descriptio* (Strasburg, 1619), trans. as *Christianopolis, An Ideal State of the Seventeenth Century*, ed. F.E. Held (Oxford, 1916). See also Miriam Eliav-Feldon, *Realistic Utopias: The Ideal Imaginary Societies of the Renaissance, 1516–1630* (Oxford, 1982).

6. For criticism of Yates's understanding of Rosicrucianism, see R.J.W. Evans in *Historical Journal*, 16 (1973), 865–8; and Charles Webster in the *English Historical Review*, 89 (1974), 434–5.

7. Frederick's forces were under the command of Christian van Anhalt (1568–1630), another important character in the story.

8. His wife Elizabeth would have become queen of England had Charles I died before marriage, but her twelfth child (born 1630 in The Hague) became Sophia of Brunswick, the electress of Hanover, friend and patroness of Leibniz, and mother of King George I of England (1714–27).

9. Dee was also a keen advocate of the Gregorian Calendar, which having been devised by papal authority was rejected by Protestants on ideological rather than scientific grounds. Although the Gregorian Calendar was devised in 1582, it was not adopted in England until 1752, at which point the date jumped forward by eleven days.

10. Yates, *Rosicrucian Enlightenment*, p. 69. For Postel, see William J. Bouwsma, *Concordia Mundi: The Career and Thought of Guillaume Postel (1510–1581)* (Cambridge, USA, 1957); Marion L. Kuntz, *Guillaume Postel: Prophet of the Restitution of All Things* (The Hague, 1981), esp. pp. 173–7.

11. See also John Dee, *The Rosie Crucian Secrets*, ed. E.J. Langford

Garstin (Wellingborough, 1985), being a transcription of British Library, MS Harl. 6485.

12. John Dee, *Monas Hieroglyphica Ioannis Dee* (Antwerp, 1564). Cf. *idem, The Hieroglyphic Monad*, ed. J.W. Hamilton–Jones (London, 1947).

13. Peter French, *John Dee: The World of an Elizabethan Magus* (London, 1972); Nicholas H. Clulee, *John Dee's Natural Philosophy: Between Science and Religion* (New York, 1990); William H. Sherman, *John Dee: The Politics of Reading and Writing in the English Renaissance* (Amherst, 1995); Lauren Kassell, *Medicine and Magic in Elizabethan London* (Oxford, 2005); Deborah E. Harkness, *John Dee's Conversations with Angels: Cabala, Alchemy, and the End of Nature* (Cambridge, 1999). More generally, see William Eamon, *Science and the Secrets of Nature* (Princeton, 1994) and Patrick Curry, *Prophecy and Power: Astrology in Early Modern England* (London, 1989). See also the novel by Peter Ackroyd, *The House of Doctor Dee* (London, 1993); and there is a good deal about Dee and the Rosicrucians in Umberto Eco, *Foucault's Pendulum* (London, 1989).

14. William Huffman, *Robert Fludd and the End of the Renaissance* (New York, 1988).

15. Michael Maier, *Arcana arcanissima; hoc est Hieroglyphica Ægyptio-Græca* (Oppenheim?, 1614?). Antoine Joseph Pernetty (1716–1800), the founder of the Avignon Society, reissued the 'Secret of Secrets' under the title *Les Fables égyptiennes et grecques dévoilées & réduites* (Paris, 1758).

16. Michael Maier, *Atalanta fugiens, hoc est, Emblemata nova de secretis naturæ chymica* (Oppenheim, 1618). See also Bruce T. Moran, *The Alchemical World of the German Court: Occult Philosophy and Chemical Medicine in the Circle of Moritz of Hessen (1572–1632)* (Stuttgart, 1991); Sally G. Allen, 'Outrunning Atalanta: Feminine Destiny in Alchemical Transmutation', *Signs*, 6 (1980), 210–29.

17. See the interesting article by Catherine Wilson, 'Visual Surface and Visual Symbol: The Microscope and the Occult in Early Modern Science', *Jnl History of Ideas*, 49 (1988), 85–108; and her *The Invisible World: Early Modern Philosophy and the Invention of the Microscope* (Princeton, 1995).

18. Susanna Åkerman, *Queen Christina of Sweden and her Circle* (Leiden, 1991); *idem, Rose Cross over the Baltic: The Spread of Rosicrucianism in Northern Europe* (Leiden, 1998); David S. Katz, 'Menasseh ben

Israel's Mission to Queen Christina of Sweden', *Jewish Social Studies*, 45 (1983–4), 57–72. See also Christopher McIntosh, *The Rose Cross and the Age of Reason: Eighteenth-Century Rosicrucianism in Central Europe and its Relationship to the Enlightenment* (Leiden, 1992).

19. Yates, *Rosicrucian Enlightenment*, chap. 8.

20. The most famous champion of this idea is F.W.C. Wigston, *Bacon, Shakespeare, and the Rosicrucians* (London, 1888). See also Mrs Henry Pott, *Francis Bacon and his Secret Society* (London, 1891). Other older writings, still interesting, include Thomas De Quincey, 'Historico-Critical Inquiry into the Origin of the Rosicrucians and the Freemasons', in *Collected Writings*, ed. D. Masson (Edinburgh, 1890), xiii. 384–448, originally published in the *London Magazine* in 1824 and drawing on the German work by J.G. Buhle published at Göttingen in 1824. De Quincey claimed that Rosicrucianism was transplanted to England by Robert Fludd, where it became Freemasonry. See also Paul Arnold, *Histoire des Rose-Croix et les origines de la Franc-Maçonnerie* (Paris, 1955), with a second edition (Paris, 1990) including a preface by Umberto Eco.

21. Tho[mas] Sprat (1635–1713), *The History of the Royal-Society of London* (London, 1667): cf. modern edn of J.I. Cope and H.W. Jones (St Louis and London, 1966): engraving printed opp. title page. Cf. Psalms 17:8, 57:1.

22. Isaac Newton himself owned a copy of the first published English translation of the *Fama* and the *Confessio*: Eugenius Philalethes [Thomas Vaughan], *The Fame and Confession of the Fraternity of R: C: Commonly, of the Rosie Cross* (London, 1652): Newton's copy is now in the Yale University library. See also, Betty Jo Teeter Dobbs, *The Foundations of Newton's Alchemy, or 'The Hunting of the Greene Lyon'* (Cambridge, 1975); *idem, The Janus Faces of Genius: The Role of Alchemy in Newton's Thought* (Cambridge, 1991).

23. Samuel Hartlib, *A Description of the Famous Kingdome of Macaria* (London, 1641); cf. Charles Webster, *Samuel Hartlib and the Advancement of Learning* (Cambridge, 1970).

24. J.A. Comenius, *The Labyrinth of the World and the Paradise of the Heart*, trans. Howard Louthan and Andrea Sterk (New York, 1998). The Rosicrucians appear in chap. 12: cf. Yates, *Rosicrucian Enlightenment*, pp. 204–6. See also his *Via lucis, vestigata & vestiganda* (Amsterdam, 1668), Englished as *The Way of Light*, ed. and trans. E.T. Campagnac (Liverpool, 1938). Generally, see the classic

H.R. Trevor-Roper, 'Three Foreigners: The Philosophers of the Puritan Revolution', in his *Religion, the Reformation, and Social Change* (London, 1967), pp. 237–93; and G.H. Turnbull, *Hartlib, Dury and Comenius* (Liverpool, 1947).

25. Alexander C. Rae, *Bluff Your Way in the Occult* (Horsham, Sussex, 1988), p. 15.

26. Yates, *Rosicrucian Enlightenment*, preface.

27. What follows leans heavily on what I wrote about Newton in *God's Last Words: Reading the English Bible from the Reformation to Fundamentalism* (New Haven & London, 2004), chap. 3.

28. William Paley, *Natural Theology* (London, 1802), p. 1.

29. Generally see F. Oakley, 'Christian Theology and the Newtonian Science: The Rise of the Concept of the Laws of Nature', *Church Hist.*, 30 (1961), 433–57; D. Kubrin, 'Newton and the Cyclical Cosmos: Providence and the Mechanical Philosophy', *Jnl Hist. Ideas*, 28 (1967), 325–346; M. Todd, 'Providence, Chance, and the New Science in Early Stuart Cambridge', *Hist. Jnl*, 29 (1986), 697–711; J.E. McGuire, 'Force, Active Principles, and Newton's Invisible Realm', *Ambix*, 15 (1968), 154–208; Keith Hutchison, 'What Happened to Occult Qualities in the Scientific Revolution?', *Isis*, 73 (1982), 233–53.

30. R.G. Collingwood, *The Idea of Nature* (London, 1946).

31. Clarke to Leibniz, 26 Nov. 1715: *The Leibniz-Clarke Correspondence*, ed. H.G. Alexander (Manchester, 1956), p. 14.

32. Gen. 9:16.

33. Isaac Newton, *The Chronology of Ancient Kingdoms Amended, To which is Prefix'd, A Short Chronicle* (London, 1728), pp. 332–46 and following three plates.

34. Isaac Newton, 'A Dissertation upon the *Sacred Cubit* of the *Jews* and the *Cubits* of the several Nations; in which, from the Dimensions of the greatest *Egyptian* Pyramid, as taken by Mr. *John Greaves*, the antient Cubit of *Memphis* is determined', in John Greaves, *Miscellaneous Works*, ed. Thomas Birch (London, 1737), ii. 405–33. John Greaves (1602–52) was professor of Astronomy at Oxford. Between 1638–40 he travelled in the Middle East and climbed the Great Pyramid twice. His work was summarised in his *Pyramidographia: or a description of the Pyramids in Aegypt* (London, 1646), including a very accurate cross-section of the Great Pyramid. See Zur Shalev, 'Measurer of All Things:

John Greaves (1602–1652), the Great Pyramid, and Early Modern Metrology', *Jnl of the History of Ideas*, 63 (2002), 555–75. For the ultimate pyramid book, see P. Lemesurier, *The Great Pyramid Decoded* (London, 1977).

35. Jewish National and University Library, Jerusalem, MS Yahuda 17.3, fos. 8–11: repr. Westfall, *Never at Rest*, p. 354.

36. I have modernized Newton's seventeenth-century spelling. For this quotation and for what follows, see King's College MS. 5, repr. Scott Mandelbrote, '"A duty of the greatest moment": Isaac Newton and the Writing of Biblical Criticism', *Brit.Jnl Hist.Sci.*, 26 (1993), 281–302.

3. Organising the Occult: Freemasons, Swedenborgians and Mormons

1. Generally see J.M. Roberts, *The Mythology of the Secret Societies* (London, 1972); D. Knoop & G.P. Jones, *The Genesis of Freemasonry* (Manchester, 1947); A.S. Frere, *The Grand Lodge, 1717–1967* (Oxford, 1967); *Early Masonic Pamphlets*, eds D. Knoop, G.P. Jones and D. Hamer (Manchester, 1945); Margaret C. Jacob, *The Radical Enlightenment: Pantheists, Freemasons and Republicans* (London, 1981); David Stevenson, *The Origins of Freemasonry* (Cambridge, 1988); Michael Baigent & Richard Leigh, *The Temple and the Lodge* (London, 1989); Jasper Ridley, *The Freemasons* (New York, 2001); cf. the official Freemasonry journal, *Ars Quatuor Coronatorum*. See also the classic Georg Simmel, 'The Sociology of Secrecy and of Secret Societies', *The American Jnl of Sociology*, 11 (1906), 441–98.

2. He also copied out an English translation of the *Fama* and the *Confessio* and actually wrote a letter of application in Latin asking to join the Rosicrucians: Bodl. Lib., MS. Ashmole 1459, fos. 280–2 (letter); fos. 284–31 (English trans.); 1478, fos. 125–9 (orig. of English trans. that Ashmole copied, not the Vaughan translation). See esp. Ashmole's *Theatrum Chemicum Britannicum* (London, 1652), a collection ('theatre') of alchemical writings written in English.

3. 1 Kings 7: 13–22.

4. 2 Kings 5; 2 Chronicles [as 'Huram the king of Tyre'] 2: 3, 11–13; 4: 11, 16; 8: 2, 18; 9: 10, 21; and yet another Huram in 1 Chronicles 8: 5.

5. The other was the Hospitallers. Generally, see Peter Partner, *The Murdered Magicians: the Templars and their Myth* (Oxford, 1982); Piers Paul Read, *The Templars* (London, 1999); *The Templars: Selected Sources*, ed. Malcolm Barber & Keith Bate (Manchester, 2002); Alain Demurger, *The Last Templar: The Tragedy of Jacques de Molay* (London, 2004).

6. The headquarters in London is now the Inner and Middle Temple, south of the Strand. The original Temple Church (1185), like other Templar churches, was modelled on the Church of the Holy Sepulchre in Jerusalem as a round building.

7. The first noble Grand Master, elected in 1721, was John, second duke of Montagu.

8. These were also the years in which English and European intellectuals tried to make sense of the radical pamphlet denouncing the 'three impostors' Moses, Jesus and Muhammad: *Les Trois imposteurs, ou l'esprit de M. Spinosa* (1719), repr. as *Traité des trois imposteurs* (Amsterdam, 1776), based on the manuscript *De tribus impostoribus*, with hundreds of copies in Latin and French circulating from about 1680–95 to the late Enlightenment. The only known copy of the 1719 printing was discovered by Silvia Berti in 1985 in the library of UCLA: see her 'Unmasking the Truth: The Theme of Imposture in Early Modern European Culture, 1660–1730', in *Everything Connects: In Conference with Richard H. Popkin*, eds James E. Force & David S. Katz (Leiden, 1999), pp. 21–36, and NB. pp. 19–20. See also *Heterodoxy, Spinozism, and Free Thought in Early-Eighteenth-Century Europe: Studies on the Traité des trois imposteurs*, eds Silvia Berti, Françoise Charles–Daubert & Richard H. Popkin (Dordrecht, 1996). English editions were published at Dundee (1844) and New York (1846), and now as *The Treatise of the Three Impostors and the Problem of the Enlightenment*, ed. Abraham Anderson (Lanham, 1997), pp. 3–42, from the 1777 edn. See *Traité des trois imposteurs*, ed. Pierre Retat (Saint-Etienne, 1973), based on the 1777 text. Generally, see Ira O. Wade, *The Clandestine Organization and Diffusion of Philosophical Ideas in France from 1710–1750* (Princeton, 1938), chap. 2; and Margaret C. Jacob, *The Radical Enlightenment: Pantheists, Freemasons and Republicans* (London, 1981), chap. 7, where she claims that the text was written by Jean Rousset de Missy (1686–1762).

9. J.M. Roberts, *The Mythology of the Secret Societies* (London, 1972), pp. 41–2.

10. Andrew Michael Ramsay, *Les voyages de Cyrus: avec un Discours sur la mythologie* (Paris, 1727). The English trans. appeared as *The travels of Cyrus. In two volumes. To which is annex'd, A discourse upon the theology and mythology of the ancients* (London, 1727).

11. Roberts, *Secret Societies*, p. 35.

12. Mark S. Dwor, 'Some Thoughts on the History of the Tracing Boards', unpublished paper, on line at the website of the Grand Lodge of British Columbia and Yukon.

13. There are two Enochs in the Bible: (1) The son of Cain (Gen. 4:16–17), who built a city 'in the land of Nod, on the east of Eden' and called it 'after the name of his son, Enoch'. This is the first 'city' mentioned in the Old Testament; (2) The son of Jared (who was Seth's great-great-grandson), and father of Methuselah (Gen. 5:18–24; Luke 3:37). This Enoch was 'the seventh from Adam' (Jude 1:14), as distinguished from the son of Cain, the third from Adam (inclusive). Enoch II's prophesying is also noticed at Jude 1:14–15. Enoch II's son Methusaleh begat Lamech, who in turn begat Noah. According to Gen. 5:24, 'And Enoch walked with God: and he *was* not; for God took him.' He is listed as well in the Epistle to the Hebrews (11:5), where it says that 'Enoch was translated that he should not see death; and was not found, because God had translated him'. Enoch II's divine translation gave rise to the belief that he was thereupon shown the secrets of the universe and the future of humankind and the world. For the Ethiopic Book of Enoch, see below, n. 69.

14. A large amount of his correspondence and papers from 1744 to 1809 is at the British Library, Add. MSS 23644–80: see Rainsford's letter from The Hague, 11 Nov. 1777, regarding the 'Baal Shem' of London (Add. MS. 23650, fos. 5–8) and a similar letter from Oct. 1782 (Add. MS. 23669, fos. 85–6). His alchemical notes and papers in eight volumes can be found at the Wellcome Library, London, MSS 4032–39; and in the private library of the Duke of Northumberland, Alnwick Castle. Other Rainsford papers can be found in the Royal Academy of Arts (correspondence with Ozias Humphry) and the Public Record Office (correspondence with F.J. Jackson). For more on Rainsford, see below, p. 97.

15. M.A. Gutstein, *The Story of the Jews of Newport* (New York, 1936),

pp. 31, 343–4; S. Oppenheim, 'The Jews and Masonry in the United States before 1810', *Publications of the American Jewish Historical Society*, 19 (1910), 3–17.

16. Gutstein, *Newport*, pp. 343–4; J.J. Lyons, 'Items Relating to Masonry in Newport', *Publications of the American Jewish Historical Society*, 27 (1920), 416. Lyons quoted the document as follows: 'On ye 5th day of ye 9th month 1658, ye 2nd Tisri A.M. 5518, we assembled at ye house of Mordecaiah Campanall and gave a degree to Abraham Moses.'

Lyons noted that it was unlikely that such a ceremony would take place on the second day of the Jewish New Year, and if it did take place in the evening it would have already been the third of Tisri. It might also have been objected that the year 5518 in Christian usage is 1758, and in that year no one named Mordecai Campanall lived in Newport, and by then the Masons were well-developed and met in the lodge, not in private houses.

17. Cemetery deed printed in Gutstein, *Newport*, pp. 37–8: facsimile copy in *Publications of the American Jewish Historical Society*, 27 (1920), pp. 174–5. The original deed is now lost: the existing copy was made in 1767 by the town clerk of Newport, William Coddington. The volume recording land evidences in Newport during the seventeenth century is also lost, so the copy is the only remaining proof of the establishment of a Jewish burial ground there.

18. Oppenheim, 'Jews and Masonry', pp. 14, 17–18.

19. Israel Finestein, 'The Jews in Regular English Freemasonry', *Transactions of the Jewish Historical Society of England*, 25 (1977), 150–209.

20. Northern Brazil was under Dutch rule between 1630 and 1654. After the reconquest of the Brazilian town of Recife by the Portuguese, the Dutch Jews living there were given three months in which to evacuate. All left, the majority returning to Holland, others to the Caribbean, and twenty-three Jews made their way to New Amsterdam. Some of these same Jews may have travelled further on to Newport, worried that not only had official permission from the Dutch authorities not been received, but a local decree had been issued actually encouraging them to leave. But the nucleus of the Newport Jewish community may have come from Barbados, drawn to Rhode Island in part because of the

large Quaker community in both places, with which the Dutch Jews had many connections. This claim is supported by the names of the principal Jewish families who lived in Newport during the first years, compared with the names of known Barbadian Jews in the middle of the seventeenth century. Some individual Newport Jews are indeed sufficiently well-known for their paths to be traced between Barbados and New England. New Amsterdam was surrendered to the English on 27 Aug. 1664, and the name of the town was changed to New York: see David S. Katz, *Sabbath and Sectarianism in Seventeenth-Century England* (Leiden, 1988), pp. 155–64.

21. Gutstein, *Newport*, p. 344.

22. Oppenheim, 'Jews and Masonry', p. 15. See also C.S. Brigham, 'Reports on the Archives of Rhode Island', *Annual Report of the American Historical Association. 1903*, 1 (1904), 605–6, where he notes that the records from the pre-revolutionary period are in a bad state because the British carried them away in 1779 in a boat that later sank. The records remained under water for several days until the governor complained to General Washington, who had them recovered and placed in a store in New York, where they were lost for a time and finally returned at the request of Newport town council in 1782.

23. Oppenheim, 'Jews and Masonry', p. 15. Others who accept 1658 as the date of the first Jewish arrivals in Newport include Carl Bridenbaugh, *Cities in the Wilderness* (2nd edn, New York, 1960), pp. 94, 104; *idem*, *Fat Mutton and Liberty of Conscience* (Providence, 1974), p. 63n.; M.J. Kohler, 'The Jews in Newport', *Publications of the American Jewish Historical Society*, 6 (1897), 61–80; S.F. Chyet, 'A Synagogue in Newport', *American Jewish Archives*, 16 (1964), 41–50. See also L. Hühner, 'The Jews of New England (Other than Rhode Island) Prior to 1800', *Publications of the American Jewish Historical Society*, 11 (1903), 75–99; J.R. Marcus, 'Light on Early Connecticut Jewry', *American Jewish Archives*, 1 (1948–9), 3–52.

24. J.M. Shaftesley, *The Lodge of Israel No. 205, 1793–1968* (London, 1968).

25. Jacob Katz, *Jews and Freemasons in Europe 1723–1939* (Cambridge, USA, 1970).

26. David Bates, 'The Mystery of Truth: Louis-Claude de Saint-Martin's Enlightened Mysticism', *Jnl History of Ideas*, 61 (2000), 635–55.

27. On Saint-Germain generally see Jean Overton Fuller, *The Comte de Saint-Germain: Last Scion of the House of Rakoczy* (London, 1988); Arthur Edward Waite, 'Comte de Saint-Germain as an Historical Personality', *Occult Review*, 37 (1923), 219–33; Isobel Cooper-Oakley, *The Comte de Saint-Germain, the Secret of Kings* (Milan, 1912; London, 1927); E.M. Butler, *The Myth of the Magus* (Cambridge, 1948), pp. 185–214. There is also the more classic Andrew Lang, 'Saint-Germain the Deathless', in his *Historical Mysteries* (London, 1904) in which he claims that the count was a bastard son of Queen Anna Maria of Spain.

28. For Madame Blavatsky, see chap. 6.

29. For contemporary views on Cagliostro, see Jean Pierre Louis Luchet, marquis de la Roche du Maine [1740–92], *Mémoires authentiques pour servir à l'histoire du comte de Cagliostro* (Paris, 1785); *idem*, *Essai sur la secte des Illuminés* (Paris, 1789); 'Lucia', *The Life of the Count Cagliostro* (London, 1787); Guillemain de St-Victor, *Receuil précieux de la Maçonnerie Adonhiramite* (n.p., 1786).

30. On Cagliostro generally, see W.R.H. Trowbridge, *Cagliostro, Splendour and Misery of a Master of Magic* (London, 1910); Butler, *Magus*, pp. 215–42; M. Harrison, *Count Cagliostro* (London, 1942); H.R. Evans, *Cagliostro and his Egyptian Rite of Freemasonry* (New York, 1930); F. Funck-Brentano, *Cagliostro and Company* (London, 1910); C. Photiades, *Les Vies du Comte de Cagliostro* (Paris, 1932); H. D'Almeras, *Cagliostro, la Franc-Maçonnerie et l'Occultisme au XVIIIe siècle* (Paris, 1904); *L'Évangile de Cagliostro, retrouvé, traduit du Latin et publié avec une introduction*, ed. Marc Haven (Paris, 1932); H.C. Schnur, *Mystic Rebels* (New York, 1949); R. Gervaso, *Cagliostro* (London, 1964); Massimo Introvigne, 'Arcana Arcanorum: Cagliostro's Legacy in Contemporary Magical Movements', *Syzygy*, 1 (1992), 117–35.

31. Jeanne, née de Saint-Remy de Valois (1756–91), married to Comte Marc Antoine Nicolas de la Motte (1754–1831).

32. The classic telling of the tale is in Thomas Carlyle, 'The Diamond Necklace', first pub. *Fraser's Magazine*, 85 & 86 (1837), and repr. in his *Critical and Miscellaneous Essays* (London, 1869), v. 3–96, which also includes his essay, 'Count Cagliostro', ibid., iv. 311–90, first pub. *Fraser's Magazine*, 43 & 44 (1833).

33. Publicity was given to these ideas in the *Vie de Joseph Balsamo*,

connu sous le nom de comte Cagliostro, Extraite de la Procédure instruite contre lui à Rome, en 1790 (Paris and Strasburg, 1791), appearing immediately afterwards in 2nd edn, being a trans. of *Compendio della vita, e delle gèsta di Giuseppe Balsamo* (Rome, 1791), which also went into 2nd edn the same year. The English trans. appeared as *The Life of Joseph Balsamo, commonly called Count Cagliostro* (Dublin, 1792).

34. A discussion of a rite taking place in Cagliostro's cell in Umberto Eco, *Foucault's Pendulum* (London, 1989 [1988]), chap. 24: Saint-Germain appears in chap. 26.

35. The Freemasons, of course, also appear endlessly in contemporary literature: see Heinrich Schneider, *Quest for Mysteries: The Masonic Background for Literature in Eighteenth-Century Germany* (Ithaca, 1947) . . . and we need hardly mention Wolfgang Amadeus Mozart (1756–91), *Die Zauberflöte* ('The Magic Flute'). This was his last opera, first performed on 30 September 1791, only a few weeks before his death. Both Mozart and his librettist, Emanuel Schikaneder (1751–1812) were Freemasons, and borrowed a good deal of the plot from Jean Terrasson (1670–1750), *Sethos*, published in French in 1731, and the following year in English as *The life of Sethos: Taken from Private Memoirs of the Ancient Egyptians* (n.p., 1732).

36. See especially the over-heated writings of Nesta Webster (1876–1960), such as *World Revolution: The Plot Against Civilization* (London, 1921) and *Secret Societies and Subversive Movements* (London, 1924). See also Richard M. Gilman, *Behind World Revolution: The Strange Career of Nesta H. Webster* (Ann Arbor, 1982); Jim Marrs, *Rule by Secrecy: the Hidden History that Connects the Trilateral Commission, the Freemasons, and the Great Pyramids* (New York, 2000); and Michael Barkun, *A Culture of Conspiracy: Apocalyptic Visions in Contemporary America* (Berkeley, 2003).

37. Roberts, *Secret Societies*, p. 124.

38. *Einige Originalschriften des Illuminatenordens* (Munich, 1787).

39. Abbé de Barruel, *Memoirs, Illustrating the History of Jacobinism* (London, 1797–8), in four vols.

40. See also Michel Riquet, *Augustin de Barruel: un jésuite face aux jacobins francs-maçons, 1741–1820* (Paris, 1989).

41. Joseph de Maistre, *Quatre chapitres inédits sur la Russie*, ed. Rodolphe de Maistre (Paris, 1859).

42. Elizabeth L. Eisenstein, *The First Professional Revolutionist: Filippo Michele Buonarroti (1761–1837)* (Cambridge, USA, 1959).

43. Filippo Michele Buonarroti, *Conspiration pour l'égalité dite de Babeuf* (Brussels, 1828). An English translation appeared as *Babeuf's Conspiracy for Equality*, ed. Bronterre O'Brien (New York, 1965).

44. What follows leans heavily on what I wrote about Swedenborg in *God's Last Words: Reading the English Bible from the Reformation to Fundamentalism* (New Haven & London, 2004), chap. 5.

45. William Blake, 'The Marriage of Heaven and Hell' (c.1790–3), in *Complete Writings*, ed. G. Keynes (London, 1957), pp. 148–60, esp. pp. 157–8. The title itself, of course, is a reference to Swedenborg's book, *Heaven and Hell*.

46. See generally Cyriel Odhner Sigstedt, *The Swedenborg Epic: the Life and Works of Emanuel Swedenborg* (New York, 1952); Ernst Benz, *Emanuel Swedenborg: Visionary Savant in the Age of Reason* (West Chester, PA, 2002) [1st pub. in German (Munich, 1948)]; Marsha Keith Schuchard, *Restoring the Temple of Vision: Cabalistic Freemasonry and Stuart Culture* (Leiden, 2002), and her earlier work, 'Swedenborg, Jacobitism, and Freemasonry', in *Swedenborg and His Influence*, ed. E.J. Brock, et al. (Penn. & London, 1988), pp. 359–79; 'Yeats and the "Unknown Superiors": Swedenborg, Falk, and Cagliostro', in *Secret Texts: The Literature of Secret Societies*, eds M. Roberts & H. Ormsby-Lennon (New York, 1995) and 'Freemasonry, Secret Societies, and the Continuity of the Occult Traditions in English Literature' (Ph.D. thesis, University of Texas at Austin, 1975). Benzelius's son-in-law Andreas Norrelius edited Kemper's MSS later on. For Benzelius's correspondence with Leibniz and others, see *Letters to Erik Benzelius the Younger from Learned Foreigners*, ed. A. Erikson (Göteborg, 1980); *Erik Benzelius' Letters to his Learned Friends*, eds A. Erikson & E.N. Nylander (Göteborg, 1983). Kemper seems to have been a secret follower of Shabtai Zvi: H.-J. Schoeps, *Barocke Juden* (Bern, 1965), pp. 60–82. See also Elliot R. Wolfson, 'Messianism in the Christian Kabbalah of Johann Kemper', *Jnl of Scriptural Reasoning*, 1 (2001), internet version.

47. For more on Falk, see David S. Katz, *The Jews in the History of England, 1485–1850* (Oxford, 1994), pp. 300–3; Michal Oron, *Samuel Falk: the Baal Shem of London* [Hebrew] (Jerusalem, 2002); Abraham G. Duker, 'Swedenborg's Attitude Towards the Jews', *Judaism*, 5 (1956), 272–6. For Rainsford on Falk, see n. 14.

48. See Robert Darnton, *Mesmerism and the End of the Enlightenment in France* (Cambridge, USA, 1968); Robert C. Fuller, *Mesmerism and the American Cure of Souls* (Philadelphia, 1982); Frank A. Pattie, *Mesmer and Animal Magnetism: a Chapter in the History of Medicine* (Hamilton, NY, 1994); Alison Winter, *Mesmerized: Powers of Mind in Victorian Britain* (Chicago, 1998); Patricia Fara, 'An Attractive Therapy: Animal Magnetism in Eighteenth-Century England', *History of Science*, 33 (1995), 127–77.

49. See generally, P.J. Lineham, 'The English Swedenborgians 1770–1840: A Study in the Social Dimensions of Religious Sectarianism' (Ph.D. thesis, Univ. of Sussex, 1978), p. 11. Cf. *idem*, 'The Origins of the New Jerusalem Church in the 1780s', *Bull. John Rylands Lib.*, 70 (1988), 109–22.

50. Emanuel Swedenborg, *The True Christian Religion* (Everyman edn, London, 1933), pp. 270, 280 (#191, 201). See also the very useful book *A Compendium of the Theological Writings of Emanuel Swedenborg*, ed. S.M. Warren (London, 1896); William Ross Woofenden, *Swedenborg Researcher's Manual: a Research Reference Manual for Writers of Academic Dissertations and for Other Scholars* (Bryn Athyn, PA, 1988).

51. For Mede and Hutchinson, see Katz, *God's Last Words*, chaps. 3 & 5.

52. Swedenborg, *True Christian Religion*, pp. 280–1, 332 (#202, 275).

53. Ibid., pp. 282–4, 335 (#204–5, 279). Swedenborg also notes that scriptural truths might be found in China: cf. David S. Katz, 'The Chinese Jews and the Problem of Biblical Authority in Eighteenth- and Nineteenth-Century England', *Eng. Hist. Rev.*, 105 (1990), 893–919. Madame Blavatsky will make great use of Swedenborg's reference to the preservation of the ancient word in Great Tartary: see below p. 165.

54. Swedenborg, *True Christian Religion*, pp. 285–6 (#209).

55. Ibid., pp. 334–5 (#278).

56. Ibid., p. 340 (#281). See also Moshe Idel, 'The World of Angels in Human Form', in *Studies in Jewish Mysticism, Philosophy, and Ethical Literature [Isaiah Tishby Festschrift]*, eds J. Dan & J. Hacker (Jerusalem, 1986), pp. 1–66, esp. pp. 64–6, where Idel argues that Swedenborg's idea of a *homo maximus* was closer to kabbalistic ideas than to the Cosmic Man of Jaina.

57. See C.D.A. Leighton, 'William Law, Behmenism, and Counter

Enlightenment', *Harv.Theo.Rev.*, 91 (1998), 301–20; A.K. Walker *William Law: His Life and Thought* (London, 1973); Paula McDowell, 'Enlightenment Enthusiasms and the Spectacular Failure of the Philadelphian Society', *Eighteenth-Century Studies*, 35 (2002), 515–533.

58. Cf. especially *Christian Perfection, The Grounds and Reasons of Christian Regeneration, Spirit of Prayer, The Way to Divine Knowledge, Spirit of Love*, and, best known of all, *A Serious Call To a Devout and Holy Life* (1728).

59. See esp. Edward Taylor, *Jacob Behmen's Theosophick Philosophy Unfolded* (London, 1691); Thomas McFarland, *Coleridge and the Pantheist Tradition* (Oxford, 1969); Désirée Hirst, *Hidden Riches: Traditional Symbolism from the Renaissance to Blake* (London, 1964), esp. chaps 3 & 7; and Alexandre Koyré, *La Philosophie de Jacob Boehme* (Paris, 1929).

60. See Ann Taves, *Fits, Trances & Visions: Experiencing Religion and Explaining Experience from Wesley to James* (Princeton, 1999).

61. John Wesley, *Journal*, ed. N. Curnock (London, 1910–17), v. 354–5 [28 Feb. 1770], 440 [8 Dec. 1771]. Wesley's fullest discussion of Swedenborg's works is dated from Wakefield, 9 May 1782, and published in the *Arminian Magazine*, 6 (London, 1783), 437–41, 495–8, 550–2, 607–14, 669–80. Cf. W.R. Ward, 'Swedenborgianism: Heresy, Schism or Religious Protest?', *Stud.Ch.Hist.*, 9 (1972), 303–9.

62. For more about Rainsford, see above, p. 77.

63. See esp. Lineham, 'Origins', pp. 112–13; M.L. Danilewicz, '"The King of the New Israel": Thaddeus Grabianka (1740–1807)', *Oxford Slavonic Papers*, n.s., 1 (1968), 49–73.

64. Lineham, *English Swedenborgians*, chap. 3; Ward, 'Swedenborgianism'. The standard history of the sect is R. Hindmarsh, *Rise and Progress of the New Jerusalem Church in England, America and other Parts*, ed. E. Madeley (London, 1861).

65. The Unitarians were also post-millennialist, and the Swedenborgians seem to have lost many followers to that less demanding sect.

66. Generally see the excellent book by John L. Brooke, *The Refiner's Fire: The Making of Mormon Cosmology* (Cambridge, 1994). The classic biography is by Fawn M. Brodie, *No Man Knows My History: The Life of Joseph Smith* (2nd edn, New York, 1971), first

pub. 1945. See also Richard N. & Joan K. Ostling, *Mormon America: the Power and the Promise* (San Francisco, 1999).

67. Emma Hale married Joseph Smith in 1827: after her husband's murder she refused to migrate to Utah. She never accepted polygamy, and campaigned against it within the church while her husband was trying to establish it. Joseph Smith eventually would have about forty wives: in the summer of 1835 he was literally caught in the act with a servant girl. In 1847, Emma Smith married Lewis Bidamon, a non-Mormon. Emma argued that her son Joseph Smith III (1832–1914) should lead the religious movement that her husband founded; failing in that, she left the Latter-day Saints and joined the Reorganized Church of Jesus Christ of Latter-day Saints (headed by her son from 1860), dying in Nauvoo, Illinois.

68. See below, p 102.

69. Richard Laurence (1760–1838), *The Book of Enoch, the Prophet: an Apocryphal Production, Supposed for Ages to have been Lost; but Discovered at the Close of the Last Century in Abyssinia; now first Translated from an Ethiopic MS. in the Bodleian Library* (2nd edn, Oxford & London, 1833): 1st pub. 1821. See the text with introduction by E. Isaac, in *The Old Testament Pseudepigrapha*, ed. James H. Charlesworth (London, 1983–5), i. 5–89. See also Edgar J. Goodspeed, *Strange New Gospels* (Chicago, 1931).

70. Egbert B. Grandin (1806–45) was the owner of a bookshop and the local Palmyra weekly, the *Wayne Sentinel.* In August 1829, he contracted to print the *Book of Mormon*, which was published the following March.

71. See, for example, the copy in the British Library: C.58.d. 10.

72. E.D. Howe, *Mormonism Unvailed . . . to which are added, inquiries into the probability that the historical part of the said Bible was written by one Solomon Spalding [sic], more than twenty years ago, and by him intended to have been published as a romance* (Painesville, printed and published by the author, 1834).

73. Howe, *Mormonism Unvailed*, pp. 240–8.

74. Much has been written about the Hofmann case, much of it sensationalist: see *Hofmann's Confession*, eds Jerald & Sandra Tanner (Salt Lake City, 1987); Linda Sillitoe & Allen D. Roberts, *Salamander: the Story of the Mormon Forgery Murders* (Salt Lake City, 1988); Steven Naifeh & Gregory White Smith, *The Mormon*

Murders (New York, 1988). Ironically, after the Hofmann case, the LDS Church discovered that some of the McLellin papers had been sitting in their archives since 1908. These have been published as: *The Journals of William E. McLellin 1831–1836*, eds Jan Shipps & John W. Welch (Urbana & Chicago, 1994).

75. Joseph Smith admitted to having read Thomas Dick, *The Philosophy of a Future State* (Brookfield, MA, 1829), which summarised Hermeticism, and in the 1830s he acknowledged that he knew the writings of Swedenborg.

76. The text of the Mormon Bible is also rather different: see Philip L. Barlow, 'Joseph Smith's Revision of the Bible: Fraudulent, Pathologic, or Prophetic?', *Harvard Theological Rev.*, 83 (1990), 45–64; *idem, Mormons and the Bible: The Place of the Latter-day Saints in American Religion* (New York, 1991).

77. Curiously, just as Joseph Smith was establishing the white race as superior to the red (in the Book of Mormon) and to the black (in the Book of Abraham), Nat Turner was reading the millennial signs quite differently as the basis for his rebellion in Virginia in August 1831.

78. Seixas produced in 119 pp., *A Manual of Hebrew Grammar for the Use of Beginners* (2nd edn, Andover, 1834 [1st edn, 1833]), a copy of which can be found in Special Collections, Marriott Library, University of Utah [PJ4563.S45 1834] and repr. in fascimile (Salt Lake City, 1981). See also Shalom Goldman, *God's Sacred Tongue: Hebrew and the American Imagination* (Chapel Hill, 2004), chap. 9.

79. See their website, www.familysearch.org.

80. Important changes for women at the temple endowment ceremony were made in 1990: no longer were they required to wear face veils, or to promise to obey their husbands, and references in regard to throat-slitting and disembowelment as punishments for revealing secrets were omitted from the set text. Generally, see R.L. Moore, 'The Occult Connection? Mormonism, Christian Science, and Spiritualism', in *The Occult in America*, eds H. Kerr & C.L. Crow (Urbana, 1983), pp. 135–61.

81. Note that the 'philosopher's stone' was the result of this sexual union, which appeared as a quintessence, the *prima materia*.

82. See also the depiction of Mormons in the works by Robert Louis Stevenson (1850–94), *More New Arabian Nights: The Dynamiter*

(London, 1885) and Zane Grey (1872–1939), *Riders of the Purple Sage* (New York, 1912).

83. Avard was born on Guernsey, and was baptised and ordained an elder by Orson Pratt in Pennsylvania in 1835, moving to Kirtland the following year, eventually leaving the faith and even testifying against Joseph Smith in 1838, which led to his excommunication in 1839. He spent the last twenty years or so of his life in Illinois.

84. Norman F. Furniss, *The Mormon Conflict, 1850–1859* (New Haven, 1960).

4. Occult Without: Re-enchanting Nature

1. The first edition was also published in 1765. The critical literature on the Gothic novel is huge. A useful beginning is the *Cambridge Companion to Gothic Fiction*, ed. Jerrold E. Hogle (Cambridge, 2002); David Punter, *The Literature of Terror: a History of Gothic Fictions from 1765 to the Present Day* (London, 1980); *Literature of the Occult*, ed. Peter B. Messent (Englewood Cliffs, NJ, 1981); and see below, n.63.

2. See Andrew Bowie, *Schelling and Modern European Philosophy* (London, 1993); Edward Allen Beach, *The Potencies of God(s): Schelling's Philosophy of Mythology* (Albany, 1994).

3. Marx was a Hegelian, but saw this process as happening not to mind or spirit, but to matter: 'dialectical materialism' . . . which is why Marx said that he had stood Hegel on his head: see Glenn A. Magee, *Hegel and the Hermetic Tradition* (Ithaca, 2001).

4. See *The Cambridge Companion to Schopenhauer*, ed. Christopher Janaway (Cambridge, 1999).

5. Thomas McFarland, *Coleridge and the Pantheist Tradition* (Oxford, 1969), esp. pp. 283–6, 303–6, 325–32; M.H. Abrams, *Natural Supernaturalism: Tradition and Revolution in Romantic Literature* (New York & London, 1971); Ernest Lee Tuveson, *The Avatars of Thrice Great Hermes: an Approach to Romanticism* (Lewisburg, 1982).

6. See the classic work by Arthur O. Lovejoy, *The Great Chain of Being: A Study of the History of an Idea* (Cambridge, USA, 1936); E.M.W. Tillyard, *The Elizabethan World Picture* (London, 1943).

7. The professionalisation of nineteenth-century life has been a focus of historiographical interest: cf. Harold Perkins, *The Rise of Professional Society* (London, 1989); Stefan Collini, *Public Moralists:*

Political Thought and Intellectual Life in Britain 1850–1930 (Oxford, 1991); Frank M. Turner, *Between Science and Religion: the Reaction to Scientific Naturalism in Late Victorian England* (New Haven, 1974).

8. E.R. Dodds, *Missing Persons: An Autobiography* (Oxford, 1977), pp. 97–8. See also his *The Greeks and the Irrational* (Berkeley, 1951).

9. Ebenezer Sibly, *A New and Complete Illustration of the Occult Sciences* (London, 1790), being a revision of his earlier book, *A Complete Illustration of the Celestial Science of Astrology: or, The Art of Foretelling Future Events and Contingencies by the . . . Heavenly Bodies* (London, 1788).

10. David de Giustiano, *Conquest of Mind: Phrenology and Victorian Social Thought* (London, 1975); Roger Cooter, *The Cultural Meaning of Popular Science: Phrenology and the Organization of Consent in Nineteenth-Century Britain* (Cambridge, 1984); *idem*, *Phrenology in the British Isles: An Annotated Historical Biobibliography and Index* (London, 1989).

11. There was also 'allopathy' (which used drugs) and 'hydropathy' (spas).

12. James Braid, *Magic, Witchcraft, Animal Magnetism, Hypnotism and Electro-Biology* (3rd edn, London, 1852). The *Oxford English Dictionary* shows that the term 'Braidism' was even used, briefly, in 1882. See also the entries for 'hypnotism' and 'mesmerism'. Generally, see Alan Gauld, *A History of Hypnotism* (Cambridge, 1992); Alison Winter, *Mesmerized: Powers of Mind in Victorian Britain* (Chicago, 1998). Also: *Animal Magnetism, Early Hypnotism, and Psychical Research, 1766–1925: An Annotated Bibliography*, ed. Adam Crabtree (White Plains, NY, 1988).

13. See below, pp. 180–3.

14. Lincoln's remarks were made at the end of his annual message to Congress, 1 December 1862.

15. See Ernest Lee Tuveson, *Redeemer Nation: the Idea of America's Millennial Role* (Chicago, 1968).

16. In *Representative Men* (1850), in *The Collected Works of Ralph Waldo Emerson*, ed. Robert Spiller et al. (Cambridge, Mass, 1971), vol. 4.

17. Esp. Catherine L. Albanese, *Corresponding Motion: Transcendental Religion and the New America* (Philadelphia, 1977). Cf. *The*

Cambridge Companion to Ralph Waldo Emerson, eds Joel Porte and Saundra Morris (Cambridge, 1999); Russell B. Goodman, *American Philosophy and the Romantic Tradition* (Cambridge, 1990); and his 'East-West Philosophy in Nineteenth-Century America: Emerson and Hinduism', *Jnl History of Ideas*, 51 (1990), 625–45; Bret E. Carroll, *Spiritualism in Antebellum America* (Bloomington, 1997); Arthur Versluis, *American Transcendentalism and Asian Religions* (New York, 1993); and *idem*, *The Esoteric Origins of the American Renaissance* (New York, 2001).

18. Samuel F.B. Morse (1791–1872) invented the telegraph (1832–5), and then the Morse Code to go with it in about 1838.

19. Earl Wesley Fornell, *The Unhappy Medium: Spiritualism and the Life of Margaret Fox* (Austin, 1964). See also Brian Inglis, *Natural and Supernatural: A History of the Paranormal from Earliest Times to 1914* (London, 1977).

20. Robert Ellwood, Jr., 'The American Theosophical Synthesis', in *The Occult in America: New Historical Perspectives*, eds Howard Kerr & Charles L. Crow (Urbana, 1983), pp. 111–34, esp. p. 126. See also I.M. Lewis, *Ecstatic Religion: A Study of Shamanism and Spirit Possession* (London, 1989), chap. 2; Clarke Garrett, *Spirit Possession and Popular Religion: from the Camisards to the Shakers* (Baltimore, 1987); Gloria Flaherty, *Shamanism and the Eighteenth Century* (Princeton, 1992).

21. . . . just as Swedenborg denied ever having read Jacob Boehme! Cf. Robert W. Delp, 'Andrew Jackson Davis: Prophet of American Spiritualism', *Jnl of American History*, 54 (1967), 43–56.

22. Andrew Jackson Davis, *The Principles of Nature, Her Divine Revelations* (3rd edn, New York, 1847).

23. Cf. Theodore Flournoy, *From India to the Planet Mars: Observations of a Case of Sleepwalking with Glossolalia*, ed. Sonu Shamdasani (Princeton: PUP, 1994), orig. 1899, a record of his sitting with medium Hélène Smith, who in trance spoke in Sanskrit and Martian, as it wasn't.

24. The magician 'Amazing Randi' similarly set up the 'James Randi Educational Foundation', which offers a prize of one million dollars to 'anyone who can show, under proper observing conditions, evidence of any paranormal, supernatural, or occult power or event'. See also Georges Charpak and Henri Broch, *Debunked! ESP, Telekinesis, and Other Pseudoscience* (Baltimore, 2004).

25. In 1886, the 'planchette' was made more efficient by printing on its face numbers and letters. 'Ouija', of course, is 'oui' + 'ja'. All rights were purchased by Parker Brothers in 1966: the sales of Ouija Boards today are second only to Monopoly.

26. *Heartbreak House* (1919), preface. For more on the special subject of the contemporary obsession with fairies, see *Victorian Fairy Painting*, ed. Jane Martineau (London, 1997); Carole G. Silver, *Strange and Secret Peoples: Fairies and Victorian Consciousness* (New York, 1999).

27. George Bernard Shaw, *Man and Superman* (1901–3), Act IV.

28. *Nature*, 10 [20 Aug. 1874]: repr. as Chapter XXXI in John Tyndall, *Fragments of Science* (6th edn, New York, [1915]), pp. 443–94.

29. John Tyndall, 'Science and the Spirits', in ibid., p. 342. He ends the essay with a quotation from Max Müller. See also in the same volume (Chapter XXIV) Tyndall's essay, 'Miracles and Special Providences', a review of J.B. Mozley (1813–78), *Lectures on Miracles* (London, 1865) [the Bampton Lectures for that year], repr. from the *Fortnightly Review*.

30. Tyndall, *Fragments*, p. 491.

31. Emma Hardinge Britten, *Modern American Spiritualism* (New York, 1870); *idem, Nineteenth Century Miracles* (New York, 1884); *idem, Faith, Fact and Fraud of Religious History* (Manchester, 1896); *idem, Extemporaneous Addresses* (London, 1866). She was editor of the American periodical, *The Western Star*, 1872, and the British *The Unseen Universe*, 1892–1893.

32. Note also that Alfred Russel Wallace (1823–1913), Darwin's co-theorist of evolution by natural selection, first attended séances in 1865, and then published a number of spiritualist writings including a pamphlet entitled 'The Scientific Aspect of the Supernatural' (1866). He twice turned down the presidency of the Society for Psychical Research at the turn of the century, although he was a great defender of spiritualism. See Martin Fichman, *An Elusive Victorian: The Evolution of Alfred Russel Wallace* (Chicago, 2003).

33. [Balfour Stewart & Peter Guthrie Tait], *The Unseen Universe: Or, Physical Speculations on a Future State* (London, 1875), with numerous later editions. Cf. their later *Paradoxical Philosophy. A Sequel to the Unseen Universe* (London, 1878). See also P.M. Heimann, 'The *Unseen Universe*: Physics and the Philosophy of

Nature in Victorian Britain', *British Journal for the History of Science*, 6 (1972), 73–9.

34. [Stewart and Tait], *The Unseen Universe*, pp. 172, 189.

35. Generally, see Alan Gauld, *The Founders of Psychical Research* (London, 1968); Pamela Thurschwell, *Literature, Technology and Magical Thinking, 1880–1920* (Cambridge, 2001); Roger Luckhurst, *The Invention of Telepathy* (Oxford, 2002); Renée Haynes, *The Society for Psychical Research 1882–1982: A History* (London, 1982); Ruth Brandon, *The Spiritualists: the Passion for the Occult in the Nineteenth and Twentieth Centuries* (London, 1983); and Janet Oppenheim, *The Other World: Spiritualism and Psychical Research in England, 1850–1914* (Cambridge, 1985).

36. According to their website, the 'Spontaneous Cases Committee of the Society for Psychical Research is interested in receiving details from anyone who had any precognition / premonition experience of the Trade Tower attack on September 11th. It is *essential* that this particular experience was notified to a witness before the attack, and the witness statement included with the details.'

37. See Bart Schultz, *Henry Sidgwick: Eye of the Universe* (Cambridge, 2004).

38. Keynes to B.W. Swithinbank, 27.3.1906: quoted in R.F. Harrod, *The Life of John Maynard Keynes* (London, 1951), p. 116.

39. Ethel Sidgwick, *Mrs Henry Sidgwick, a Memoir by her Niece* (London, 1938), p. 66n.

40. Over 3,000 scripts survive (some of them mediated by Rudyard Kipling's sister Alice), known collectively as the 'Palm Sunday Case'.

41. She was Annie Marshall, his cousin's wife, whom he loved but could not marry: she committed suicide in 1876. Myers himself eventually died in Rome in January 1901. Myers's wife's sister was married to the explorer Henry Morton Stanley (1841–1904), who was also connected with the SPR. Cf. Myers's posthumous two-volume study, *Human Personality and its Survival of Bodily Death* (London, 1903), which also appeared in an abridgement first published in 1919 and now (Norwich, 1992), and in a new abridgement ed. Susy Smith (New Hyde Park, 1961).

42. Gurney would be found dead in Brighton at the Royal Albion Hotel in June 1888, from an overdose of chloroform. He may have been experimenting with trance states; another theory is that

he committed suicide upon discovering that his two prize tele-pathic case studies (Blackburn and Smith: see below, p. 129) were frauds: Trevor H. Hall, *The Strange Case of Edmund Gurney* (London, 1964).

43. Podmore was also found dead, on 19 August 1910, in New Pool, Malvern. According to Hall, *Strange Case*, Podmore committed suicide in the wake of financial ruin and accusations of homo-sexuality. His study of *Modern Spiritualism* (London, 1902) is still very useful as an historical source: cf. the reprint (London, 2000).

44. Home was the model for Robert Browning's 'Mr Sludge, "The Medium"': see below, p. 134. He was born in Scotland, came to the United States in the 1840s, and worked as a medium there in the early 1850s. From 1855 until the 1870s he was the medium in demand for the rich and famous in both England and Europe, giving his séances free, but accepting generous gifts. One of his most celebrated moments came in December 1868, the 'Ashley House levitation', when he went out one window and came in another. See J. Burton, *Heyday of a Wizard: Daniel Home the Medium* (London, 1948); Earl of Dunraven, *Experiences in Spiritualism with D.D. Home* (London: SPR, 1924); Mme Dunglas Home, *The Gift of D.D. Home* (London, 1890); D.D. Home, *Lights and Shadows of Spiritualism* (New York, 1877). Interestingly, Madame Blavatsky met Home in Paris in 1858.

45. Cook was a teenaged medium from Hackney: she was nearly unmasked in 1873 when a sitter grabbed her spirit manifestation. Katie retired *c.* 1875, but joined up again with the spirit world from about 1880 with a new spectre called 'Marie', although her career as a medium ended for all but the very credulous after the famous eccentric (and, later, father to Edith, Osbert and Sacheverell) Sir George Sitwell (1860–1943) grabbed her at a séance held under the auspices of the British National Association of Spiritualists in January 1880. See Trevor H. Hall, *The Spiritualists: the Story of Florence Cook and William Crookes* (London, 1962).

46. Oliver Lodge, *Raymond: Or, Life and Death* (London, 1916). See also J.M. Winter, 'Spiritualism and the First World War', in *Religion and Irreligion in Victorian Society*, eds R.W. Davis & R.J. Helmstadter (London, 1992), pp. 185–200.

47. Printed in his *Traffics and Discoveries* (London, 1904). See Carolyn Marvin, *When Old Technologies Were New: Thinking About Electric*

Communication in the Late Nineteenth Century (New York, 1988); Richard J. Noakes, 'Telegraphy is an Occult Art: Cromwell Fleetwood Varley and the Diffusion of Electricity to the Other World', *Brit. Jnl Hist. Science*, 32 (1999), 421–59; Laura Otis, 'The Metaphoric Circuit: Organic and Technological Communication in the Nineteenth Century', *Jnl History of Ideas*, 63 (2002), 105–28; Nicholas Royle, *Telepathy and Literature: Essays on the Reading Mind* (Oxford, 1991).

48. See the French novel by Auguste Villiers de l'Isle-Adam, *Tomorrow's Eve* (1886), narrated by a fictional Thomas Edison (Urbana, 1982).

49. Cf. Avital Ronell, *The Telephone Book: Technology, Schizophrenia, Electric Speech* (Lincoln, 1989). See also *idem, Dictations: On Haunted Writing* (Bloomington, 1986).

50. See Graeme J.N. Gooday, *The Morals of Measurement: Accuracy, Irony, and Trust in Late Victorian Electrical Practice* (Cambridge, 2004).

51. In 1906, Thomson was awarded the Nobel Prize in physics for his researches into the discharge of electricity in gases. In 1918 he was chosen Master of Trinity College, and held this post until his death in 1940.

52. Cf. *Conceptions of Ether: Studies in the History of Ether Theories, 1740–1900*, eds G.N. Cantor & M.J.S. Hodge (Cambridge, 1981); P.M. Harman, *Energy, Force, and Matter: the Conceptual Development of Nineteenth-Century Physics* (Cambridge, 1982).

53. See, for example, Phyllis Mack, *Visionary Women: Ecstatic Prophecy in Seventeenth-Century England* (Berkeley, 1992).

54. In 1894, Charles Richet (1850–1935), the distinguished French physiologist who won the Nobel Prize in 1913, produced the concept of 'ectoplasm', said to be 'an unfamiliar form of matter' which he believed was exuded by certain mediums, especially Eusapia Palladino. This ectoplasm could be modelled like living clay into human forms and body parts.

55. For much more on William James, see chap. 5 below.

56. See below, p. 165.

57. Thurschwell, *Literature, Technology and Magical Thinking*, p. 35. See also Logie Barrow, *Independent Spirits: Spiritualism and English Plebeians 1850–1910* (London, 1986); Ann Braude, *Radical Spirits: Spiritualism and Women's Rights in Nineteenth-Century America* (Boston, 1989).

58. Peter Gay, *The Naked Heart* (London, 1995), p. 35 [*The Bourgeois Experience*, vol. iv].

59. After the Creery sisters were unmasked, Blackburn wrote *Thought-Reading, or, Modern Mysteries Explained* (London, 1884), moved to South Africa and became a novelist, producing one of the first secret service/spy novels, albeit anonymously: *Kruger's Secret Service, By One Who Was In It* (London, 1900): other novels followed, under his own name. Smith became one of the most important figures in the pioneering Victorian cinema, and was the first to use trick photography to produce 'ghosts'.

60. *Oxford English Dictionary*, s.v. 'telepathy'; and ibid., s.v. 'empathy', which was coined in 1904 as a translation of the German *Einfühlung*.

61. Edmund Gurney, F.W.H. Myers, Frank Podmore, *Phantasms of the Living* (London, 1886), a two-volume compilation of SPR evidence for telepathy: the case for the Creery sisters is made at i. 20–31.

62. His medium was the long-active Geraldine Cummins (1890–1968), who published the results as *The Road to Immortality: being a description of the after-life purporting to be communicated by the late F. W. H. Myers through Geraldine Cummins, foreword by Sir Oliver Lodge* (London, 1932); *idem, Beyond Human Personality, being a detailed description of the future life purporting to be communicated by the late F. W. H. Myers, containing an account of the gradual development of human personality into cosmic personality* (London, 1935); *idem, Swan On a Black Sea; A Study in Automatic Writing, the Cummins-Willett Scripts*, transmitted by Geraldine Cummins, ed. Signe Toksvig, with a foreword by C.D. Broad (London, 1965).

63. As with the Gothic, so too is there a huge bibliography for later supernatural writing. See, for example, Howard Kerr, *Mediums, and Spirit-Rappers, and Roaring Radicals; Spiritualism in American Literature, 1850–1900* (Urbana, 1972); Fred Kaplan, *Dickens and Mesmerism: the Hidden Springs of Fiction* (Princeton, 1975); Russell M. and Clare R. Goldfarb, *Spiritualism and Nineteenth-Century Letters* (Rutherford, NJ, 1978); Stoddard Martin, *Orthodox Heresy: The Rise of 'Magic' as Religion and its Relation to Literature* (New York, 1989); Michael Wheeler, *Death and the Future Life in Victorian Literature and Theology* (Cambridge, 1990); Glen

Cavaliero, *The Supernatural and English Fiction* (Oxford, 1995); Kathleen Brogan, *Cultural Haunting: Ghosts and Ethnicity in Recent American Literature* (Charlottesville, 1998); *The Haunted Mind: The Supernatural in Victorian Literature*, ed. Elton E. Smith & Robert Haas (Lanham, MD & London, 1999).

64. For background, see Leslie Mitchell, *Bulwer Lytton: The Rise and Fall of a Victorian Man of Letters* (London, 2003).

65. A Scotsman named John Lawson Johnston (1837–1900) invented 'fluid beef' in about 1873, building a factory for its production in Quebec and rechristening it 'Bovril'. He returned to London in 1884, bought and lived in Kingswood House, Dulwich, and was even the subject of a caricature in *Vanity Fair* (1897).

66. Joan Bulman, *Jenny Lind, A Biography* (London, 1956); Daniel Pick, *Svengali's Web: The Alien Enchanter in Modern Culture* (New Haven & London, 2000).

67. Bram Stoker, *Dracula* (Penguin edn, London, 1993), pp. 35, 405, 431, 450. The multi-narration technique was effectively previously in Wilkie Collins's spooky novel, *The Woman in White* (1860). The classic nineteenth-century artistic portrayal of the vampire figure is that by Philip Burne-Jones (1862–1926), 'The Vampire' (1897), itself inspired by the painting by the Swiss artist Henry Fuseli (1741–1825), *The Nightmare* (1781). See also David Glover, *Vampires, Mummies, and Liberals: Bram Stoker and the Politics of Popular Fiction* (Durham, 1996).

68. See Jill Galvan, 'Glass Ghosting "In the Cage"', *Henry James Rev.*, 22 (2001), 297–306.

69. Cf. Helen Sword, 'Necrobibliography: Books in the Spirit World', *Modern Language Qly*, 60 (1999), 85–112; and *idem, Ghostwriting Modernism* (Ithaca, 2002).

70. Theodora Bosanquet, *Henry James at Work* (London, 1924), p. 6.

71. Joseph Conrad, *Heart of Darkness* (Signet edn, New York, 1950), pp. 95, 105, 119, 120, 147, 155, 157.

5. Occult Within: Psychologising the Esoteric

1. The other extreme of false religion was to be a 'formalist', someone who had the form of religion without the power or the experience. Both formalism and enthusiasm were two unacceptable alternatives.

2. Frank Manuel, *The Eighteenth Century Confronts the Gods* (Cambridge, Mass., 1959), p. 71. See also the excellent Ann Taves, *Fits, Trances & Visions: Experiencing Religion and Explaining Experience from Wesley to James* (Princeton, 1999); Michael Heyd, *'Be Sober and Reasonable': The Critique of Enthusiasm in the Seventeenth and Early Eighteenth Centuries* (Leiden, 1995); Clement Hawes, *Mania and Literary Style: the Rhetoric of Enthusiasm from the Ranters to Christopher Smart* (Cambridge, 1996). Cf. Clarke Garrett, *Spirit Possession and Popular Religion: from the Camisards to the Shakers* (Baltimore, 1987); D.P. Walker, *Unclean Spirits: Possession and Exorcism in France and England in the Late Sixteenth and Early Seventeenth Centuries* (London, 1981); B. Robert Kreiser, *Miracles, Convulsions, and Ecclesiastical Politics in Early Eighteenth-Century Paris* (Princeton, 1978).

3. The book was first published in 1621, with revised editions in 1624, 1628, 1632, 1638 and 1651. It was reprinted in 1660 and 1676, and then not until 1800. The most famous edition is the Everyman (London, 1932) although newer editions were published by OUP (1989–94) and the New York Review of Books (2001) being a one-volume reprint of the Everyman.

4. This Casaubon was the son of the more famous Isaac Casaubon (1559–1614), who had unmasked the more modern origins of the hermetic writings: see above, p. 28–9. Henry More was the Cambridge Platonist, under the patronage of Anne Conway (1631–79).

5. See also Sang Hyun Lee, *The Philosophical Theology of Jonathan Edwards* (Princeton, 2000); Robert E. Brown, *Jonathan Edwards and the Bible* (Bloomington, 2002); Avihu Zakai, *Jonathan Edwards's Philosophy of History: The Reenchantment of the World in the Age of Enlightenment* (Princeton, 2003); Rhodri Hayward, 'Demonology, Neurology, and Medicine in Edwardian Britain', *Bulletin of the History of Medicine*, 78 (2004), 37–58.

6. Mary Baker Eddy, *Retrospection and Introspection* (Boston, 1891), pp. 47, 77. Interestingly, *Science and Health* was published in the same year that Madame Blavatsky founded the Theosophical Society, although Blavatsky rejected Christian Science as a crude occultism. See also R.L. Moore, 'The Occult Connection? Mormonism, Christian Science, and Spiritualism', in *The Occult in America*, eds H. Kerr & C.L. Crow (Urbana, 1983), pp. 135–61, esp. p.145; Raymond J. Cunningham, 'The Impact of Christian

Science on the American Churches, 1880–1910', *Amer.Hist.Rev.*, 72 (1967), 885–905; and the standard Willa Cather & Georgine Milmine, *The Life of Mary Baker G. Eddy and the History of Christian Science* (New York, 1909).

7. Especially Swedenborg's *A Dictionary of Correspondences, Representatives and Significatives Derived from the Word of the Lord* (1st printed in Boston in 1847).

8. Sigmund Freud also studied with Charcot.

9. F.W.H. Myers, 'General Characteristics of Subliminal Messages', *Proc.Soc.Psych.Res.*, 7 (1891–2), 301; Thurschwell, *Literature*, p. 18.

10. William James, *The Varieties of Religious Experience: A Study in Human Nature* (New York & London, 1902), based on his Gifford Lectures of 1901–2. The standard edition of the book includes the revisions that he made between the first publication (June 1902) and the revised edition (August 1902). These quotations, pp. 233, 511–12n. Recent relevant general books on William James include the monumental biography by Gerald E. Myers, *William James: His Life and Thought* (New Haven & London, 1986); *The Cambridge Companion to William James*, ed. Ruth Anna Putnam (Cambridge, 1997); Richard M. Gale, *The Divided Self of William James* (Cambridge, 1999); David C. Lamberth, *William James and the Metaphysics of Experience* (Cambridge, 1999); Wesley Cooper, *The Unity of William James's Thought* (Nashville, 2002); Charles Taylor, *Varieties of Religion Today: William James Revisited* (Cambridge, MA, 2002).

11. James, *Varieties of Religious Experience*, pp. 94, 133.

12. Ibid., pp. 9, 234, 242.

13. Ibid., pp. 431, 483–4, 508, 511–12.

14. Ibid., pp. 431, 519.

15. William James, *The Principles of Psychology*, i. 393–400: repr. in *William James on Psychical Research*, ed. Gardner Murphy & Robert O. Ballou (New York, 1960), p. 55.

16. Ibid., p. 58.

17. See the mass of material in ibid., pp. 95–210; and above, page 128.

18. William James, 'Frederic Myers's Service to Psychology', *Proceedings of the Society for Psychical Research*, xvii (Part xlii) (May 1901): repr. in his *Memories and Studies* (New York, 1911); and in Murphy and Ballou, *William James*, pp. 219–20.

19. Adam Phillips, *Terrors and Experts* (London, 1995), chap. 1, esp.

pp. 18–22. See also James P. Keeley, 'Subliminal Promptings: Psychoanalytic Theory and the Society for Psychical Research', *American Imago*, 58 (2001), 767–91; Adam Crabtree, *From Mesmer to Freud: Magnetic Sleep and the Roots of Psychological Healing* (New Haven, 1993); and even Stefan Zweig (1881–1942), *Mental Healers: Franz Anton Mesmer, Mary Baker Eddy, Sigmund Freud* (London, 1933).

20. *Oxford English Dictionary*, s.v. 'telepathy'. See Stephen Braude, 'Telepathy', *Nous*, 12 (1978), 267–301; Roger Luckhurst, *The Invention of Telepathy* (Oxford, 2002).

21. For Freud's view that Jewish males menstruate, see David S. Katz, 'Shylock's Gender: Jewish Male Menstruation in Early Modern England', *The Review of English Studies*, n.s., I (1999), 440–462. See also *The Cambridge Companion to Freud*, ed. J. Neu (Cambridge, 1991), esp. pp. 267–308.

22. Gustave Le Bon, *The Crowd: A Study of the Popular Mind* (London, 1896); Frederick Morgan Davenport, *Primitive Traits in Religious Revivals* (New York, 1905).

23. Ernest Jones, *The Life and Work of Sigmund Freud* (London, 1954–7), iii. 375.

24. Jones to Freud, 25 February 1926, from London: *The Complete Correspondence of Sigmund Freud and Ernest Jones, 1908–1939*, ed. R. Andrew Paskauskas (Cambridge, USA, 1993), pp. 592–3 (letter #476). Jones later noted the negative effects that solar mythology had on the study of folklore: Jones to Freud, 20 October 1928: ibid., pp. 650–1 (letter #530).

25. Freud to Jones, 7 March 1926, from Vienna: ibid., pp. 596–7 (letter #478).

26. Sigmund Freud, 'The Uncanny', in *The Standard Edition of the Complete Psychological Works*, ed. James Strachey (London, 1953–74), xvii. 218–56. The article was first published in *Imago*, 5 (1919), 297–324. Cf. Terry Castle, *The Female Thermometer: Eighteenth-Century Culture and the Invention of the Uncanny* (New York, 1995), esp. chap. 1; Dorothea E. von Mücke, *The Seduction of the Occult and the Rise of the Fantastic Tale* (Stanford, 2003).

27. *The Collected Works of C.G. Jung*, eds G. Adler, M. Fordham, H. Read & W. McGuire (Princeton, 1953–91) is the standard collection.

28. Niles R. Holt, 'Ernst Haeckel's Monistic Religion', *Jnl History of Ideas*, 32 (1971), 265–80.

29. Cf. Vincent Brome, *Jung* (London, 1978); *Lingering Shadows: Jungians, Freudians, and Anti-Semitism*, eds Aryeh Maidenbaum and Stephen A. Martin (Boston & London, 1991); Richard Noll, *The Jung Cult: Origins of a Charismatic Movement* (Princeton, 1994); *idem, The Aryan Christ: The Secret Life of Carl Jung* (New York, 1997); Michael Palmer, *Freud and Jung on Religion* (London, 1997); Sonu Shamdasani, *Jung and the Making of Modern Psychology* (Cambridge, 2003).

6. The Occult Passage to India

1. Charles François Dupuis, *Origine de tous les cultes, ou religion universelle* (Paris, 1795). Cf. the extract printed as *Christianity a Form of the Great Solar Myth* (London, n.d.); and the reply to Dupuis by John Prior Estlin, *The Nature and the Causes of Atheism* (Bristol, 1797).

2. (Henri-) Benjamin Constant (de Rebecque), *De la religion: considérée dans sa source, ses formes et ses développements* (Paris, 1824–1831).

3. David Friedrich Strauss, *The Life of Jesus Critically Examined* (London, 1846), iii.425.

4. Ernest Renan, *La Vie de Jésus* (Paris, 1863). Cf. Alan Pitt, 'The Cultural Impact of Science in France: Ernest Renan and the *Vie de Jésus*', *Hist.Jnl*, 43 (2000), 79–101. Cf. H.W. Wardman, *Ernest Renan: A Critical Biography* (London, 1964). This emphasis on self-development gave Jesus an appeal for working-class radicals: cf. Edward Berenson, *Populist Religion and Left-Wing Politics in France, 1830–1852* (Princeton, 1984); Judith Devlin, *The Superstitious Mind: French Peasants and the Supernatural in the Nineteenth Century* (New Haven, 1987). Mussolini knew Renan's work well, and used it to argue that a superior individual has the right to infringe upon the rights of his supposed inferiors (although Renan himself believed in liberal democracy).

5. Edward B. Tylor, *Primitive Culture: Researches into the Development of Mythology, Philosophy, Religion, Art and Custom* (London, 1871), i. 129, 141, 384–7; Chapter IV deals with the occult. The book also appeared in different editions under the titles of *The Origins of Culture* and *Religion in Primitive Culture*. Note also the obvious

reference to Mrs Piper: see pp. 128 and 145 above. Cf. the later influential book by Max Nordau (1849–1923), *Degeneration* (1892). Herbert Spencer, *Study of Sociology* (1870), also argued that the worship of dead ancestors was the origin of the belief in ghosts.

6. E.B. Tylor, *Anthropology* (London, 1881), esp. p. 344, and Chapter XIV generally. Tylor sometimes preferred the expression 'rude philosopher' (p. 343). Cf. George W. Stocking, Jr., 'Animism in Theory and Practice: E.B. Tylor's Unpublished "Notes on 'Spiritualism'"', *Man*, n.s., 6(1971), 88–104, and his classic works, *Victorian Anthropology* (New York, 1987) and *After Tylor: British Social Anthropology* (Madison, 1995). See also Henrika Kuklick, *The Savage Within: The Social History of British Anthropology, 1885–1945* (Cambridge, 1991).

7. See generally, Eric J. Sharpe, *Comparative Religion: A History* (2nd edn, London, 1986); John Drew, *India and the Romantic Imagination* (Delhi, 1987); *Exoticism in the Enlightenment*, eds G.S. Rousseau & Roy Porter (New York, 1990); Peter Bishop, *The Myth of Shangri-La: Tibet, Travel Writing and the Western Creation of Sacred Landscapes* (Berkeley, 1990); Thomas R. Trautmann, *Aryans and British India* (Berkeley, 1997).

8. See Lytton Strachey's long article in the *Dict.Nat.Biog.*; A. Vidler, *Witness to the Light: F.D. Maurice's Message for Today* (New York, 1948); *idem, F.D. Maurice and Company* (London, 1966); D. Young, *F.D. Maurice and Unitarianism* (Oxford, 1992). Older works include Florence Higham, *Frederick Denison Maurice* (London, 1947) and Claude Jenkins, *Frederick Denison Maurice and the New Reformation* (London, 1938).

9. Frederick Morgan Davenport, *Primitive Traits in Religious Revivals* (New York, 1905), p. 258.

10. Frederick Denison Maurice, *The Religions of the World and their Relations to Christianity* (London, 1847), pp. 2–3: his Boyle Lectures.

11. Ibid., pp. 8–9. It is for this reason that people like Allan Bloom, *The Closing of the American Mind* (New York, 1987) and Alasdair Macintyre, *Whose Justice? Which Rationality?* (London, 1988), accuse among others the early anthropologists for encouraging the fall of absolute moral standards.

12. Maurice, *Religions*, p. xiii.

13. Georgina Max Müller, *The Life and Letters of the Rt. Hon. Friedrich*

Max Müller (London, 1902), i. 1, 28–9, 47, 57–8, 74, 211, 217; ii. 48, 409. See also Max Müller's *Auld Lang Syne* (London, 1898), which includes an amusing portrait of the author in uniform and armed with a sword; and his *My Autobiography: A Fragment* (London, 1901). His collected essays appeared as *Chips from a German Workshop* (London, 1867–70). See also, J.H. Voight, *Max Müller: The Man and His Ideas* (Calcutta, 1967); N.C. Chaudhuri, *Scholar Extraordinary: The Life of Professor the Rt. Hon. Friedrich Max Müller, P.C.* (London, 1974); R.M. Dorson, *The British Folklorists: A History* (London, 1968), and Philippa Levine, *The Amateur and the Professional: Antiquarians, Historians and Archaeologists in Victorian England* (Cambridge, 1986).

14. Max Müller, *Life and Letters*, i. 241–5.
15. Max Müller to Stanley, 17 Apr. 1861: ibid., i. 246–7. The testimonials for Max Müller are preserved in the Bodleian Library as G.A. Oxon. c.76 (181–3); and G.A. Oxon. 8° 179 (26, 26*, 26**, 26***, 27).
16. Max Müller, *Life and Letters*, i. 242, 350.
17. Ibid., i. 499; ii. 2–6.
18. Ibid., ii. 9.
19. F. Max Müller, 'Preface to the Sacred Books of the East', in *The Sacred Books of the East*, ed. F. Max Müller (Oxford, 1879–1910), I. ix–xxxviii, esp. pp. ix–xi.
20. The dispute began in 1886, and had a revival in 1895: Max Müller, *Life and Letters*, ii. 194–5. Curiously, Copleston was greatly admired by Andrew Lang when they were up at Oxford together: Andrew Lang, *Adventures Among Books* (London, 1905), p. 34.
21. Max Müller, *Life and Letters*, i. 468; cf. his letter to Darwin on the same subject, 7 Jan. 1875: i. 476 and his 'Address to the Anthropological Section of the British Association at the Meeting Held at Cardiff in August, 1891', *Jnl Anthropological Inst. of Great Brit. & Ireland*, 21 (1892), 172–92. Generally, see Gillian Beer, 'Darwin and The Growth of Language Theory', in *Nature Transfigured: Science and Literature, 1700–1900*, eds J. Christie & S. Shuttleworth (Manchester, 1989), pp. 152–70; *idem, Darwin's Plots: Evolutionary Narrative in Darwin, George Eliot and Nineteenth-Century Fiction* (London, 1983); Robert M. Young, *Darwin's Metaphor: Nature's Place in Victorian Culture* (Cambridge, 1985); Peter J. Bowler, *The Invention of Progress: The Victorian and*

the Past (Oxford, 1989); David Spadafora, *The Idea of Progress in Eighteenth-Century Britain* (New Haven, 1990). See also J. Winternitz, 'The "Turanian" Hypothesis and Magyar Nationalism in the Nineteenth Century', in *Culture and Nationalism in Nineteenth-Century Eastern Europe*, eds R. Sussex & J.C. Eade (Columbus, 1985), pp. 143–58.

22. For solarism, see Robert Ackerman, *J.G. Frazer: His Life and Work* (Cambridge, 1987), pp. 76–7; Richard M. Dorson, 'The Eclipse of Solar Mythology', *Journal of American Folklore*, 68 (1955), 393–416: repr. *Myth: A Symposium*, ed. T.A. Sebeok (Bloomington, Ind., 1958), pp. 25–63 and also *The Study of Folklore*, ed. Alan Dundes (Englewood Cliffs, NJ, 1965), pp. 57–83; S. Connor, 'Myth and Meta-myth in Max Müller and Walter Pater', in *The Sun is God: Painting, Literature and Mythology in the Nineteenth Century*, ed. J.B. Bullen (Oxford, 1989), pp. 199–222; G. Schrempp, 'The Re-Education of Friedrich Max Müller: Intellectual Appropriation and Epistemological Antinomy in Mid-Victorian Evolutionary Thought', *Man*, n.s., 18 (1983), 90–110. Cf. Robert Brown, *Language and Theories of Its Origin* (London, [1881]); *idem*, *Researches into the Origin of the Primitive Constellations of the Greeks, Phoenicians and Babylonians* (London, 1899–1900).

23. See the wildly funny and exciting book by Geoffrey Lewis, *The Turkish Language Reform: A Catastrophic Success* (Oxford, 1999), chap. 5, where he does not connect the Turkish end of the story with Max Müller, although he does mention the latter's cousin George A. Müller (p. 45), whose ideas on language development were equally creative. As it happens, the theory that Turkish is the original language of Europe may not be entirely wrong, if by Turkish we mean Hittite, which was deciphered only in 1917, and is an Indo-European language: see Jay Jasanoff, *Hittite and the Indo-European Verb* (Oxford, 2003); and Russell D. Gray & Quentin D. Atkinson, 'Language-tree divergence times support the Anatolian theory of Indo-European origin', *Nature*, 426 (2003), 435–9. I look more closely at these issues in a forthcoming article.

24. Andrew Lang, *Custom and Myth* (London, 1884), dedicated to E.B. Tylor; *idem*, *The Making of Religion* (London, 1898).

25. Andrew Lang, *Cock Lane and Common Sense* (London, 1894).

26. Andrew Lang, *The Making of Religion* (London, 1898), his Gifford Lectures.

27. See, generally, James Kissane, 'Victorian Mythology', *Victorian Studies*, 6 (1962), 5–28; Robert Crawford, 'Pater's *Renaissance*, Andrew Lang, and Anthropological Romanticism', *English Literary History*, 53 (1986), 849–79; and *The Myth and Ritual School: J.G. Frazer and the Cambridge Ritualists*, ed. Robert Ackerman (New York & London, 1991).

28. William James, *The Varieties of Religious Experience: A Study in Human Nature* (New York & London, 1902), p. 421.

29. On Blavatsky generally, see Bruce F. Campbell, *Ancient Wisdom Revived: a History of the Theosophical Movement* (Berkeley, 1980); Peter Washington, *Madame Blavatsky's Baboon* (London, 1993); Joscelyn Godwin, *The Theosophical Enlightenment* (Albany, 1994); Sylvia Cranston, *HPB: The Extraordinary Life and Influence of Helena Blavatsky* (New York, 1993); Maria Carlson, '*No Religion Higher than Truth': A History of the Theosophical Movement in Russia, 1875–1922* (Princeton, 1993); K. Paul Johnson, *The Masters Revealed: Madame Blavatsky and the Myth of the Great White Lodge* (Albany, 1994); Joy Dixon, *Divine Feminine: Theosophy and Feminism in England* (Baltimore, 2001), Diana Basham, *The Trial of Woman: Feminism and the Occult Sciences in Victorian Literature and Society* (Basingstoke, 1992). See also *Theosophy in the Nineteenth Century: An Annotated Bibliography*, ed. Michael Gomes (New York & London, 1994).

30. Olcott wrote a long and detailed study of the Eddy brothers, published as *People From the Other World* (Hartford, CT, 1875).

31. See Charles Allen, *The Buddha and the Sahibs: The Men Who Discovered India's Lost Religion* (London, 2003); Isaac Lubelsky, '"Celestial India": Theosophical Activity in India, 1879–1919' [Hebrew], (Ph.D. thesis, Tel Aviv University, 2005).

32. A.P. Sinnett, *Esoteric Buddhism* (1883); *idem, The Occult World* (2nd edn, London, 1882).

33. Emanuel Swedenborg, *The True Christian Religion* (Everyman edn, London, 1933), p. 335.

34. See Alvin Boyd Kuhn, *Theosophy, a Modern Revival of Ancient Wisdom* (New York, 1930), pp. 206, 232–52; Robert S. Ellwood, *Theosophy: A Modern Expression of the Wisdom of the Ages* (New York, 1933).

35. In Swedenborgianism, the afterlife is a process of continuing education: in heaven, souls are not punished for their sins, but are

confronted with realities that they have created for themselves by their spiritual attitudes. That is to say, their heavenly environment is a mirror of their own state of mind, and can be changed once in heaven as spiritual understanding progresses.

36. NB that a hierarchy of elect Lemurians became the Lemuro-Atlantean dynasty of priest-kings who lived on the island of Shamballah in the Gobi Desert.

37. For Atlantis, see the classic Ignatius Donnelly, *Atlantis: The Antediluvian World* (New York, 1882). Donnelly also wrote a book on *The Great Cryptogram: Francis Bacon's Cipher in the so-called Shakespeare Plays* (London, 1888). See also L. Sprague de Camp, *Lost Continents: The Atlantis Theme in History, Science, and Literature* (New York, 1954), who also wrote the series of numerous 'Conan' books, which inspired the film by Oliver Stone and starring Arnold Schwarzenegger: *Conan the Barbarian* (1982).

38. Cf. Besant's book, *Esoteric Christianity or the Lesser Mysteries* (London, 1898, 1901, 1902). See also Arthur H. Nethercot, *The First Five Lives of Annie Besant* (Chicago, 1960); *idem, The Last Four Lives of Annie Besant* (Chicago, 1963).

39. See esp. *The World's Parliament of Religions*, ed. John Henry Barrows (Chicago, 1893); Richard H. Seager, *The World's Parliament of Religions* (Bloomington, 1995); *The Dawn of Religious Pluralism: Voices from the World's Parliament of Religions, 1893*, ed. Richard H. Seager and Diana Eck (Chicago, 1993); John P. Burris, *Exhibiting Religion: Colonialism and Spectacle at International Expositions, 1851–1893* (Charlottesville, 2001). See also Richard H. Seager, *Buddhism in America* (New York, 2000); Thomas A. Tweed, *The American Encounter with Buddhism, 1844–1912: Victorian Culture and the Limits of Dissent* (Bloomington, 1992).

40. See generally, S.F. Walker, 'Vivekananda and American Occultism', in *The Occult in America*, eds H. Kerr & C.L. Crow (Urbana, 1983), pp. 162–76.

41. William James, *Pragmatism: A New Name for Some Old Ways of Thinking: Popular Lectures on Philosophy* (New York & London, 1907), Lecture Four [(New York, 1955), p. 102], being lectures delivered at the Lowell Institute in Boston in Nov.–Dec. 1906, and in Jan. 1907 at Columbia University. Vedanta is one of the six major philosophies of Hinduism. Vedanta teaches that man's real nature is divine, and that the aim of human life is to realise

that divinity through selfless work, devotion to God, control of the inner forces, and discrimination between the real and the unreal. It recognises that Truth is one and accepts all religions, properly understood, as valid means of realising the truth.

42. *Karma-Yoga* was published in America in 1896, and *Raja-Yoga* appeared later that year in England. Yoga became more widely known through the work of Paramahansa Yogananda [Mukunda Lal Ghosh] (1893–1952), who published his famous *Autobiography of a Yogi* (New York, 1946) and lived and taught in California from 1920 until his death.

43. Vivekananda, *Complete Works* (Calcutta, 1970–1), iv. 318; Walker, 'Vivekananda', p. 165.

44. Gregory Tillett, *The Elder Brother: A Biography of Charles Webster Leadbeater* (London, 1982).

45. Mary Lutyens, *Krishnamurti, His Life and Death* (New York, 1990); Roland Vernon, *A Star in the East: Krishnamurti, the Invention of a Messiah* (New York, 2001).

46. For what follows, I am greatly endebted to Mark Bevir, 'Theosophy as a Political Movement', in *Gurus and their Followers: New Religious Reform Movements in Colonial India*, ed. A. Copley (Delhi, 2000).

47. See also [Anna Blackwell], *The Probable Effect of Spiritualism Upon the Social, Moral, and Religious Condition of Society* (London, 1876).

48. See generally Christopher McIntosh, *Eliphas Lévi and the French Occult Revival* (London, 1972).

49. Ellic Howe, *The Magicians of the Golden Dawn: A Documentary History of a Magical Order 1887–1923* (London, 1972); R.A. Gilbert, *The Golden Dawn: Twilight of the Magicians* (San Bernardino, CA, 1986); *idem, The Golden Dawn Scrapbook: the Rise and Fall of a Magical Order* (York Beach, ME, 1997). See also Patrick Curry, *A Confusion of Prophets: Victorian and Edwardian Astrology* (London, 1992).

50. Cf. S.L. MacGregor Mathers, *Kabbala Denudata, the Kabbalah Unveiled* (London, 1887), his most famous work. Mathers married the sister of the celebrated philosopher and Nobel Prize winner (literature) Henri Bergson (1859–1941) and settled in Paris in 1894.

51. There is a good deal about Yeats and the occult: see, for example, George Mills Harper, *Yeats's Golden Dawn* (London, 1974);

Kathleen Raine, *Yeats, the Tarot, and the Golden Dawn* (Dublin, 1972); *idem, Yeats the Initiate* (London, 1986); Frank Kinahan, *Yeats, Folklore, and Occultism* (Boston, 1988); Timothy Materer, *Modernist Alchemy: Poetry and the Occult* (Ithaca, 1995); William T. Gorski, *Yeats and Alchemy* (Albany, 1996).

52. R.A. Gilbert, *A.E. Waite: Magician of Many Parts* (Wellingborough, 1987); *idem, A.E. Waite: A Bibliography* (Wellingborough, 1983).

53. John Symonds, *The Great Beast: the Life of Aleister Crowley* (London, 1951); *idem, The Magical Record of the Beast 666: the Diaries of Aleister Crowley, 1914–1920* (London, 1972); *idem, The Confessions of Aleister Crowley: an Autohagiography* (London, 1979); Charles Cammell, *Aleister Crowley* (London, 1951); Timothy D'Arch Smith, *The Books of the Beast: Essays on Aleister Crowley, Montague Summers and Others* (Oxford, 1991); Gerald Suster, *The Legacy of the Beast: the Life, Work and Influence of Aleister Crowley* (London, 1988). See also the important new book by Alex Owen, *The Place of Enchantment* (Chicago, 2004) and her earlier work, *The Darkened Room: Women, Power, and Spiritualism in Late Victorian England* (Philadelphia, 1990).

54. 'Papus', *Le Tarot des bohémiens: le plus ancien livre du monde* (1889); *idem, Le Tarot divinatoire; clef du triage des cartes et des sorts* (1909). Generally, see Richard Decker, Thierry Depaulis and Michael Dummett, *A Wicked Pack of Cards: The Origins of the Occult Tarot* (London, 1996); Ronald Decker & Michael Dummett, *A History of the Occult Tarot, 1870–1970* (London, 2002). Another scholar of the occult was Montague Summers (1880–1948). After an education at Trinity College, Oxford, in 1909 he became a Roman Catholic priest, and wrote extensively about witchcraft and Satan. He famously disagreed with the view of Margaret Alice Murray (1863–1963) that witchcraft was a harmless relic of an original pre-Christian medieval religion: see Timothy d'Arch Smith, *A Bibliography of the Works of Montague Summers* (London, 1964); and cf. Margaret A. Murray, *The Witch-Cult in Western Europe: a Study in Anthropology* (Oxford, 1921).

55. One could also add, perhaps, Charles Fort, who wrote those huge compendia of unexplained happenings, the *Book of the Damned* (1919) and *New Lands* (1923).

56. The most important secondary work on this subject is Nicholas Goodrick-Clarke, *The Occult Roots of Nazism: Secret Aryan Cults*

and their Influence on Nazi Ideology: The Ariosophists of Austria and Germany, 1890–1935 (New York, 1992). See also his *Hitler's Priestess: Savitri Devi, the Hindu-Aryan Myth, and Neo-Nazism* (New York, 1998); *Black Sun: Aryan Cults, Esoteric Nazism and the Politics of Identity* (New York, 2002). Other books of varying quality include: Ellic Howe, *Astrology and Psychological Warfare During World War II* (New York, 1967) [pub. in the UK as *Urania's Children*]; Ken Anderson, *Hitler and the Occult* (Amherst, 1995); Francis King, *Satan and Swastika* (London, 1976); Louis Pauwels & Jacques Bergier, *The Morning of the Magicians* (New York, 1964); J.H. Brennan, *The Occult Reich* (New York, 1974); Gerald Suster, *Hitler and the Age of Horus* (London, 1981), repr. as *Hitler: Black Magician* (London, 1996); Dusty Sklar, *The Nazis and the Occult* (New York, 1977); Trevor Ravenscroft, *The Spear of Destiny: the Occult Power behind the Spear which Pierced the Side of Christ* (London, 1973); Jean-Michel Angebert, *The Occult and the Third Reich: the Mystical Origins of Nazism and the Search for the Holy Grail* (New York, 1974); Michael Howard, *The Occult Conspiracy: Secret Societies, their Influence and Power in World History* (New York, 1989); Mattias Gardell, *Gods of the Blood: the Pagan Revival and White Separatism* (Durham, 2003).

57. Von List derived the term 'Armanen' from the name 'Hermiones', which appears in Tacitus, *Germania*. Whereas Tacitus used the term to describe tribes that lived in the interior of the country, von List fantasised that these were the priest-kings: Goodrick-Clarke, *Occult Roots*, p. 56.

58. The swastika appeared for the first time on 20 May 1920 as the flag of the new NSDAP: black, in a white circle on a red background.

59. Reginald H. Phelps, '"Before Hitler Came": Thule Society and Germanen Orden', *Journal of Modern History*, 35 (1963), 245–61.

60. Rudolf von Sebottendorff, *Bevor Hitler kam: Urkundliches aus der Frühzeit der nationalsozialistischen Bewegung* (Munich, 1933), preface: quoted in ibid., 245.

61. Nevertheless, Phelps claims that Sebottendorff disappeared in 1933, possibly killed by the Nazis: ibid., p. 247 (basing himself on a personal letter from Hans Georg Grassinger).

62. G.L. Mosse, 'The Mystical Origins of National Socialism', *Jnl of the History of Ideas*, 22 (1961), 81–96, esp. p. 81.

63. For some of the larger religious issues involved, see Richard

Steigmann-Gall, *The Holy Reich: Nazi Conceptions of Christianity, 1919–1945* (Cambridge, 2003).

7. The Occult (Re-)Turn to Religion: Fundamentalism and New Age

1. Generally, see E.R. Sandeen, *The Roots of Fundamentalism: British and American Millenarianism 1800–1930* (Chicago, 1970); G.M. Marsden, *Fundamentalism and American Culture: The Shaping of Twentieth-Century Evangelicalism 1870–1925* (New York, 1980); Paul Boyer, *When Time Shall Be No More: Prophecy Belief in Modern American Culture* (Cambridge, USA, 1992); David S. Katz & Richard H. Popkin, *Messianic Revolution: Radical Religious Politics to the End of the Second Millennium* (New York, 1999); Stephen Prickett, *Narrative, Religion, and Science: Fundamentalism versus Irony, 1700–1999* (Cambridge, 2002).

2. Miller appears briefly above, pp. 118–19.

3. Of course, Miller might have also have pondered 2 Peter 3:8: 'But, beloved, be not ignorant of this one thing, that one day *is* with the Lord as a thousand years, and a thousand years as one day.'

4. See the classic Whitney R. Cross, *The Burned-over District: The Social and Intellectual History of Enthusiastic Religion in Western New York, 1800–1850* (Ithaca, 1950); David L. Rowe, *Thunder and Trumpets: Millerites and Dissenting Religion in Upstate New York, 1800–1850* (Chico, CA, 1985); Michael Barkun, *Crucible of the Millennium: the Burned-Over District of New York in the 1840s* (Syracuse, 1986).

5. For some wonderful Victorian biblical mathematics, see David S. Katz, *God's Last Words: Reading the English Bible from the Reformation to Fundamentalism* (New Haven & London, 2004), chap. 7.

6. 'And I heard the number of them which were sealed: *and there were* sealed an hundred *and* forty *and* four thousand of all the tribes of the children of Israel': Rev. 7:4.

7. Russell also borrowed from the followers of Great Pyramidism, in proclaiming that the measurements of that Egyptian monument contain the key to predicting all of mankind's greatest events until the end of the world. Rutherford would abandon Pyramidism entirely. For more on Pyramidism, see below, pp. 193–4.

8. A young woman biology teacher in Arkansas brought a case in

1965 against a state law forbidding the teaching of evolution, and won, with the backing of the ACLU and the American Jewish Congress. In 1968, the Supreme Court declared unconstitutional any law banning the teaching of evolution in public schools, and in 1987 it ruled that it was unconstitutional to compel public schools to teach so-called 'creation science', since religion is not a science. Nevertheless, in 1989, the California Board of Education ruled that evolution will also be taught as a theory rather than as scientific fact. In 1999, Kansas removed evolution as a subject in high school biology classes. See generally Edward J. Larson, *Summer for the Gods: The Scopes Trial and America's Continuing Debate over Science and Religion* (New York, 1997).

9. B.A. Kosmin & S.P. Lachman, *One Nation Under God: Religion in Contemporary American Society* (New York, 1993), pp. 9, 15–17, 197: still the most comprehensive and reliable statistical survey of American religion. See also 'America and Religion: The Counter-Attack of God', *The Economist* repr. *National Times* (Oct-Nov. 1995), 29.

10. A.C. Gaebelein, *The History of the Scofield Reference Bible* (New York, 1943).

11. Rev. 20: 12–16.

12. Dan. 2:31–45.

13. Tim LaHaye & Jerry B. Jenkins, *Left Behind: A Novel of the Earth's Last Days* (Wheaton, IL, 1995), and numerous sequels.

14. For more on this issue, see Katz and Popkin, *Messianic Revolution*, chap. 8.

15. Bob Woodward, *Plan of Attack* (New York, 2004), p. 421.

16. Bruce Lincoln, *Holy Terrors: Thinking about Religion after September 11* (Chicago, 2003), pp. 30–32. Bush's address is printed on pp. 99–101, and is also easily available online.

17. For James Frazer's inadequate distinction between religion and magic, see above, pp. 12–13.

18. See generally Grant Wacker, *Heaven Below: Early Pentecostals and American Culture* (Cambridge, USA, 2001); David Martin, *Pentecostalism: Their World Their Parish* (Oxford, 2002).

19. See the voluminous writings of Adam Rutherford of the 'Institute of Pyramidology' at Stanmore, London, in the 1930s, especially his monumental *Anglo-Saxon Israel or Israel-Britain* (4th edn, Stanmore, 1939) [1st edn, 1934], subtitled 'A Call to all the Anglo-

Saxon, Celtic, Dutch and Scandinavian nations with A Special Call to Iceland'. Iceland, indeed, was one of his favourite subjects, on which he published many books on everything from that country as the key to biblical prophecy to its transportation system. The predictions cited above are on pp. 556, 569, 579–89, 613, 615, 620, 630, 655, 656, 676.

20. See generally the ultimate pyramid book, Peter Lemesurier, *The Great Pyramid Decoded* (London, 1977), esp. p. 181.

21. Rutherford, *Anglo-Saxon Israel*, p. 329.

22. Wouter J. Hanegraaff, *New Age Religion and Western Culture* (Leiden, 1996).

23. This would also include the tendency of reducing spirit to matter, so that spirit becomes merely an 'epiphenomenon' of essentially material processes.

24. J.C. Smuts, *Holism and Evolution* (New York, 1926), p. 317.

25. See the *Oxford English Dictionary*, s.v. 'holism', 'holistic medicine'.

26. David Bohm, 'Hidden Variables and the Implicate Order', *Zygon*, 20 (1985), 111–24. See also his joint books with Jiddu Krishnamurti, *The Ending of Time* (London, 1985) and *The Future of Humanity* (The Hague, 1986).

27. Karl H. Pribram, *Brain and Perception: Holonomy and Structure in Figural Processing* (Hillsdale, NJ, 1990).

28. Erich Jantsch, *The Self-Organizing Universe: Scientific and Human Implications of the Emerging Paradigm of Evolution* (Oxford, 1980).

29. Rupert Sheldrake, *A New Science of Life: the Hypothesis of Formative Causation* (London, 1981); *idem, The Presence of the Past: Morphic Resonance and the Habits of Nature* (London, 1988)

30. J.E. Lovelock, *Gaia: A New Look at Life on Earth* (Oxford, 1979).

31. Generally, see esp. Eileen Barker, *The Making of a Moonie: Choice or Brainwashing?* (Oxford, 1984); John Lofland, *Doomsday Cult: A Study of Conversion, Proselytization, and Maintenance of Faith* (rev. edn, New York, 1977).

32. The term 'Black Muslims' was coined by C. Eric Lincoln, *The Black Muslims in America* (Boston, 1961). See also Martha F. Lee, *The Nation of Islam: an American Millenarian Movement* (Lewiston, 1988); Mattias Gardell, *Countdown to Armageddon: Louis Farrakhan and the Nation of Islam* (London, 1996); Gilles Keppel, *Allah in the West: Islamic Movements in America and Europe* (Cambridge, 1997).

33. See, for example, Russell Miller, *Bare-Faced Messiah: The True Story of L. Ron Hubbard* (New York, 1987); Jon Atack, *A Piece of Blue Sky: Scientology, Dianetics and L. Ron Hubbard Exposed* (Secaucus, 1990); Roy Wallis, *The Road to Total Freedom: A Sociological Analysis of Scientology* (London, 1976); Marco Frenschkowski, 'L. Ron Hubbard and Scientology: An Annotated Bibliographical Survey of Primary and Selected Secondary Literature', *Marburg Journal of Religion*, 4 (1999), 1–12; Stephen A. Kent, 'The Creation of "Religious" Scientology', *Religious Studies and Theology*, 18 (1999), 97–126; Josef Joffe, 'Germany vs. the Scientologists', *New York Rev. Books*, 24 Apr. 1997, 16–21.

34. J.G. Frazer, *The Golden Bough*, ed. Robert Fraser (Oxford, 1994), pp. 54–6.

35. Ibid., p. 55.

36. This wonderful passage has been omitted from Robert Fraser's 'Oxford World's Classics' edition of *The Golden Bough*, along with many other gobbets of J.G. Frazer's characteristic purple prose. Robert Fraser's justification for producing a new abridgement of the multi-volume original is that the 'hastily undertaken abridgement of 1922' went 'to extreme lengths not to offend', and left out passages which were 'risky', 'deliciously irreverent' or mere 'speculations', and, in any case, most of the actual editing was carried out by Lady Frazer on rather idiosyncratic principles: 'Note on the Text', pp. xl-xli. While readers will be grateful, for example, to have J.G. Frazer's idiotic discussion of the crucifixion back in place, they will dearly miss Frazerian writing at its worst. For the passage quoted above, see the *The Golden Bough* (London: Macmillan, 1922), p. 64.

INDEX

INDEX

Weishaupt, Adam 83–4
Weisz, Erik 'Harry Houdini' 121
Wells, H. G. 132–3
Wesley, John 96
Wesley brothers 94, 95
Westcott, Dr William Wynn 172
Wewelsburg castle, near Paderborn 176
Weyer, Johann 36
Whigs 69, 72, 74, 75, 84
White, Ellen Harmon 181
White, James 181
Whitmer, David 101
Wicca movement 196
Wilde, Oscar 111, 132
Wildman, John 69
Wiligut, Karl Maria 176
Wilkins, John 54–5
Willermoz, Jean Baptiste 80
William of Ockham 58, 60
Williams, Charles 123

Williams, William Carlos 36–7
witchcraft 3, 36, 54
Wittgenstein, Ludwig 114
Woodman, Dr William Robert 172
Woodruff, Wilford 108
Woodward, Bob 190
world soul 16, 18, 21, 35, 37
Wotanism 173
Wundt, William 124, 139
Wyclif, John 182

Yagel, Abraham 45
Yates, Frances 2–3, 14, 43–4, 50–51, 52, 55–6
Yeats, William Butler 172
Young, Brigham 107

Zionism 184
zodiac 20, 21, 27, 35
Zoroaster 22